KNUD S. LARSEN has dedicated his life to the optimistic hope that peace between nations can be achieved. An associate professor at Oregon State University since 1974, he also is a research associate of the International Peace Research Institute of Oslo, Norway. He serves on the Board of Social Issues of the Oregon State Psychological Association and is a permanent corresponding member of the editorial committee of the *Bulletin of Peace Proposals.*

He also is a research fellow in psychology of the Australian Institute of Aboriginal Studies, Canberra, and currently is conducting studies in aboriginal decision-making processes.

Dr. Larsen received his early education in Denmark's schools and came to California in 1956, where he attended high school. He received B.A. and M.A. degrees from California State University at Los Angeles and a doctorate in social psychology from Brigham Young University.

He was a probation counselor for Los Angeles County while attending school and in 1968 went to Oslo as a researcher for the International Peace Research Institute.

His research paper on "Images of the World in the Year 2000" was read at the plenary meeting, Year 2000 Project, held in Prague. He has published widely in scientific journals on the subjects of peace and conflict research, social cost, social judgment and discriminatory behavior, attitude change, and on varied other subjects.

AGGRESSION
Myths and Models

Knud S. Larsen

AGGRESSION
Myths and Models

BIP-87

Nelson-Hall Chicago

Library of Congress Cataloging in Publication Data

Larsen, Knud S.
  Aggression.

  Bibliography: p.
  Includes index.
  1. Aggressiveness (Psychology)   2. Aggression
(International law)   I. Title.
BF575.A3L37   301.6'3   76-5882
ISBN 0-91102-71-0 (hardbound)
ISBN 0-91102-452-0 (paperback)

Copyright © 1976 by Knud S. Larsen

Manufactured in the United States of America

for
Jens Sonderhede Larsen

Contents

Isolated, a man may well be a cultivated
individual; in a crowd he is a barbarian.
—Gustave LeBon

Preface

Today is an ordinary day. As I look out the window, I see the
rolling hills in the distance. Hardly a wind is stirring. This quiet
pastoral scene is complemented by the early evening sun, generously
spilling its rays on the horizon as it prepares to join the Pacific — a
scant fifty miles away. The peace of an evening in Oregon on an
Indian summer Sunday is overwhelming. As I sit back in my chair,
the notes of Beethoven's Ninth Symphony fill the air: "Alle menschen
werden bruder, wo dein sanfter flugel weilt." Yes, all men will be
brothers.

I pick up the Sunday paper and read of war and peace. In "new"
Mozambique, security stays tight at the swearing-in ceremony of the
new independence government. The white settlers' rebellion is at
least temporarily suppressed. In the Middle East, the Palestinian
Liberation Organization is in conflict with Jordan about who should
represent the Palestinian people in upcoming peace talks with Israel.
President Marcos of the Philippines is in China trying to reach out for
that portion of humanity (and resources) which has been inaccessible
for reasons of ideology. Meanwhile, back in the Philippines, martial
law continues because of the "threats" of underground communist
organizations. Even World War II gets into the act today with the
death sentence of a Canadian citizen in the Soviet Union for participating with the Nazis in the execution of more than three thousand
Soviet citizens. In Cyprus, the Turk and Greek Cypriots are exchang-

ing prisoners from the latest war; and in Ethiopia, Emperor Selassie has been ousted by the army.

Here at home, violence is expressed in the first murder of a policewoman in the nation's history. The people and politicians are discussing the pros and cons of amnesty for resisters to the nation's longest war. The Evel Knievel Snake River jump of the past week is characterized as a "bizarre spectacle, garnished with machismo and the threat of death." At the site, crowd violence was the order of the day. Yes, today is an ordinary day in September, but the peace of my Oregon hide-away has not been shared by the world.

The events of one day in the history of the world indicate eloquently the need to understand and control aggression and violence. For that purpose this book was written.

Several theorists have attempted to define aggression. For Buss (1961) aggression is "a response that delivers noxious stimuli to another organism." For Carthy and Ebling (1964) an organism "acts aggressively when it inflicts, attempts to inflict, or threatens to inflict damage on another animal." The intent or anticipation of aggression expressed in the Carthy and Ebling formulation is deemed of great importance. However, I will not further define aggression here, as that is a major purpose of the book, especially of Chapter 7, which discusses types of aggression.

Man's potential to destroy, not only other men, but also nature itself, is increasing rapidly. Psychology, as a discipline, has a particularly important contribution to make in explaining aggression as it focuses directly on man's behavior. Seventeen years ago, McNeil (1959), in reviewing the literature on aggression, noted the study of this area had commanded an inordinate amount of energy from social scientists. Since that time, literally hundreds of studies have been completed by psychologists all over the world. Many of these studies have drastically changed our conceptions about aggression. For that reason alone, there is a need for an up-to-date review focusing especially on the work of the last decade.

Other books have been written about aggression. However, past reviews of aggression have limited their focus to particular issues. The accompanying table may be used as a convenient guide to the range of literature on aggression.

Authors and Approaches to the Study of Aggression

Author	*Models*
Berkowitz	A social-psychological analysis based on frustration-aggression hypothesis
Buss	Selective emphasis on previously unpublished material
Feshbach and Singer	Field experiment on effect of television on aggression — reduced aggression in some groups
Johnson	Interdisciplinary viewpoints
Kaufman	The aggression-altruism model
Maple and Matheson	The nature versus nurture question
Megargee and Hokanson	Major theories and supporting research in original presentation
Scott	Extrapolation from animal studies to human behavior
Storr	Psychoanalytic instinct theory
Toch	Study of violent man

These authors represent the range of thinking about aggression from psychoanalytic instinct theory to the frustration-aggression hypothesis. However, nowhere are these issues summarized within the covers of one book. A major ambition of this work is to develop a comprehensive analysis of aggression, including a survey of recent literature.

The various viewpoints represented by the authors cited in the table indicate the complexity of the subject of aggression and, therefore, the necessity of studying violence within relevant levels. Aggression at the infrahuman level requires an examination of its own, or we may fall into the error of anthropomorphizing animal behavior. Likewise, violence between individuals is different from the kind of violence which exists in a conflict between nations. This, then, is my purpose: to present a comprehensive review of models on aggression at the levels of recent animal and human experimentation, individual human aggression, and international conflict.

But, how do I organize this mass of data which has accumulated during the past few decades? What is the emphasis or theoretical line of this book? This book argues an approach which recognizes the gregarious nature of man and his unique dependence on those who have power over him, that is, his significant others. Man is largely motivated by his fear of rejection and his desire for approval by significant others. On the whole, the development and maintenance of human aggression and international conflict are functions of the inhibiting and facilitating effects of the social environment. Social aggression, as expressed in gang killings, intergroup prejudice, and international conflict, is largely caused by conformity needs based on social cost. By social cost I mean the approval or disapproval anticipated from significant others as a result of a person's interaction with another person from a different group or category. The interaction we are concerned with is aggression.

This theoretical framework is applied to human aggression and international hostility in topics as varied as aggressive personalities and hostile international images. For the convenience of the reader, each chapter has an insert which summarizes the relationship of social cost to the variables discussed in the chapter. I have used social cost as an umbrella concept to tie the data together and to develop models of human aggression and hostile international images.

Understanding the variables which predict human aggression and international hostility is important primarily for the application of this understanding to conflict management and resolution. Throughout the chapters, emphasis is placed on the amelioration or resolution of aggression; and the last three chapters focus directly on this problem.

What issues are we concerned with in a comprehensive review of models on aggression? The nature versus nurture of human aggression has been debated from early instinct theorists following Freud to the modern school of ethology. Is aggression a result of the carnivorous nature of man; or does the individual learn aggression by observation and imitation of an aggressive person who is rewarded for his behavior? To what extent may we extrapolate from animal experiments in developing a human model on aggression? Is there such a thing as aggressive personalities? These and many other issues are covered in the systematic building of models on aggression. In creating these models, I criticize much of the literature which is based on fictions and myths.

This book is divided into three sections. Part I, devoted to experiments on animals and humans, is organized around the type of stimuli which facilitate or elicit aggression whether found internally in the organism or in its environment. Part II is aimed at developing a comprehensive theory of human aggression. In approaching this goal, I discuss theories of aggression (and frustration), aggression as a personality construct, the social psychology of aggression, and two major types of aggression. Part III is on international hostility. A review of the literature is presented, leading to two models which explain the development and maintenance of hostile international images. The discussion which follows focuses on conflict management, *i.e.*, the prevention of overt conflict and conflict resolution. In moving toward conflict resolution, the importance of developing a peace ideology, *i.e.*, a systematic presentation of the values which will bring a lasting and just peace, is recognized. The final chapter of the book is a report of a large-scale, international survey of images of the future. I invite you to think of the future while reading this book, for whether we are its captives or its architects may depend in great measure upon our comprehension of human aggression — and its individual and international implications.

I am acutely aware of the contributions that many former teachers and friends have made which directly or indirectly are reflected in this work. Those teachers who supervised my work during my undergraduate days amalgamated my concern for social justice with a desire to study conflict. Professors Henry Minton and Vernon Kiker planted seeds of scientific curiosity. — I would like them to know it.

I owe special thanks to Professor Kenneth Hardy. My world of concepts has been enlarged as a result of my contact with this generous friend and teacher. His constructive criticisms of early drafts of this book were invaluable. My sincere thanks go to Professor Milton Rokeach for evaluating research on social cost. My work on the social cost concept stems from a seminar on racial prejudice with

Professors Rokeach and Pettigrew at Oregon State University.

A bouquet of roses goes to my students, Ken Pierce and Don Langenberg, who labored with me many hours, painstakingly reviewing the book page by page. Theirs was a labor of love.

Finally, to my wife Kathy, who typed the manuscript and reviewed it for grammatical errors, I give sincere and deepfelt thanks.

I.

EXPERIMENTS ON ANIMALS AND HUMANS

In this section, I emphasize the recent literature on animal and human experiments, organized by the nature of stimuli which elicit, moderate, or inhibit aggressive behavior. Chapter 1 focuses on the factors in the organism's external environment. External stimuli include population density, concepts of territory, monotonous environments, isolation, and power relationships. Chapter 2, on the other hand, looks within the organism. What are the internal stimuli which predict aggression? The genetic, hormonal, and physiological controls of aggression are examined.

Rapid advances in research have made contributions toward mapping the control areas of the brain; some of these areas are important in aggression. This section, then, represents the most active concerns of recent years in the experimental work on aggression. The information outlined here will constitute an important basis for understanding human aggression.

1.

External Aversive Stimuli and Aggression

If social scientists can discover the causes (predictors) of aggression, presumably society can take steps toward alleviating or eliminating hostile behavior. The search for predictors has inspired many ingenious experiments investigating either situational-environmental factors or causes within the organism itself. Research with animals has a special value, as it is possible to carry out certain experiments which could not be tried on humans. There will always be those who argue against experimenting on animals, but few can deny the great progress achieved in the areas of medical research and the understanding of behavior as a result of animal research.

The underlying assumption of animal research is that analogies exist between the physiology and behavior of animals and of man. The closer the animal and man, on the evolutionary scale of development, the closer the analogy. However, it is also generally recognized that man is more plastic than animals in his behavior, and that he is more easily influenced by the environment. Animals, especially lower forms, are directed more by hormones and other intra-organism causes.

Any analogy from animal behavior to human behavior must therefore always be made with caution. In the past, many researchers have made the error of attributing human qualities (such as thinking or feeling processes) to animals. We have no way of knowing the non-physiological internal processes of animals. This does not mean that analogies are not useful. The opposite error is to assume that animal and human behaviors are discrete, separated by a gulf so wide as to make any comparisons meaningless. A reasonable position is that analogies are useful in the extent to which animals and humans share comparable internal and external environments. In other words, if the physiology is roughly similar, then we may assume that the organs involved in aggression among animals probably also play a function in aggression in humans. If the environment contains similar elements, such as painful stimuli, we may expect that some animal reactions probably also are characteristic of humans. A human whose foot has been stepped on may not act much differently (depending on other socially constraining factors) from a rat whose foot has been painfully pinched.

INDIVIDUAL AVERSIVE STIMULI

Individual aversive stimuli are those which impinge directly upon the organism without major alteration or mediation by the environment; other stimuli are chiefly functions of the organism's physical or social environment. This twofold classification does not represent a hard and inflexible rule, but it is useful for convenience in organization.

Pain. What might be a predictable reaction if someone administered a painful stimulus to an animal? — The animal would attack either the source of the pain or some substitute target. If the aggression occurred at the human level, the selection of such substitute targets would be called "scapegoating." The only connection substitute targets have with pain is that they are present and handy.

The learning of aggression as a result of pain follows a simple association paradigm. The painful stimulus elicits an aggressive reaction which is associated with the most convenient target for attack. Tedeschi, Tedeschi, Mucha, Cook, Mattis, and Fellows (1959), exposing mice to mild foot shocks, were able to elicit fighting episodes among the mice. As early as 1951, Scott and Frederickson noted pain may cause fighting behavior. A pain threshold which must be exceeded before attack behavior occurs may operate in animals and humans. Pain below this level may not elicit attack, whereas pain exceeding this minimum intensity may elicit hostile behavior.

Azrin, Hutchinson, and Sallery (1964) produced attack behavior in squirrel monkeys by applying electrical shock. Not only did the shock elicit attack upon other monkeys, but also upon rats, mice, and even inanimate objects, such as a stuffed doll. Attack behavior in the Azrin study was found to be directly related to the shock intensity as was the duration of the attack. Up to the point where an animal is incapacitated by painful stimuli, the more pain it suffers, the greater the ferocity and duration of its attack. Azrin, Hake, and Hutchinson (1966) partially replicated these results by using tail pinches rather than shock. The tail pinches were administered to the animals in the presence of a cloth-covered ball. Once again, the greater the force of the tail pinch, the more ferocious the attack — a direct function between these two variables.

In another study, Hutchinson, Azrin, and Renfrew (1968) exposed squirrel monkeys to tail shocks in the presence of a rubber tube. The longer the time interval from the time the shock was applied, the less intensely the squirrel monkeys bit on the tube. The more intense the shock and the longer it lasted, the more intensely the monkeys bit. In short, biting attack was discovered to be a decreasing function of time since shock delivery and a direct function of shock intensity and duration. Further support for these findings may also be found in a study by Dreyer and Church (1968).

Azrin, Hutchinson, and McLaughlin (1965) suggested that aggression is a distinct motivational state which is produced by aversive stimulation and which can be used to condition and maintain new behavior. These studies have shown that the administration of pain to animals will produce aggression as a function of the amount and duration of the aversive stimuli.

While the most natural response to pain is probably counterattack, the target for aggression as noted will often be irrelevant. However, in all of the studies just reviewed, the possibility for counterattack was minimal or nonexistent. Counterattack is the normal response when the organism has the possibility of attacking the source of the pain and when the source is equal or inferior in strength. Logically, counterattack would rarely occur if the organism risks greater pain or damage by doing so. It would appear, from what we know of the literature on scapegoating activities of humans, that animal and human behavior is similar in this respect. — Aggression derived from frustration or pain is displaced to other targets, which may or may not be relevant, if direct attack is not possible or the direct target is more powerful.

Deprivation. Another individual aversive stimulus is deprivation. In order for an animal to experience deprivation, it must first have experienced something of positive incentive value. Many objects have positive incentive value, including those satisfying the basic needs of life, such as food, water, and sex. By association with these drive-reducing (or hedonistic) properties, other variables, such as territory and population, may also achieve positive incentive value. Incentives result in one of two reactions: positive incentives, such as food, suggest approach; negative incentives, such as pain, suggest avoidance. They imply a directional orientation for the organism toward or away from a condition that is either attractive or repulsive. In the past, psychology, due to the enormous influence of tension reduction theory, has mainly considered negative incentives (escape from pain, anxiety, and tension); however, animals will avoid deprivation as well as seek positive rewards. Deprivation results in tension, frustration, and eventually pain.

Initially deprivation will produce searching behavior on the part of the organism. For example, a dog deprived of food may search the garbage cans of the neighborhood for sustenance. Assuming that these contain no food or are perfectly sealed, and assuming that the food deprivation has reached a certain threshold level, the domesticated dog may begin hunting.

Among humans, food deprivation can cause the ultimate in intra-species aggression — cannibalism. Although many cases of human cannibalism are associated with symbolic mythology, there are recorded cases of cannibalism derived from starvation. It is likely that cannibalism as a cultural practice was originally motivated by food deprivation; however, because of the anxiety over the taking of human life, different mythological rationales were developed. The myth that eating a human heart gives that person's strength to the consumer may have derived from the original motivation of gaining strength to survive food deprivation. Regardless of the truth of this explanation, even with humans, deprivation is experienced as unpleasant, may initiate searching behavior, and, in the presence of consistent goal blocking, will produce aggression.

The general procedure of a deprivation and aggression study is to start by rewarding the animal (usually with food) for performing some task. After expectation for the reinforcement has been developed, the reward is withheld and opportunities for aggression are presented. Performing the task without reinforcement is assumed to be experienced as deprivation. Such nonreinforced trials may produce overt aggression. Gallup (1965) employed albino rats in a learning task (making a correct choice in a straight alley experiment) and noted that more aggression occurred following nonreinforced trials, when compared to reinforced trials. Thompson, Travis, and Bloom (1966) indicated in their report that discontinuing positive reinforcement of rats elicited fighting. Azrin, Hutchinson, and Hake (1965) found that pigeons became more aggressive during the transition from food reinforcement to extinction.

Extinction may be defined as the weakening of a learned response following non-reinforcement of that response. As noted, such non-reinforcement is experienced as deprivation. Consequently, varying amounts of extinction or non-reinforcement of responses lead to varying levels of aggression. Davis and Donenfeld (1967) found various types of aggression ranging from postured threat to chasing another animal from the cage under different degrees of extinction. The type of aggression was related to the amount of extinction (deprivation) for each pair of animals. Hutchinson, Azrin, and Hunt (1968) showed that such extinction-induced aggression effects occur also in primates. These results all appear to be quite consistent; depriving animals of some type of reinforcement after expectation for such has developed produces aggression.

ENVIRONMENTAL AVERSIVE STIMULI

Certain factors, such as pain, may affect an organism directly; other factors may affect the organism as mediated by the immediate environment. To classify certain stimuli as possessing only environmental characteristics is somewhat difficult. The stimuli with which we are concerned under this classification are mediated indirectly by the environment and not directly by some agent.

Monotony and novelty. The variables pain and deprivation tend to affect the organism's internal environment by producing physiological disequilibriums upsetting the homeostatic balance in the animal. This is not to suggest all aversive environmental stimuli affect only physiology. Some aversive stimuli are primarily social in origin and relate to social needs — not physiological drives.

A number of investigators have challenged the traditional drive reduction theory of motivation. Harlow (1953, 1954) has especially emphasized *curiosity* as a motive for behavior. In his well-publicized studies of monkeys, he has demonstrated the willingness of these animals to take apart rather complicated devices without any obvious reinforcement. In other cases, monkeys have worked hard on problems merely for the opportunity to solve them. Since there was no obvious drive reduction taking place, Harlow concluded curiosity itself is a motive.

Montgomery (1952) has carried out a series of experiments on rats which would tend to indicate the presence of exploratory drives. These experiments cannot be explained solely in terms of hunger or thirst drives. They suggest that a novel stimulus — even if it arouses fear — may itself produce exploratory behavior. In 1947, Woodworth came to the conclusion that a "motive to perceive" is prevalent. He suggested that making sense of, or ordering, the social environment is a primary motive of organisms. Consequently, there are social factors which affect an organism's behavior apart from needs of homeostatic balances.

On the basis of these investigations, one may assume the presence of needs for novel and/or complex experience. Therefore, an environment which tends to be uniform and monotonous will frustrate the individual organism and produce aggression; however novel stimuli may also have shock value and produce fear. If the new stimuli are too discrepant from the old or known (such as a polar bear being transferred from the Arctic to the San Diego Zoo), the discrepancy may produce disorientation and fear. Objects which are feared are often attacked.

The relationship between people and foreign cultures may provide an analogy on the human level. People who fear the foreign or discrepant often display an impulse to aggress. Cultural discrepancy is known at the human level as cultural shock, and it is felt by many a traveler who visits an exotic country for the first time. Initially, the traveler may experience a period of bewilderment, disorientation, and fear, which in turn support all the negative stereotypes he may have of the native inhabitants. It is possible to assume that an analogous process takes place in lower organisms; a highly novel and discrepant environment produces disorientation and fear and, consequently, aggressive behavior.

It is clear, therefore, that each organism has an optimal level of novel stimuli. This level may be defined as a band on the stimulus continuum having threshold properties. Below the band, the lack of novel stimuli produces frustrated searching behavior and aggression. In the band itself the amount of stimuli is just right to satisfy curiosity needs. Above the band, the stimuli are too discrepant and intense, and they produce disorientation, fear, and aggression.

Population density. Too many organisms can also be an environmental aversive stimulus. Usually, the more organisms there are per unit of space, the less food, water, and recreation area is available, and the more noise, threat, chaos, and other tension-producing stimuli abound. A number of species seek to protect rather well-defined territories, suggesting that a minimum living space is required. If individuals external to the group cross these lines, conflict usually follows. Even a domesticated dog has a rather definite notion what constitutes "his" yard and the neighbor dog's yard, and dogs will chase strangers — humans or animals — away (as many a mail carrier will testify). Although aversive stimuli from population density include deprivations such as lack of food and water, sex may be readily available, and thus mass starvation may occur until the population density is re-established at a supportable level.

A few recent studies have investigated the relationship of living space and aggression. Rood (1958) found that there was an increase in fighting among male shrews when they were placed together in small cages. Willis (1966) showed that fighting among pigeons also increased with a decrease in available space, and Southwick (1967) found that a combination of reducing cage space and introducing new monkeys to an established group of monkeys tended to increase aggression.

The lack of space *per se* is not the only factor which may influence aggressive behavior, as lack of space may be indicative of a host of aversive environmental variables. Population density leads to an overload of stimuli resulting in anxiety and high levels of tension. Being crowded into a small space forces an organism to be cognizant of more factors per unit of time. Some factors, such as the power hierarchy, are more acute when space is limited. Furthermore, animals crowded into a small space often have less opportunity to escape even from the usual stresses.

Presumably, each species has an optimal level of population density above which the overload of stimuli leads to tension and conflict. It is not likely that a low population density would lead to aggression. However, for those species who depend on social cooperation to survive; too few animals per unit of space may lead to low levels of food production and of mutual protection. This, in turn, might encourage intra-species competition and aggression. The optimal level of population density may therefore be defined as enough individual organisms to make social cooperation efficient and productive, but not so many as to produce high levels of tension or to encourage competition and aggression.

Social versus environmental changes. Southwick (1967) concluded from his study that "Social changes . . . had a far greater impact on levels of intra-group aggression than did environmental changes." In other words, a change in social relationships, such as a disturbance in the power hierarchy, is more crucial than a change in the objective environment, such as population density. The introduction of new animals into an established group produced several results in the Southwick study. The reestablishment of the power hierarchy caused considerable fighting among the animals. We may suggest that tension derived from social changes will remain until the pecking order is stable once again and the social order secure. The introduction of new animals represents a fracture of the old order, the secure and ordered sequences of life that the animals are accustomed to. The disturbance will move the animals (both the old and new group members) toward stabilizing a new social order dependent in part on changed power relationships.

Castell and Plogg (1967) found results similar to those of Southwick. The initial phase of integrating two groups of monkeys produced a collective expression of aggression in the new group. Wolfe and Summerlin (1968) showed that aggression was lower in naturally organized populations, when compared to groups composed of strangers, Two reasons may be suggested to explain these findings. The mere presence of other organisms will increase the tension level, due to an increased stimulus load. When the stimulus load reaches a certain point, the tension is released in a cathartic fashion. In this case, increased tension results in nondirective aggression, or, to put it in other words, blind rage. The introduction of new organisms could tend to disrupt the pecking order. Aggression is then the natural element in the formula which produces a new order and, with that, a new stability. In this case, the aggression may be directive and instrumental and involve either a challenge upward in the pecking order or a reassertion downward.

Stress. There is a stress factor derived simply from the presence of the other animals. Evidence that the presence of other organisms produces stress is suggested by the study of Siegel and Siegel (1961). They compared the adrenals of birds who lived in groups with birds who lived in individual cages. The results showed that birds who lived in groups had heavier adrenals than those raised individually. The adrenal gland produces epinephrine (adrenalin) which increases the sugar output by the liver and increases the heart rate. The role of the hormones is primarily for emergency functions enabling the organisms to respond rapidly to potential danger. If it can be assumed that the weight of an adrenal is related to its use in excreting adrenalin, the Siegel and Siegel result could be explained as a result of higher levels of social tension; but perhaps this stress factor is related to an optimal stimuli level, as previously suggested. There were presumably no other differences between the two groups of pigeons.

Stress may be defined as the rate of wear in the body. Aggression is not the only reaction to tension stress. The organism may adapt to the level of stress, or stress may lead to disease and a breakdown of the body. Some stress is normal, and it is an expected part of all life.

Selye (1956) calls the change which follows stress the general adaption syndrome (G.A.S.) which he says develops in three stages: (1) the alarm reaction, (2) the stage of resistance, and (3) the stage of exhaustion. The first phase is the call to defense by the various bodily mechanisms. Since no living organism can stay perpetually in a state of alarm, the first phase is followed by a stage of resistance. If the noxious stimuli persist, this acquired adaption is eventually lost, and the animal enters the stage of exhaustion.

Aggression will most likely occur during the first phase, when the organism is healthy and well integrated. The tension derived from small living spaces (or high population density) can produce the general adaption syndrome with aggression occurring mainly during the alarm reaction. The stage of resistance is concerned mainly with adaption to the existing noxious stimulus (e.g., the adrenal cortex does not secrete adrenalin; blood is diluted, not concentrated as in the alarm stage). The symptoms of the final stage are much like the initial phase, only the animal is no longer capable of resistance.

Many factors may produce stress. Some are individual noxious stimuli such as pain, and some are mediated by the environment such as population density. Stress may produce aggression primarily as part of its alarm reaction, and secondarily as part of adaptive strategies for survival. If the stress persists, it will eventually produce a stage of exhaustion, a breakdown of health, and death.

Power and hierarchical relations. There are many definitions and concepts of power at the human level. Traditionally, social power has been defined as the ability to influence the behavior of others. Power is based on certain attributes, such as being able to mete out rewards or punishment. Minton (1967) suggested a conceptual differentiation between manifest and latent power, in which manifest power is exemplified by the *exercise* of social power, and the latent power refers to an *attitude* of power (i.e., how powerful one feels). Most studies of power and aggression among animals are concerned with the actual exercise of power (manifest power). In a certain sense, animals may also possess latent power. Latent power among animals may refer to differences such as amount of male hormone (or in general the hormonal balance in a particular animal).

What role does the object of power play in interaction with the holder of power? Do perceptions of the object interact with the subject's latent power and exercise of power? And, if so, what is the nature of this interaction? Larsen and Minton (1971) suggested that the perceptual approach (the organism's perception of the object of power) is important to understanding social power. Their basic assertion is that no power is power unless it is perceived to be power. How can an organism have a feeling of power unless this feeling is derived by means of some environmental reinforcement? If the object did not attribute power to the subject, the social relations among the species would be in constant disruption, as each meeting of the individuals would become an occasion for confrontation and challenge. Through meting out reward and punishment, the organism not only expresses latent power as manifest power, but also defines the amount of power which resides in and may be attributed to the object. Aggression is avoided as a result of attributed power. High attributed power produces deference and, consequently, stable social relations.

Power and aggression. If the rationale of attributed power is correct, larger or more powerful organisms would tend toward more aggressive behavior when compared to weaker organisms. Ono and Uematsu (1958) observed pairs of fish placed in separate containers. In pairs of opposite sex, males were dominant, whereas, in same-sex pairs of fish, the larger one tended to be dominant. Other evidence may be found in the study by Rood (1958) who showed that young female shrews tended to be less pugnacious than adult males. Carpenter (1960) observed greater dominance in male lizards which were large and active.

Successful aggression may contain its own reward. Lagerspetz (1964) demonstrated the reward value of aggressive behavior when he showed aggressive mice crossed a painful electric grid more readily if permitted to begin fighting before the trial began. Hautojarvi and Lagerspetz (1968) showed high aggressiveness in mice was induced by repeated victories over mice that have not experienced aggressive contact. In the Watten and Marony (1958) study on rhesus monkeys, the correlation between aggressiveness and success in food getting was a high .77. Aggression may be so rewarding as to support other learning in the conditioning paradigm. Myer and White (1965) showed the opportunity to kill mice reinforces killer rats in a discrimination learning task; and in a classical conditioning experiment, Vernon and Ulrick (1966) demonstrated that aggression was produced by using classical conditioning procedures between paired rats. Apparently, power or dominance leads to aggression, and successful aggression leads to higher levels of aggression.

Møller, Marlow, and Mitchell (1968) did a study on the factors which affected dominance (and consequently aggression) in rhesus monkeys. Age was a factor, as dominance displays, such as yawning or threats, increased with age, while fear responses (grimaces and vocalizations) decreased with age. Age may also be related to other variables, such as increased strength. Older monkeys may have a clearer picture of whom to aggress toward successfully, or be capable of directing aggression so it will be frequently rewarded. Younger monkeys may proceed more cautiously until they have derived estimates of their latent and manifest power and attribute objectively these components to other members of their group. Once the hierarchy of power is established, it is predictable that aggression proceeds downwards. Aggression also exists between individuals who are still jockeying for positions at the top of the hierarchy.

There is some evidence for the function of attributed power in the Møller study. The displays of dominance or submission were dependent upon certain characteristics of the social partner, such as size, age, and level of hostility. This suggests the importance of the social stimulus of all the members of the troop. The display of dominance is rewarded only if the social partner is weaker. That a considerable amount of testing occurs in the "newness" phase of a relationship is suggested by the decrease of dominance behavior as the animal becomes more familiar with a strange social partner.

Sex is also related to dominance. Dominance displays occurred more often in males than in females, and fear grimaces occurred less often in males. These differences may, for a good part, be attributed to hormonal differences, with males having a larger share of the so-called male hormone.

The dominance hierarchy has been reported in a number of studies. Crook (1968) noted that, among Japanese and rhesus macaques, troops tended to be divided into central controlling cores and weaker peripheral sections. The result of this division had practical consequences, as high status animals tended to gain prior access to food. The offspring of dominant animals also tended to show the attributes of assertiveness. Baldwin (1968), in particular, emphasized the importance of the mating season on aggression. As the mating season approached, his squirrel monkeys became increasingly more active, excitable, and aggressive, and established a dominance hierarchy. Approximately forty percent of the mating season interactions involved dominance. A peculiar ritual had been established during the periods when the males were contesting their status. If the individuals did not come to rest in a pile-up in a position compatible with their social status, violent fights occurred.

Isolation. Another environmental factor is social isolation (i.e., the removal of parental or peer contact). Investigators have studied the effect of social isolation among primates. Seay, Alexander, and Harlow (1964) noted that female rhesus monkeys who had been separated from their mothers at birth became abusive or indifferent mothers. In a follow-up study, Arling and Harlow (1967) found support for these results. The motherless mothers were deficient in maternal behavior. They displayed considerably fewer nurturing responses, such as cradling, nursing, or retrieving, which are generally observed in normally reared mothers. Arling and Harlow also observed the infants of motherless mothers engaged in greater amounts of infant to infant aggression, such as clapping, pulling, or biting responses. Sackett (1965) also found such infants were hyperaggressive, as compared to infants of normally reared mothers.

Mitchell (1968) suggested that total social isolation has both immediate and long-term negative effects on the social behavior of rhesus monkeys. Isolated animals become fearful, disturbed, and socially inactive. The fights of isolated monkeys are more frequent, longer in duration, and of greater severity; and they are at times characterized by suicidal attacks against huge males or by brutal beatings of infants. Etkin (1964) notes that the normal expression of dominance often depends on appropriate restraint of aggression. The dominance orders of isolated monkeys are, however, abnormally unstable (Mitchell, 1968).

These studies all seem to suggest a sequence of behaviors ending

SOCIAL COST AND STRIKING OUT

Social cost refers to the potential or perceived rejection or acceptance of significant others as a result of a social interaction. More broadly, social cost may also include two additional interlocking variables. The power or strength of the administrator of aversive stimuli and the potential threat to physical survival that the administrator represents are aspects of this broader concept of social cost. Thus it is expected that the response of an organism to pain or deprivations, for example, would depend on the power and threat of the administrator. Displacement or substitute aggression is indicative of social cost. In such scapegoating aggression, two possibilities exist: (1) the administrator of the aversive stimuli was not available for counter-aggression, or (2) the administrator was too powerful and represented too great a threat to permit direct aggression.

External aversive stimuli may instigate aggression, but social cost will, to some extent, define the type and intensity of the response. The social cost of aggression would predict that aggression will be directed downward in a power hierarchy. Thus, although the organism may seek some equity between aversive stimulation and response, even rage reaction may be moderated to some extent. Those monkeys capable of suicidal rage attacks were those who were socially isolated and had therefore not learned to attribute power and threat to other monkeys. Social cost would also explain the type and intensity of instrumental aggression. The organism would select the course of action which would represent the least social cost. Social cost is a hedonistic concept. At the broadest definition, social cost refers to the avoidance of pain and the attainment of pleasure.

in aggression as a result of mother or peer deprivation. Initially, isolated animals respond with fear and withdrawal; however, these characteristics eventually are combined with an abnormal degree of aggression. Normal infants grow up learning a proper balance between fear and assertive responses. By "proper" is meant "socially realistic" (i.e., knowing the consequences of a behavioral action). Deprived infants grow up not learning the proper balance between fear and exploration. Suicidal attacks on adults and beating of infants are both examples of how isolated infants strike out without a sense of social reality.

THE IMPORTANCE OF THE EXTERNAL ENVIRONMENT

The studies mentioned suggest that the aggression is goal oriented (i.e., aimed at removing the source of individual or environmental aversive stimuli). Aggression may also be reactive in nature. However, in reviewing the animal research literature, Berkowitz (1961) observed there is little empirical evidence to suggest a continually active aggressive drive in animals. In other words, to explain aggression on the basis of intra-organism factor (drives) is less than a complete rendition of the facts.

In discussing hormonal factors and aggression, Beeman (1947) suggested some alternate social motivations for the aggressive behavior in animals. These motivations include struggles for social rank. The ability to achieve high rank is related to the amount of male hormones, as well as other strength factors in the animal. High social rank also has incentive values, such as having the first choice in foods and females. Thus, competition for social rank may be a learned motivation. Another social reason for aggression, previously discussed, is the requirement of a minimum amount of living space. Animals will become aggressive if they do not possess minimum territory.

The point is simply that animals, like humans, are not closed systems; they respond to their environment. When aggression occurs, there must be some stimuli from the external environment. This is even more true for the higher animals, where hormones play less important roles and behavior is more plastic. Zuckerman (1932) studied aggression among baboons, noting in the cases of serious fighting that aggression appeared to be goal oriented. Most frequently, the fighting concerned objectives important to life itself, such as food, sex, or territory.

Bevan, Daves, and Levy (1960) castrated animals to observe the effect of the loss of male hormones. Since the amount of male hormones has been related to aggression, one might assume that castration should produce lower levels of aggression. However, the interesting finding of this study was that previous fighting experience (learning) has a more powerful effect than whether the animal is castrated. The study indicates the powerful role of learning as compared to hormonal factors. These studies indicate external motivation is an important variable in the cause of aggression.

A strong environmental point of view is expressed by Scott (1958), who stated there is no need for fighting, either aggressively or defensively, apart from factors in the external environment. This is an extreme point of view. Aggression is probably a function of *both* the internal and the external environments (i.e., it is learned in some cases, drive reactive in others, and frequently a response to both drives and learning combined). When an animal reacts to pain, for example, the reaction may be attributed partly to the noxious stimuli (or the implied frustration derived from the stimuli). On the other hand, aggression may be viewed also as instrumental, in the sense that the animal seeks to eliminate the source or reduce the impact of the pain. In short, aggression in response to pain may be either a learned instrumental and goal-oriented response, or an automatic association to a variety of targets.

A WORD ON DRIVE REDUCTION VERSUS HEDONISM

Overall, the effect of drive reduction motivation is recognized among animals. They will become aggressive if deprived of basic physiological stimuli, such as food and water. Drive reduction, however, does not explain the whole story, as a lack of novel stimuli or too many stimuli may also result in hostile behavior. Such need for novel stimuli is adequately understood within the framework of McClelland's (1951) theory of affective arousal. The definition of a motive in this theory is "a strong affective association, characterized by an anticipatory goal reaction and based on past association of certain cues with pleasure or pain" (p. 466). It is basically a pleasure/pain theory of motivation in which stimuli take on emotional (affective) properties due to past pleasure/pain experience and induce movement toward or away from goals. In the case of social needs, certain stimuli (such as too little or too much novelty) take on emotional properties associated with pain and are "avoided" if possible by searching behavior. This may lead to frustration or aggression if the searching is blocked.

While this theory particularly applies to social needs, it may also explain the motivation typically attributed to drive reduction. The internal stimuli of hunger, for example, may be experienced as unpleasant (receive a negative emotional valence) due to past pleasure/pain experience and thus induce movement toward food goals. There is no need to postulate a drive reduction mechanism, as movement may occur regardless of drive reduction. Hedonism is a more parsimonious explanation for aggression. The hedonistic principle (approach toward pleasure and the avoidance of pain) explains aggression which might be attributed to drive reduction, as well as aggression which has no drive reducing function.

INSTRUMENTAL AGGRESSION AND THE LAW OF EQUITY

There are several possible explanations for why the external aversive stimuli described in this chapter lead to aggression. These stimuli may be experienced as frustrating and unpleasant in a hedonistic sense. Thus the animal may simply "strike out" in response to the unpleasant internal stimulation. Also, in cases where instrumental responses are not feasible, aggression is the only response possible. For example, in the case where the rat is given a painful shock, biting a rubber tube may be the only response the situation permits. The deprivation experienced from extinction produces stimulation leading to goal-oriented behavior. But, when the organism cannot make the response which would produce stimulus reduction, alternate "strike out" responses are made.

Responses without drive reduction may be satisfying in themselves, and it is clear that aggression need not be reinforced for it to be displayed. In some cases, aggression is instrumental in leading to goals which are drive or tension reducing and therefore reinforcing. Alternately, instrumental aggression may also lead to hedonistic states which are characterized by pleasure or the avoidance of pain. In other cases, aggression is motivated by what appears to be the need to make a counter-response. One can only speculate on the internal processes of animals, but perhaps there is some law of equity operating, a law of just distribution summed up in the concept "an eye for an eye." In this view, each organism responds to the environment in a balanced fashion. If the organism is subjected to pain or deprivation, it returns in kind. The same is true for benign stimuli.

The model proposes that the type of aggressive response made to aversive external stimuli follows a hierarchal continuum which is dependent on the possibilities of making instrumental responses. The top of the hierarchy consists of direct instrumental responses leading to immediate drive reduction or desirable hedonistic states; the bottom, of haphazard responses governed by the law of equity as previously defined.

To illustrate, let's consider a member of the species Homo sapiens. A student may wish an A grade for a given course. On the first exam he gets an F. However, it is still possible through increased effort to get an A in the course. The student burns the midnight oil for the next several weeks and confidently takes the next exam. Again he gets an F. Furthermore, it is now past the drop date for the course. He begins to make snide remarks in class. Not only does the instructor irritate him, but so do his fellow students. One day he slams the door as he leaves the class. When the course is evaluated at the end of the term, he rates the class, instructor, and the fairness of grading him as F's.

This is an example of an organism (in this case a student) initially making an instrumental response to his deprivation (desire for an A grade). However, as his options for instrumental responses close and he becomes locked into his frustrations (no A grade and can't drop the course), his responses gradually follow the law of equity. He strikes back at his instructor with snide remarks, shows his dislike to fellow students, and slams the door on the class. Finally, he attributes an F to the instructor in student evaluation, thus "getting even." If this possibility of "getting even" had not existed, we might expect his aggression to take several haphazard indirect forms, such as irrelevant comments, sending paper planes around, and so forth.

Thus, depending on the possibilities of instrumental responses, an organism will progress from direct instrumental responses to law of equity responses. If our sample student was locked into the same teacher term after term, his responses might all be haphazard equity, as shown in the curvilinear function in Figure 1.1. Then we would have the case of the school bully or habitual troublemaker.

Figure 1.1
The relationships between the possibility of making
instrumental responses, duration of aversive stimuli and the
type of aggressive response made (instrumental or equity)

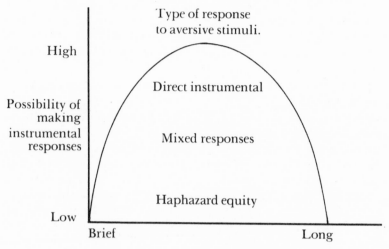

Between the extreme instrumental and extreme equity responses, combinations of the two responses may be found. The intensity of the aggressive responses is dependent upon the duration of the aversive stimuli. The relationship between the type of response and the duration of the aversive stimuli interaction is also essentially a curvilinear function, as indicated in Figure 1.2.

As a rule, if any organism is exposed to aversive stimuli only briefly, it will respond mildly to the stimuli. This is a second aspect to the law of equity. Above a certain threshold, brief durations of aversive stimuli will cause a low intensity response. If a tempting banana is held in front of a satiated monkey, he will make a half-hearted attempt to take it. His response will be considerably more vigorous after twenty-four hours of food deprivation. The law of equity states there will be a balance between stimuli and response, in

Figure 1.2

The relationship between intensity of response and duration
of aversive stimulation

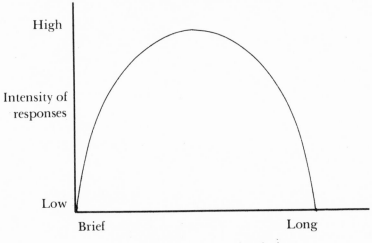

Duration of aversive stimulation

that the response will match the stimuli in *type* and *intensity*, all
other factors kept equal.

The possibilities of making instrumental responses and the
duration of aversive stimulation, combined, explain the type of
aggressive response (instrumental or equity) and the relative intensity
of the response. These relationships may be summarized in Figure
1.3.

From these figures, the following predictions can be made:
(1) instrumental responses will be made at middle levels of duration
of aversive stimulation, (2) high intensity responses will be made
near middle levels of duration of aversive stimulation, and (3) the
type (instrumental, equity) and intensity of responses will vary
according to levels of possibilities of instrumental responses and
duration of aversive stimulation.

The model suggests that a minimum amount of aversive

Figure 1.3

The relationship between the possibility of making
instrumental responses and duration of deprivation
to type and intensity of responses made to deprivation

	Brief	Long
High	Instrumental: Manipulation, Reasoning	Instrumental: Direct violence
Possibility of Instrumental Response **Low**	Equity: Mild generalized irritation	Equity: Indirect violence, scapegoating

Duration of aversive stimulation

stimulation must occur before the aggressive behavior becomes
instrumental. Prior to this time the behavior may be experienced as
annoying and therefore lead neither to goal activity nor intense
responses. Above this level the responses become direct and somewhat
more intense, until the duration produces disorganization. Long-
term exposure to aversive stimuli will cause the organism to become
goal-disoriented but maintain levels of intense, haphazard responses
until it becomes weakened.

SUMMARY

We have been concerned with the relationship of external,
individual, or environmental stimuli, and the aggressive behavior of
animals. Individual aversive stimuli impinge directly on the organism, whereas environmental stimuli are mediated by the physical or
social environment. Individual aversive stimuli, such as pain and
various types of deprivations, were shown to be directly related to

aggression. Environmental aversive stimuli producing aggression include monotony, population density, stress, power and hierarchal relations, and social isolation.

We discussed the question of whether aggression is learned or reactive in nature. Toward the lower end of the phylogenetic scale (e.g., insects), the role of reactive aggression is of greater importance. As we move up the scale, behavior becomes more plastic and the role of learning takes on increased importance. However, we have hypothesized that *both* external and internal stimuli play some role in the aggressive behavior of *all* organisms.

Does aggression occur because it reduces some drive or because it enables the organism to avoid pain and achieve pleasure? Drive reduction cannot explain the whole story, and the hedonistic principle is more parsimonious. Nevertheless, both factors undoubtedly play a role in most organisms.

We concluded with a discussion of two types of aggressive responses which are made as a function of two variables: (1) the relative possibility of making instrumental responses aimed at removing some goal blockage, and (2) the duration of the aversive stimulation. The model makes it possible to make predictions concerning the type of response (instrumental or equity), and the relative intensity of the response.

This chapter focused on the relationship between external aversive stimuli and aggression. We turn now to a consideration of internal stimuli and aggressive behavior.

2.
Internal Stimuli and Controls of Hostile Behavior

Control of aggressive behavior cannot be ignored by a society concerned about the welfare of a majority of its citizens. However, some difficult questions must be answered. For example: Do we have the right to perform brain surgery on extremely violent criminals? Or is it a lesser evil to risk that they may commit violent crimes? Which is the lesser evil, to castrate a repeated sexual offender or to have him spend large portions of his life behind bars?

A man's body is his property; and, based on the ethics of our civilization, it should be under his total control. Yet, by placing a person in prison, we place limits on this freedom. Is this condition fundamentally different from placing limits by means of surgery? Is prison more humane than surgery? As we consider the findings of experimental research, we may ponder these questions.

Any social policy used for the advantage of society could also as easily be turned around and used against society. Aldous Huxley (Andrews and Karlins, 1971) noted that all past revolutions were "trivial by comparison with the psychological revolution toward which we are rapidly moving. That will really be a revolution. When it's over, the human race will give no further trouble" (p. 1). Andrews and Karlins speak of the brave new behavior controls as the final revolution.

Not by any means is brain experimentation done solely on animals. The human brain is being probed extensively using electrical stimulation and refined surgical techniques. The moral dilemma of this final revolution is discussed toward the end of the chapter.

FACILITATING AGGRESSION

Looking inside the organism, we know there are certain factors which can appropriately be named as facilitators of aggression. From experiments, we know, for example, if certain brain structures were not present, aggression would not occur. In several areas (such as the relationship of genes to aggression), we have only begun to scratch the surface. Internal aggression facilitators are one variable in the complex formula causing aggression in man and animals.

Genetic factors. Genetic factors may predispose some people more than others to hostility. Genes determine the structure and the specific function of organs. Thus the influence of genes on aggression is revealed through the function of brain centers and hormones. Karli (1961) concluded from his study that there appeared to be a genetic basis for the aggression trait. Further evidence is found in a study by Lagerspetz (1961), who showed there were significant differences in aggressiveness and non-aggressiveness for animals who had been selectively bred for these traits. These differences were evident as early as the second and third generation of selective breeding.

Brain facilitators. The brain has an important function to play in all behavior, including aggression. Anatomists have localized several areas in the brain which have specific functions for specific behaviors. There are areas in the brain which facilitate aggression and without which aggressive response cannot occur.

In recent years, research has focused on locating the specific areas of the brain which may facilitate or inhibit aggressive responses. The functional relationship between these brain centers and aggression is chiefly found in their mediating of incoming stimuli. Karli and Vergnes (1963) carried out a series of lesions in the forebrain of rats and concluded that the amygdaloid complex facilitates aggression. The amygdaloid complex is in the allocortex. In an evolutionary sense, this is the older section of the cerebral cortex.

The hypothalamus is in the diencephalon; it primarily controls autonomic functions. Roberts and Keiss (1964) found stimulation of the hypothalamus induced normally non-aggressive cats to make predatory attacks on rats. They concluded the hypothalamus controlled both motivational and cue properties important to predatory attack. Levison and Flynn (1965) also observed attack behavior in cats during hypothalamic stimulation. There are areas within the hypothalamus whose primary function is the mediation of aggression. Roberts, Steinberg, and Means (1967), who mapped some of these areas, found electrical stimulation of these special zones in the opossum caused biting attacks. Ellison and Flynn (1968) showed that cutting parts of the hypothalamus affected aggressive behavior. We can see that the hypothalamus has important functions concerning aggression.

Experiments with electrodes. Delgado (1963, 1967) has used stereotaxically implanted electrodes to evoke aggressive behavior. This methodology opens up a powerful new approach in the study of the brain. The possibility of behavior control by means of brain implants is outlined in his book *Physical Control of the Mind* (1969). His accomplishments include staging a bullfight where the matador (Delgado) stopped the bull dead in his tracks by the mere touch of a button transmitting signals to implanted electrodes in the bull's head. Normally loving mother monkeys stimulated in this way violently attacked their offspring.

Delgado has also experimented with humans, producing some extraordinary behavior by means of brain stimulation. He has brought about uncontrollable motor reactions, fear that a "horrible disaster" was about to occur, sexual excitement, and even sex role reversals. In one case, assaultive behavior was elicited in a young female with a history of uncontrollable rage. This brain-stimulated rage was similar to those she had experienced spontaneously. Heath (1963) has found both pleasure and pain centers in man. Penfield (1959) stimulated areas of the cerebral cortex, enabling his patients to recall moments from their pasts. Evidently the possibility of behavior control by means of brain implants is as real for man as it is for animals.

Chemicals and hormones. We are living in a psychedelic age which has witnessed an explosion of mind-altering drugs on and off the market. The current generation has grown up experimenting with drugs. LSD, a hallucinogenic drug, has created sensations, producing nightmares for some and ecstatic experiences bordering on the religious for others. Many have read of the exploits and problems of former Harvard professor Timothy Leary who created a cult of drug worship. LSD, however, affects the metabolism of the brain in unpredictable ways, and people experimenting with it may be "strung out" for life. Drugs and hormones are capable of drastically altering behavior.

Hormones are chemical agents of genes; ingestion of such substances can drastically change behavior. Male rats have been known to engage in nest building when injected with female hormones, and the amount of sex hormones has been related to aggression (Levine and Conner, 1969).

Unfortunately, knowledge of the relationship of chemicals and hormones to aggression is limited; but we do have a few leads. McDonald and Heimstra (1964) found that LSD-25 increased the number of attacks made by otherwise submissive fish on other fish. Although the widely known effects of alcohol are influenced by many social factors (e.g., social status or sex roles may inhibit a person), alcohol consumption often leads to aggression.

Several explanations can be offered to account for the relationship between alcohol and aggression. Alcohol may be causing a depression of cerebral cortex activities (demonstrated as a lack of inhibition) releasing the more primitive functions of the old brain (food, sex, and aggressive behavior). In addition to this physiological explanation, and directly related to it, we may also offer some psychological explanations. Alcohol interferes with judgment, and the consequences of an action may not be properly evaluated. The social-psychological cause of aggression in the alcoholic or heavy-drinking person could also be thought of as the need for power. He may use alcohol to help fantasize himself as having status he has found difficult or impossible to obtain in real life. Corresponding with these fantasies is an increased sensitivity to insults. A feeling of power coupled with a loss of judgment and a paranoid sensitivity to insults is a formula which may easily lead to aggression. Many violent crimes have occurred under the influence of alcohol. However, we should hasten to note there are great individual variations in the effect of alcohol on behavior.

Indirect evidence of hormonal control may be found in a study by Bronson (1964), which showed that aggressive interactions depend upon the season. We know that the various sex related hormones fluctuate with seasons of the year. Were there no hormonal controls, we would expect aggressive interactions to be approximately constant all year.

REDUCTION OF AGGRESSION

One major reason to study the relationship between internal stimuli and aggression is the hope that such research may lead to an understanding of factors which may reduce or control aggression. Such control factors span the scope from brain inhibitors and displacement of energy to hormones and genetic surgery. These controls could herald a new world of sanity — or perhaps the Big Brother of 1984 will become a reality.

Electrodes. Brain stimulation is an exciting and challenging field which offers new explanations for many old riddles. Andrews and Karlins (1971) have reviewed the accomplishments of brain stimulation research. They discuss a number of human psychological characteristics which have been modified or reversed. Depending upon the area stimulated, a person may become more docile or savage, more alert or lethargic, more dominant or submissive. This technology can also be used to control extreme aggressiveness.

We have only seen the beginning of this research. It is not too farfetched to predict that, within a few decades and at the discretion of social policy, the use of such brain implants may be common in the control of hostility. Comparative physiology indicates the more primitive brain structures controlling emotional behavior are the same in man and animals. Since extensive research on animals has shown the effectiveness of brain stimulation in controlling emotional behavior we may assume that similar control is possible in man.

The work on brain mechanisms facilitating aggression logically leads to the possibility that there are specific brain areas which inhibit aggression. Several researchers (Bard and Mountcastle, 1964) have established that dogs or cats who have the cortex (a brain center the function of which is to inhibit aggression) surgically removed display behavior patterns best described as rage. Hostility is expressed with less provocation in chronically decorticate animals than in normal animals. Decorticate animals display intense rage reactions to stimuli which would seem insignificant: cats went into violent fits when lifted off the floor, and a dog became enraged by the mere presence of a fly on its nose.

The usual explanation for this behavior is that decortication leads to hyperexcitability. The class of stimuli which elicit rage is broader, the intensity of the stimuli necessary to bring forth the rage reaction is lower. Thus, the cerebral cortex must serve as an inhibitor for preventing dysfunctional reactions (e.g., inhibiting aggression against inappropriate targets at inappropriate times). If the cortex serves this inhibitory function and is a relatively recent evolutionary development, at one point in time these low threshold rage reactions must have been common — truly a dog-eat-dog world.

Delgado (1963) studied a monkey who was dominant in his social hierarchy. He found that stimulating the caudate nucleus of the brain inhibited the monkey's aggressive behavior. Interfering with the functioning of areas which elicit aggression (e.g., the hypothalamus) may also reduce the probability of its occurrence (Ropartz, 1968). Affecting the brain centers by administering reserpine and phenothiazine or meprobamate may suppress fighting behavior (Tedeschi, Tedeschi, Mucha, Cook, Mattis, and Fellows, 1959). These results may be attributed either to the interference with the perception of relevant aggression cues or to the interference with the motor centers which facilitate aggressive behavior.

Displacing energy. Diverting some of the organism's energy would reduce the amount left over for aggressive behavior. Indirect evidence may be cited from the Dilger (1960) experiment with redpolls which showed that, during the reproductive season, females became dominant over males. The Ono and Uematsu (1958) study demonstrated fight behavior among fish decreased with an increase in sexual behavior. Conversely, Lagerspetz and Hautojarvi (1967) showed previous aggressive behavior tended to decrease sexual behavior of inexperienced male mice toward females in heat.

Other factors may also divert energy. For example, Komai and Guhl (1960) found a relationship of egg production, tameness, and feeding to decreased aggressive behavior in the cod, although aggression was renewed with increased vigor later.

Hormones and chemicals. Levine and Conner (1969) have demonstrated the amount of aggression exhibited by animals is related to the amount of sex hormones in the blood stream. Hormones and drugs are powerful controls of behavior. Hormone injections have the ability to moderate many basic drives, including hunger and thirst. Will it be possible to control aggression by hormone injections?

Andrews and Karlins (1971, p. 29) report a prediction that we will soon have an anti-aggression pill. This pill would reduce hostility by neutralizing the effect of sex hormones in certain cortical parts of the brain. The day may indeed not be far off when our knowledge of the brain and its metabolism will enable scientists to control or manipulate many types of behavior, including aggression.

If this seems far-fetched, then consider the events of the last couple of decades in the area of pharmacology. Disturbed and potentially violent people, who were formerly confined, are now administered tranquilizers, enabling them to live fairly normal social lives. In the space of about twenty years since the first tranquilizer (chlorpromazine) entered the market, tranquilizers have become common far beyond the mental hospitals.

Also, regardless of the positive or negative consequences of the use of LSD, the social problem it has created has diverted new research funds to investigate how LSD affects the metabolism of the brain. As this question unravels, we'll probably learn a great deal about the control of human behavior. Perhaps within a few years tranquilizers may be replaced with a variety of pills which affect specific psychological functions. The anti-aggression pill may be as common for hyperaggressive people as "the pill" is as a birth control technique today.

Genetic surgery. Using these powerful techniques indeed makes total control of the mind a real possibility in the not-too-distant future. Is it also possible to control future generations and thereby permanently change the human psychology and culture? The answer, based on recent scientific advances, is affirmative. It is not only possible, but also likely, that "genetic surgery" will be carried out, especially in the case of pathological hereditary diseases.

Genetic surgery has become possible by the discovery of DNA, the basic chemical code of the genes. In addition, scientists have isolated and obtained pictorial records of the single gene, making it possible to alter its composition. Muller (1965) reports that research-ers have already succeeded in transferring chromosomes in mammal-ian cells. Another possibility in altering the gene is to let viruses and bacteria invade the gene and destroy certain parts, without destroying others or the cell as a whole. Once genetic surgery becomes feasible, it is almost unlimited what can be achieved in the way of controlling the human organism. We could create pretty much the "ideal" human being: happy, content, and intelligent — or perhaps a programed robot.

The idea of genetic intervention is nothing new. All kinds of utopian philosophers, including Plato and Thomas More, have advocated selective breeding. The technique of selective breeding has advanced to a considerable extent by the innovation of techniques of freezing spermatozoa and the establishment of frozen sperm banks. Parents of tomorrow could select the qualities they desire in a child, order these characteristics from the sperm bank, and accomplish pregnancy by means of artificial insemination. Conversely society could also order these characteristics for all human beings. While the aforementioned techniques have been described as general behavior controls, they may be applied specifically to the control of interper-sonal aggression (i.e., the aggression which occurs between people in dyads and other small groups).

THE MORAL QUESTION OF BEHAVIOR CONTROL

At the very root of human civilization is the notion of freedom. This even includes the freedom to err; but does it include the freedom to commit evil? Thus, behavior control has aroused controversy among those concerned with maximizing the human potential and those concerned with minimizing crime and violence. A number of arguments, both pro and con, could be raised regarding behavior control. One could argue that all men are subject to psychological laws and that man's behavior is determined often in haphazard and arbitrary ways. However, the evil resulting from this is minor in comparison to the hazards to freedom if such control is exercised on a

SOCIAL COST AND BEHAVIOR CONTROL

The social cost concept plays a small role with respect to the variables considered in this chapter. However, the objective pressure from significant others in the organism's environment will, to some extent, moderate both the facilitation and reduction of aggression. Eventually the moral question of behavior control will be determined by the prevalent social norms. Whether behavior control becomes public policy or is only used in individual therapy is dependent upon the social norms supporting or opposing these alternatives. The norms or values of society in turn receive their motivating power from social cost. Only if the norms have strong approval or sanctions from significant others will they effect behavior.

mass, society-wide basis. If behavior control is elevated to the status of social policy, is there a potential that behavior control may become a form of elite dictatorship? Could this happen? Indeed it could! Man is uniquely dependent upon social approval for his behavior and is, as Fromm (1941) states, trying to escape from the responsibilities of freedom.

The governments of most countries, including the United States, tend toward authoritarianism, characterized by the willingness of the people to submit to authority — the willingness to let "the experts" (those in power) make decisions. Is the decision to implement behavior controls on a nation-wide basis any different from other educational programs? Is the diversity of parliamentary democracy a bulwark against such a policy? The decision is a political decision; and we all need to keep in mind how readily public opinion is swayed on almost any issue, as long as the appeal is backed by appropriate sources of status and power.

However, control is not necessarily evil, and man is controlled by laws of which he is often unaware. Why not decide what we as humans want to be and, having made that decision, implement the behavior controls which will enable us to reach these goals? Controls are not good or evil. Whether they become good or evil depends on their relationship to moral laws. Behavior controls do not involve an evaluation of free will versus determinism. For the great masses of people, there is no such thing as free will, since their behavior is rigidly controlled by various motivators. The question is, can we trust any elite, regardless of how benevolent, to decide the ultimate and desirable form of human nature? Under the present social structures in the world, man will not decide his destiny — rather, elitist experts will. Is it not best to work to establish a social structure where the great mass of people are not dependent upon elites? When such a society is created, it will make sense to evaluate behavior controls as a social policy.

Behavior controls used on an individual basis, however, are entirely appropriate in consultation with such individuals. Individuals who are dissatisfied with their behavior or individuals controlled by unhappy events of the past may benefit greatly from a program in behavior control. The individual dying from cancer will not object to surgical intervention which may save his life. Likewise a person who is mentally incapacitated would not object to behavior controls being applied which might enable him to live free to make decisions. Therapeutic behavior control does not threaten social freedom and, if applied properly, may advance individual freedom. It is not different in nature from physical therapy. If the human mind is ill or dysfunctional, should it not be treated with the best method possible?

To the argument that the great mass of people are alienated and dysfunctional, behavior control is not the answer. Rather let us take a critical look at the structure which causes such all-pervading unhappiness. Behavior control on a social basis fits in with the bureaucratic model, the fundamental goal of which is the smooth and unruffled maintenance of the status quo. Let us change social structure to fit human needs, not change human nature to fit bureaucratic structural requirements.

SUMMARY

This chapter surveyed the literature on the relationship of genetic, hormonal, and physiological factors to aggression. The first section of the chapter covered aggression facilitators. Although the evidence points to a larger role of genetic determination of behavior at the lower phylogenetic levels, man is not totally exempt. Certain areas of the brain, especially the allocortex and the hypothalamus, are important to facilitating aggression. Furthermore, research on the human brain shows that a host of complex behaviors can be elicited by electrical stimulation. Through research on chemicals and hormones, brain metabolism is being understood and a new means for eliciting behavior is being discovered.

Research on reduction of aggression in animals has shown that stimulation or interference with certain areas of the brain may inhibit aggression. The literature also suggests that aggression will be reduced if the organism's energy is diverted into other areas. Research on humans, as well as animals, has demonstrated powerful new physical behavior controls. Brain stimulation can produce a variety of behaviors, including dominance, alertness, and docility. In the future lies the possibility of aggression control by hormone administration and genetic surgery. Pharmacological research has taught us much about brain metabolism, and the day may not be far off when anti-aggression pills will be produced. Genetic surgery and selective breeding may also be used to control aggression as well as other types of behavior.

The final section of the chapter was concerned with the moral questions involved in behavior control. As envisioned in *1984* and *Brave New World,* behavior controls could be used as part of social policy. It is true that all people are subject to psychological laws and many individuals are exposed to capricious and arbitrary conditioning — both of which can result in unproductive and unhappy lives. Nevertheless, the structure of most societies prevents the intelligent participation of all citizens in helping to formulate what an ideal person is; and this question is too important to be left in the hands of an elite — regardless of how benevolent. Therefore, until high levels of awareness are achieved in a society (at which time behavior modification will probably not be needed), the various behavior controls are probably best administered on an individual basis as part of a therapeutic program.

II.
HUMAN AGGRESSION

In this section of the book we focus on the topics which are important to the understanding of human aggression. A great deal of the literature on aggression is mythological. A critique of aggression myths is primarily a critique of those theorists who emphasize instincts or the innate nature of human aggression. The literature shows the preponderant importance of learning and the corresponding less importance of innate factors in human aggressive behavior. In this section we systematically analyze the personality and social factors which lead to aggression.

Chapter 3 then, is a critique of traditional approaches to aggression, focusing on the mythological nature of instinct theory. The next logical consideration is the traditional frustration-aggression hypothesis covered in Chapter 4. The frustration-aggression approach has dominated, and continues to dominate, the thinking on human aggression. In Chapter 5 we look at the personality factors which are crucial to understanding hostility; and, in the process, we develop models of aggressive personality types. Next, we consider the human environment in Chapter 6. The importance of modeling successful aggression consumes a large part of this chapter. Also, we consider the relative importance of personality versus the situation. Can a nonaggressive person become aggressive in order to survive in an aggressive environment? The final chapter of this section outlines a two-factor theory of human aggression: Due credit is given to the innate nature of emotional-reactive aggression; learning, however, plays a primary role in the *type* of aggression, determined by social cost.

3.
Theories of Human Aggression—Myths and Models

From the beginning of recorded history, scholars, researchers, and laymen alike have been concerned about human aggression. Every man, woman, and child is affected by aggressive behavior; millions have died or are dying from the ultimate form of mass aggression — war. It is no wonder that a considerable amount of literature has been written about aggression. Various approaches to the study of aggression have been employed by scholars, depending upon discipline and theoretical orientation. Some writers have been concerned about aggression from an ethical or moral point of view, while others have tried to define the determinants of hostile behavior.

Theoretical approaches have ranged from instinct theories to elaborate models based on learning. Instinct theory makes claims for the innate nature of aggression. Drive theory proposes a motivational analysis, which emphasizes learning, the internal stimulus, and energy properties which impel an individual to be aggressive. Although aggression theories have generated much supporting research, they have often overlooked cognitive factors which are important at the human level of behavior. Instinct and drive theories do not account for such factors as expected reward or punishment derived from a particular interaction. Behavioristic theories disregard the internalized values of an individual which help define the limits of behavior. Yet at the human level, such cognitive-emotional factors are very important and may override other factors which motivate hostile behavior.

Myths may be defined as imaginary and fictitious conceptualizations which are spoken of as if they were real. Historically these fictions have filled important needs for security in explaining natural phenomena not otherwise understood. Greek myths, among others, sought to define man's existence, the origins of life, and many other questions with which humanity has struggled since time immemorial. Myths are cognitively circular in the sense that they can be neither proved nor disproved. What cannot be scientifically measured cannot be tested empirically and must, therefore, depend on internal criteria for validity and must be accepted on faith.

A scientific model, on the other hand, is based on testable hypotheses. Models may take the form of either inductive or deductive theories. There are no pure inductive or deductive systems, since all theories must of necessity contain elements of both. It is more a matter of emphasis, that is, the approach to the data collection which sustains or develops the theory. Deductive reasoning proceeds from a known and general principle to the unknown or specific; inductive reasoning produces general or known principles on the basis of specific interrelated facts. Despite attempts to polarize these reasoning procedures as mutually exclusive or incompatible, they do in fact complement each other. In a dialectic fashion, science progresses from the general to the specific and from the specific to the general, despite futile chicken-or-the-egg controversies; both approaches are useful.

Science emphasizes the collection of theory relevant data. ("Theory relevant" means employing hypothesis testing procedures capable of replication.) Myths rely upon either grandiose armchair theorizing or subjective case histories which are very malleable to the expectations of the experimenter. It is well known that all people selectively filter for attention only those information elements considered relevant. This may be a hazard in all theory building, but it is a particularly faulting element in "theories" which depend on subjective data collection procedures to confirm the "known" propositions. These conceptualizations are not scientific theories, they are better classified as myths.

PSYCHOLOGICAL MYTHS: INSTINCT THEORIES OF AGGRESSION

Some theorists have relied on instincts as explanatory constructs in human aggressive behavior. As the following discussion shows,

instincts are not theoretical constructs but possess mainly mythological qualities when used to explain human aggression. In this section
we will consider not only those theorists who relied upon instincts in
their theories but also those (e.g., Neo-Freudians) who departed
somewhat from instinct positions, since they used similar subjective
data collection procedures.

Freud has undoubtedly made notable and lasting contributions
to psychological theory, but his instinct theory possesses only mythological properties. His early conception of aggression (1920, 1925)
viewed such behavior as a function of frustration. At that time Freud
thought that aggression was a primordial reaction against the
thwarting of either pleasure seeking or pain avoiding responses.
Later (1950) he formulated the problem in terms of instincts, of which
there are two basic types: the eros, or life instinct (i.e., sexual energy
broadly defined, expressed, or sublimated in socially approved ways)
and the thanatos, or death instinct. Man is impelled not only by
attempts to maintain life, but also by the search for quiescence. The
primary function of the death instinct is to bring man to an inanimate
state. Aggression is the manifestation of the thanatos, or destructive,
forces. Freud's hope of solution to aggression relied on human reason
to counterbalance the destructive energy.

Freud's death instinct notion, the desire to return to a state of
nothingness, is consistent with all instinct theories which suggest
that organisms seek to conserve energy and desire to move toward a
tensionless state. The stronger this death instinct, the more direct the
aggression. Freud's ideas suggest a hydraulic pump model; that is,
aggression built up gradually over time must eventually be released
in some fashion. If aggression is not turned outward, it is eventually
turned on oneself. Freud viewed instinctive behavior as a constantly
driving force, the energy of which must be expressed. Aggressive
behavior does not depend on the presence of an appropriate stimulus;
it is simply discharged, either directly or indirectly. McDougall's
(1906) conception of instincts differs from Freud's. McDougall also
viewed aggression as an instinct. However, whether or not aggressive
response is actually elicited depends on the presence of some appropriate stimulus.

Freud on inhibiting aggression. Freud (1959) made some suggestions
regarding the reduction of inter-group conflict. Since aggression is a

result of energy which must be expressed, it is useless to try to eliminate man's aggressive tendencies directly. Rather, he proposed to bring eros into play against the antagonistic forces (thanatos) by encouraging emotional ties between people. To prevent war, people should establish relations which are loving and promote common identifications. Whatever helps people to share common interests produces a community of feeling which is the best safeguard against war. While instincts are powerful, they may be modified. Cultural evolution dictates a progressive displacement of instinctive aims (sublimation, for instance) and a restriction of instinctive impulses.

Freud also made an elitist proposal for educating an upper stratum of man. He wanted the people in this elitist group to have independent minds and to refuse to be intimidated. The elite should direct the dependent masses and lead them to peace. Freud's ideal society would be some form of benevolent dictatorship, where people have subordinated their instinctual impulses to the dictatorship of reason. By means of such a community, Freud hoped to compensate for the lack of inhibitions against aggression which has characterized so much of man's history.

Criticism of Freud. Hopefully we will maintain our skepticism of benevolent dictatorships. Often such governments turn out to be less than benevolent and more concerned with maintaining the status quo. A ranked society is incapable of resolving conflict; although the power of the status quo forces may prevent conflict from becoming overt, lasting peace, that is, peace with social justice, is not possible in a ranked society, regardless of the benevolence of the dictatorship. The elimination of aggression and conflict must begin with the restructuring of societies and the elimination of social rank — the root cause of most conflict within and between nations. Freud's elitism would perpetuate social rank, the major cause of conflict.

Freud's theory has had world wide impact and, whether directly acknowledged or not, has affected much contemporary research. However, his propositions are not scientifically provable and suffer from serious data collection problems (Hall and Lindzey, 1970, p. 69). His contribution to the problem of nominalism in psychology cannot be overestimated. Nominalism is the terminal solution which names some internal element, usually an instinct, in place of the search for predictors of behavior. This limits research to the confirmation of the instinct. Confirmation, however, is only possible by questionable subjective interview procedures, which, since they are unique, cannot be duplicated. The sole task of the investigator is to define the behavior and name it. Instinct theory as a form of nominalism obviously begs the question it seeks to answer.

The main criticism of psychoanalytic theory remains the vagueness and untestability of its concepts. As Cofer and Appley (1964) noted:

> Within science, the criticism [of psychoanalytic theory] has focused on the untestability of the many poorly defined analytic concepts and the limited evidence on which the system rests. Unfortunately for its acceptance as scientific theory, many of its practitioners and supporters, themselves largely untrained in the rigors of scientific evidence accumulation, defend their positions either by rejecting the very notion of and need for independent testing, or by presenting voluminous subjective case records as "proof" of their points of view. (P. 655)

Neo-Freudian approaches to aggression. The psychoanalytic tradition has produced other prolific writers. Adler, an early follower of Freud, later deviated somewhat from orthodox psychoanalytic tradition. Ansbacher and Ansbacher (1956) discuss his early writings. Adler saw aggression as a drive. The drive was instrumental in achieving satisfaction of basic human needs. In his later writings, he renounced the drive conception but retained the idea that aggression has goal-oriented utility. At times, aggression is conscious, but it may also be an irrational reactive tendency. As conscious behavior the aggressive tendencies serve to overcome obstacles in the way of achieving everyday tasks. Adler took into account the importance of learning and emphasized the goal-oriented utility function of aggression.

Horney (1939, 1945) proposed that basic anxiety is the basis of all motivated behavior. Basic anxiety is the feeling a child has of being abandoned, isolated, and helpless to cope with a potentially hostile world. The response to basic anxiety takes one of three forms: The child may learn to move *toward* people, that is, to be open and acceptant of communication; to move *against* people and show hostile behavior; or to move *away* from people by avoiding potential conflict altogether. For Horney, the genesis of aggression lies in the rejection of the child. Rejection may result in sadism, the experience of pleasure achieved by inflicting pain on others, which in turn is derived from a sense of hopelessness and futility. She emphasizes the importance of early child-rearing procedures and, in particular, the critical importance of warm and protective parents. Parents may aid the child in coping with basic anxiety, thereby creating interaction patterns of moving toward people.

Adler and Horney both made thought-provoking contributions to psychoanalytic theory. In contrast to the Freudian view of aggression as innately determined, both Adler and Horney emphasize learning factors. Adler has drawn attention to the instrumental function of aggression, whereas Horney has pointed to the genesis in early child rearing procedures. However, these writers share the common difficulty of psychoanalysis; they depend on subjective data collection procedures or no data collection at all. Nevertheless, Adler and Horney, along with Freud, have had a heuristic effect on psychology.

Recent psychoanalytic contributions: Storr on aggression. Storr (1968) has followed traditional psychoanalytic concepts in formulating a theory of human aggression. He sums up the psychoanalytic approach by stating that the death instinct is the personification of the second law of thermodynamics (all living organisms return to an inanimate state). Aggression is an expression of the death instinct, "an inborn, automatic possibility which is easily triggered" (p. 14). In support of this proposition, he points to a physiological mechanism, the hypothalamus, which, when stimulated, "gives rise to both subjective feelings of anger, and also to physical changes which prepare the body for fighting" (p. 11).

According to Storr, the aggressive drive serves a biological function in terms of preserving the individual and the species. He points to three specific functions. Aggression is necessary under conditions of competition; only those with strong aggressive drives will survive. Aggression provides for the sexual selection of the strongest males, helping to perpetuate the species. Aggression ensures peace and order by means of a hierarchy of dominance; without such a hierarchy intra-species conflict would be constant. Storr also suggests that aggression is an essential element in the psychology of the child. Without this drive it would be impossible for the child to break the ties of dependency and strike out on its own. Pathological aggressiveness characterizes individuals who have developed in such a way that they are unable to come to terms with their own aggressive drive. This leads to schizoid, paranoid, or psychopathic reactions.

In evaluating Storr's theory it must be observed that the presence of a physiological mechanism for aggression is no proof of its innate nature. The triggering of this mechanism still depends upon some external stimulus, as noted by Scott (1958, p. 62). Secondly, the "survival of the fittest" world which Storr describes is a social artifact. Competitive attitudes and competitive social conditions are neither innate nor natural, but are the result of the particular economic organization of our society.

The policy implications of psychoanalytic theory are clearly fascistic. To establish peace and order by means of a hierarchy of dominance is wrong from the point of view of justice, and naive in historical terms. One needs only to observe the numerous rebellions under heavy odds undertaken by dominated people against those who dominate them. Finally, Storr appears to equate the term "aggression" with "active, independent strivings." Such strivings, learned in interaction with the environment, are surely important in overcoming dependency. Paradoxically, Storr's definition of aggression as active, independent striving appears to be in direct contradiction to the death instinct which is fundamental to Freud's aggression theory. The purpose of the death instinct is to return the organism to an inanimate stage. Aggression as strivings for survival reflects the eros and would appear to contradict the death instinct, which is the basis of psychoanalytic theory.

The ethologists on the evolution of behavior and aggression. In recent years the work of Lorenz (1966) has received wide attention. Lorenz points out the evolution of species-specific behavior patterns. In addition to the varying learned behavior patterns of a given species, the species also inherits unvarying motor patterns. Lorenz maintains that these unvarying motor patterns characterize a species as much as bodily structure. An example of a motor pattern is the scratching movements of dogs and birds. A dog scratches its jaw in the same manner as a bird preens its head feathers. Only with great difficulty can learning change or inhibit the behavior. Lorenz points out that it is easy for a bird to move its claw directly to the head, yet it will lower its wings (which lie folded out of the way) and reach its claw forward in front of the shoulders. In short, before a bird scratches, it reconstructs the spatial relationships of the limbs of its fourlegged ancestors. These inborn traits are rooted in the genetic inheritance of a species.

Lorenz reports on comparative hybridization studies. By studying the behavior traits of existing species and then mating these with compatible but different organisms, it is possible to observe the transmission and combination of traits in hybrid offspring. These behavior patterns, which distinguish species from each other, can be duplicated in the offspring. The studies have shown convincingly that not only physiological characteristics, but behavior patterns also, are inherited. Lorenz also maintains that aggression is inherited. Some species move through attack patterns which appear to be innate and unmodifiable through learning. Aggression is elicited upon the presentation of very specific cues. Most species have inherited inhibitions against aggression toward members of their own species. Man, however, is peculiar in lacking such inhibitions.

Lorenz suggests that the aggressive instinct is the force, or drive, necessary for survival or evolution. Were it not for the aggressive instinct, no one would protect territory against intrusion, and consequently the species would perish. Defending the young and selecting the strongest specimens for procreation are also functions of the aggressive instinct which are indispensable for survival. Instincts must find outlets; man, in particular, suffers from an insufficient discharge of his highly aggressive instincts. The basic instincts making man capable of love and hate developed at an early time, but the development of man's inhibitions against aggression lagged. For example, most species show inhibitions if faced with a potential victim who shows submission. However, human aggression, especially massive warfare, occurs at such a distance that the victims have no chance to model submissiveness — the victims are simply not seen. Man shows an incredible lack of aggression inhibitions.

Lorenz has made vital contributions to the study of animal behavior. The question which remains is how much of man's animal ancestry actually affects his behavior. Has man a genetic inheritance similar to that of the animals Lorenz studied? What is the evidence for the existence of this inheritance in man, and to what extent is it possible to generalize from animal to human behavior? Unfortunately these questions are not answered by Lorenz. Tinbergen (1968) suggests that the uncritical explanation of human behavior patterns by analogies to lower animals fails to recognize the distinctive differences between the species. In effect, Lorenz is making an error which is the reverse of anthropomorphizing animal behavior: he is animalizing human behavior. If there is one thing which characterizes human behavior, it is the variability and flexibility of man's actions. To a large extent Lorenz ignores these individual and group differences.

There are several common factors underlying aggression, including motivation, that is, the factors which impel an organism toward destructive behavior. Aggressive motivation is produced by the combined effects of internal factors and external cues. Of particular importance to human motivation are the factors defined by the situation in which an individual finds himself. Situational factors may facilitate or inhibit aggression. The particular importance of social motivators at the human level is overlooked by Lorenz.

MODELS OF HUMAN AGGRESSION:
THE IMPORTANCE OF LEARNING

The differences between Homo sapiens and other species are not discrete. To the extent that animals and human beings share the same internal and external environment, we may extrapolate from animal studies to predict human aggression. It is important to realize that behavior becomes more plastic and dependent on learning as we move up the phylogenetic scale and approach the primates. To predict human aggression on the basis of studying species whose behavior is largely a function of genetic internal releasers is a grievous error. Learning is of primary importance in human aggression.

Aggression in man and lower animals is characteristically different. The relationship of predator to prey cannot be called aggression. Such behavior is for food-gathering purposes. The aggressive behavior which occurs in the lower animals between members of the same species is mainly for the maintenance of territory or dominance.

Carthy and Ebling (1964) state that aggression for most animals is ritualized into displays of threat, submission, and appeasement. Most intra-species fighting stops short of serious damage because, in the course of evolutionary development, animals have learned to predict the outcome of fighting by means of threats and posturing.

Carthy and Ebling see in war much that is ritualistic. Propaganda and martial artifacts are indications of ritualistic attempts to deal with aggression. Yet, as they point out, the destructive outweighs the ritualistic in human warfare. Man is different from animals; he is an exception to the rule of ritual display which prevails in the animal kingdom. Human beings do not solve conflict by means of ritual display. Man also apparently has no built-in inhibitions. Fighting and warfare between humans seem only inhibited by social custom, especially by the sanction of authority. It is clear therefore, if we are to understand human aggression, we must focus on the human social environment and not extrapolate from animal behavior which is governed by fundamentally different laws.

The learning of aggression. The importance of the role of learning in aggression is emphasized by Scott (1958). His book focuses on the application of animal studies to human behavior and is concerned with aggression between individuals as a function of learning and frustration. He makes it clear that fighting is learned behavior based on the principle of reinforcement. Scott notes that defensive fighting can be stimulated by the pain of an attack, but aggression in the strict sense of an unprovoked attack can only be produced by training. Scott concludes that a happy and peaceful environment should automatically produce a child with strong habits of being peaceful (p. 22). Scott emphatically states that there is no such thing as an instinct for fighting. There is no need for fighting in either the aggressive or defensive sense apart from what happens in the external environment

(p. 62). The results of his work can be summarized in these principles: motivation for fighting is increased by success; frustration leads to aggression; and all so-called physiological causes can be traced to external stimulation.

The nature versus nurture question. The nurture of human aggression has largely been argued by instinct theorists from McDougall to Freud to the modern European school of ethology. They advocate essentially a hydraulic system that accounts for behavior by means of energy reserved for specific actions. As Maple and Matheson (1973) point out, "instinct is an inherited tendency to action of a specific kind, usually set off by a limited range of stimuli, and having definite survival or biological value in the struggle for existence" (p. 11). This energy is localized in the central nervous system and is released when the innate releasing mechanism (IRM), in the analogy of a lock, is opened by a specific releasing stimulus.

Perhaps the ultimate form of instinct theory is found in the proposition that aggression is the result of the carnivorous nature of man. The following section from Dart (1953) poetically describes this point of view:

> The blood-bespattered, slaughter-glutted archives of human history from the earliest Egyptian and Sumerian records to the most recent atrocities of the Second World War accord with early universal cannibalism, with animals and human sacrificial practices or their substitutes in formalized religions and with the world-wide scalping, headhunting, body-mutilating, and necrophilic practices of mankind in proclaiming this common bloodlust differentiator, this predaceous habit, this mark of Cain that separates man dietetically, from his anthropoidal relatives and allies him rather with the deadliest of carnivora. (P. 33)

In answer, Maple and Matheson point out that man's closest relatives, the apes, are true vegetarians. Ritual cannibalism, often based in desperate food environments, certainly does exist; however, there is not an iota of proof that this behavior is innately based. On the other hand, there is ample proof of the role of learning in human and animal aggression.

The amount of variance accounted for by genetic innate releasers in animals and humans. Learning is a factor in all organisms, and particularly in humans. Scott and Fredericson (1951, p. 240), in particular, note that the *acquisition* of animal fighting behavior depends on hormonal factors, but the *habit* of fighting depends on previous learning. Genetic aggressive motor patterns may be a part of some organisms' behavior repertory, but whether they are expressed depends on learning. Instinct theory, however, assumes the opposite: aggression is universal, unlearned behavior. This is a most difficult proposition to prove, and the literature as a whole tends to support the overwhelming importance of learning factors in human aggression. One small piece of evidence is that attack behavior in humans occurs no earlier than talking and walking; this supports the assumption that aggression must be learned.

Lorenz's suggestion explaining why aggression occurs frequently in man is a form of a "cultural lag" proposition. Man's rapid technological achievements have out-paced the slowly evolving innate inhibitions. Like other hydraulic myths, Lorenz suggests man must have an outlet, that is man must be provided with opportunities for discharge of aggressive energy through sports and other competitive activities. The assumption is that lower levels of aggression will occur, since presumably lower levels of energy will remain after such discharge. This instinct explanation overlooks the possibility that competitive activities may in fact strengthen a habit of aggression. Originally aggression may have been instrumental in trying to remove obstacles. Suppose the behavior is then rewarded by removing the obstacles — a habit may have been created. Thus, competition, if successful, may strengthen rather than weaken, a habit.

This is not an argument to disregard physiological considerations in the study of aggression. However, such factors must be put in proper perspective as to their relative importance. At lower levels of phylogenetic development, genetic controls account for the largest proportion of behavior; but such genetic controls are of less importance for primates and, especially, humans. Here the laws of learning achieve primary importance, in particular as applied to motivation. As Hardy (1964) noted, for primates, particularly for humans, there is an increasing relaxation of genetic and endocrine controls. Substituted in their place we find greater plasticity of behavior and an increasing importance of the role of learning and of emotional processes as regulators of conduct. This relationship is shown in Figure 3.1.

Figure 3.1

The striped portions reflect the theoretical amount of
behavior attributed to genetic innate releasers.
The unmarked portions reflect the role of learning
and plasticity in the organism.

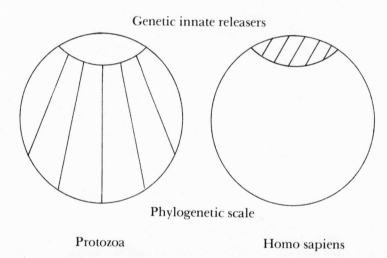

Genetic innate releasers

Phylogenetic scale

Protozoa   Homo sapiens

To develop a theory of human aggression dependent upon analogies to lower animals may be grossly misleading. No one has, as yet, made a strong case for an instinctive position at the human level which could survive close scientific scrutiny. Such positions are based either on subjective data collection procedures or on vague analogies between animals and human behavior. It is very tempting to "solve" the problem in such global terms, but the evidence shows that the complexity of behavior increases as one moves up the phylogenetic scale. This logically implies the need to approach the study of aggression by taking into account multiple variables, whereas instinct theory seeks to reduce the issue to the localization and naming of an instinct.

Another problem of instinct theories concerns solutions to destructive behavior. Instinct theories, which posit unchanging and unmodifiable internal releasers, leave the area of conflict resolution without a place to go. Since it is impossible, or extremely difficult, to modify instincts, the result and sense of futility finds its ultimate expression in the notion of "letting nature run its course." Statements, such as "There have always been wars, and there will always be wars" echo the futility of global, innate ideas. By contrast, what is learned *can* be unlearned. If we can accept the plasticity of human behavior, and especially its subordination to the many social factors affecting learning and behavior, the task is obvious, though complex. To control aggression, we must define the antecedent conditions and contemporary inhibitors. The complexity of these conditions and inhibitors depends on the phylogenetic level of the organism.

Social learning theories. A number of researchers have been interested in the learning parameters of hostile behavior. Social learning theorists characteristically show less concern for the antecedents of aggression and are more involved with understanding the reinforcement factors in the environment which reward aggressive responses, once made. Aggression may be learned as a function of frustration. The frustration-aggression relationship will be discussed in Chapter 4.

The individual may learn aggressive behavior from parents and other significant others. Parents may exhibit behavior models for children to follow and, in addition, may reward or punish aggression. Aggressive behavior may, therefore, be acquired directly through the reinforcement contingencies which parents apply to their childrens' behavior. Some researchers (Davis, 1943; Davis and Havighurst, 1947) have shown that lower-class parents encourage and reward aggression to a greater extent than middle-class parents, and a higher degree of aggressiveness was found among children of the lower classes. While child-rearing procedures have changed since the 1940s, the results do show the importance of parental influence.

SOCIAL COST AND THEORIES OF HUMAN AGGRESSION

Any theory of human aggression must first and foremost take into account the significant variables which motivate human behavior. In the past, the emphasis has been on internal releasers of various kinds. As we have indicated in this chapter, instinct formulations of human aggression are largely myths with little scientific backing. A scientific model on the other hand requires testable hypotheses. Social cost as an inhibitor and facilitator of human aggression is a testable variable and is, therefore, a possible component in model building. Whether it remains a part of a model of human aggression depends on the scientific evidence and the predictive, generic, heuristic, and parsimonious nature of this theoretical construct. The succeeding chapters will be addressed to this question. However, one thing is quite certain at this point; aggression, apart from predator activity, is largely a learned phenomenon. Therefore, the parameters of learning, whether by imitation or reward, take on special importance. For human beings, a person's significant others (whether parents, teachers, or powerful leaders) play a primary role in the learning process. Social cost motivation is essentially an optimistic view; after all, what has been learned can also be unlearned. Human aggression can be moderated and eliminated by knowing the parameters of social cost.

Since Wordsworth and Freud, the impact of child socialization on aggression has been recognized by layman and researcher alike (see Larsen and Schwendiman, 1968). Early studies (Dollard, Doob, Miller, Mowrer, and Sears, 1930) demonstrated that the intensity of aggression training (punitiveness) is related to the amount of frustration experienced and hence to aggression. Whiting and Child (1953) found cross-cultural evidence for a relationship between severity of aggression training and projected aggression. However, Bandura and Walters (1959) noted that both high permissiveness and severe aggression training produced aggressive behavior. The reason is clear: parents perform the dual function of acting as a model for aggressive behavior and rewarding such behavior. Thus Radke's (1946) study indicates that children prescribe for others the same type and intensity of punishment which they receive from their parents.

The research clearly suggests that severe punitiveness by the parents is a potent variable in determining frustration and aggressive behavior. Authoritarian personalities display symptoms thought to have been derived from punitive child-rearing experiences. Larsen and Schwendiman (1970) demonstrated moderately strong relationships between the perceived severity of parental aggression training and dogmatic and chauvinistic attitudes. This indicates that such child-rearing procedures may affect even broader social attitudes and lead to closed mindedness and rejection of potential out-groups. In brief, the parents may model and reinforce hostility, and they may also present an aggressive model to the child by extreme punitiveness. The modeling of aggression will be discussed further in Chapter 5.

Learned aggression also may be reflected in the personality of the individual. Aggression as a personality construct will be discussed in Chapter 6. Chapter 7 ends the section on human aggression with a discussion of two basic types of aggression.

SUMMARY

This chapter presented a critical overview of the major mythological theoretical concepts concerning aggression from Freud to the present. Freud and those who followed him in the psychoanalytic traditions undoubtedly made signal contributions to psychological knowledge. However, all of the proposed psychoanalytic concepts suffer from lack of empirical validation. Freud moved from considering aggression as a function of frustration to seeing the thanatos (death instinct) as chiefly responsible.

To demonstrate an instinct, one must indicate its universality in the population specified; this Freud and other instinct theorists have failed to do. Horney sees anxiety as the chief motivation of all things human. How the helplessness of the child is handled determines whether the child moves toward, against, or away from people. Adler rejects any instinct notion and views aggression as partly conscious and partly reactive and irrational. Storr builds his theory of aggression on traditional psychoanalytic concepts. Ethologists like Lorenz maintain that aggression is innate and species-specific behavior.

There is little proof that instincts have an extensive influence at the human level. On the contrary, as Hardy points out, human behavior is characterized by plasticity, flexibility, and complexity. This does not exclude a genetic basis for human behavior, but such a role is probably minor and modifiable by experience. The important point is that human aggression and animal aggression are different. Genetic factors are of greater importance in the lower animals than in man, for whom learning and the social environment are the significant variables.

4.
Frustration and Aggression

A learning model for human aggression is found in the famous frustration-aggression hypothesis. The classic work of the Yale school (Dollard, Doob, Miller, Mowrer, and Sears, 1939) presents the most systematic approach to the study of the frustration-aggression relationship. Their approach became the basis for treatment of the hypothesis in other writings, for example, Berkowitz (1962). Man has basic needs, such as hunger, which will, if unsatiated, produce goal-oriented behavior aimed at satisfying them. This behavior is described by Dollard et al. as "an instigated goal response," and frustration is "interference with this response at its proper time in the behavior sequence" (p. 7). The original hypothesis stated frustration always leads to aggression. As it became clear that aggression is one of several responses which may be made to frustration the hypothesis was modified. In this chapter, the accumulated evidence on the frustration-aggression hypothesis will be discussed. First, let us examine some propositions derived from the hypothesis.

PROPOSITIONS DERIVED FROM THE FRUSTRATION-AGGRESSION HYPOTHESIS

The Yale school and a number of other researchers developed a considerable body of literature both supportive and critical of the frustration-aggression hypothesis. In the course of these investigations, the theory was refined and research branched out in several directions. In this section, we shall examine the evidence pertaining to three areas of research built on the work of Dollard. First the factors which relate to the strength of a predisposition to aggress are reviewed. Then variables which may intervene between frustration and aggression are discussed. Finally, the evidence for and against catharsis, the idea that the expression of aggressive energy will lower the instigation of aggression, is discussed.

Strength of instigation to aggression. Dollard suggested the strength of the instigation to aggression is determined by three principles. First, the strength is a direct function of the strength of the frustrated response. Second, aggression is a function of the degree of frustration. Finally, repeated frustrations tend to summate and lead to higher levels of aggression. The evidence for and against these propositions has led to some modifications, especially in employing expectancies of reward (see Berkowitz, 1962). These modifications were necessary due to an inadequate coverage of the importance of goal expectancies. We may add to this the equally critical modifier: the expectancies of punishment and reward derived from social interaction — the degree of social cost. Inhibition may be postulated to be a direct function of the anticipated social cost. The more severe the cost, the more inhibited the aggressive response.

SOCIAL COST AND AGGRESSION INHIBITION

Social cost affects the strength of the instigation to aggression primarily as an inhibitor of aggression responses. As such, social cost is an intervening variable between the frustrating stimulus and the response. Social cost is a more or less conscious evaluator of alternative courses of action. Social cost also determines the impact of frustration on the individual. Individuals high in approval-seeking are more willing to tolerate frustration and tend to inhibit direct aggressive responses. Frustration of approval-seeking goals tends to produce more sad than angry responses in high approval-seeking individuals. The avoidance of direct aggression may also influence other responses. High approval-seeking persons are more apt to reject minorities and out-groups. After basic survival needs are met, social approval is a primary incentive for most people. Thus, social cost is both a general social motivator of the vast majority of mankind and also a personality variable in the sense that there are individual differences in the need for approval.

Intervening variables. Berkowitz (1962) suggests there are two classes of variables intervening between the objective situation and the person's aggressive reaction. One element is the emotion of anger. This emotion underlies the aggressive energy and is regarded as the motivational construct serving to heighten the likelihood of aggression. Anger is conceived as an inborn reaction to goal blockage. The second factor is the interpretation of the situation. Prior learning may influence how a given situation is perceived and, therefore, define the appropriateness of behavior. A person who has achieved positive incentives as a result of aggression will behave very differently from a person who, for various reasons, has generally received punishment. Since so much aggression is instrumental or goal oriented, rather than injury seeking, the utility of actions takes on importance, specifically in terms of the social cost to the individual. The expected social cost of the aggressive interaction is one important intervening variable.

Catharsis. A substitute response, for example masochism or scapegoating, may to some extent reduce the strength of the aggressive response, as does the direct aggressive act. This weakening of the strength to instigation is called catharsis. Catharsis may occur with either direct or indirect responses. Since aggression following frustration must find some means of expression (note analogy to Freudian and allied instinct conceptions), the solution to violence is to divert these responses into socially acceptable areas. In other words, we must try to sublimate (direct behavior in socially approved ways) the cathartic activities of the individual.

The basic idea of catharsis is that aggressive energy is consumed as a result of the aggressive act; consequently, less energy is available and the aggressive drive should be lessened. The experimental literature is, at best, ambiguous. Feshback (1955), Thibaut (1950), and Thibaut and Coules (1952) showed less aggression following catharsis; but the Kenney (1953) and DeCharms and Wilkins (1963) studies showed aggression increased following catharsis. Expressing aggression may not only release energy, but may, if rewarded, maintain and increase the aggressive habit.

Allied with the idea of catharsis is the notion of displacement. Displaced aggression is the phenomenon of focusing on a target different from the instigator of frustration. Reasons for displacement include fear of punishment following the aggressive act. Displacement is more likely if threat of punishment is strong. Displacement may be based on perceptual similarity; that is, the more similar the substitute target is to the original target, the more likely it is to be selected as a target for aggression. The basic idea is that displacement will result in a draining off of energy, lowering the aggressive drive. However, as the above research indicates, the evidence is not clear — there is no one-to-one relationship between displacement and lowered energy; any cathartic activity may lead to stronger habits of aggression if rewarded.

FRUSTRATION OF NEEDS

Frustration means the interference, thwarting, or obstruction of some goal response. Dollard et al. suggested that the stronger the instigated goal response (drive or need) which is frustrated, the more intense the aggression. This idea can also be expressed in terms of a hierarchy of needs. The incentive value of the goal is directly related to this need system. The more intense the need, the greater the incentive value of the goal. Needs differ somewhat from person to person, but there is probably a hierarchy common to most members of a society. As the needs of each level of the hierarchy are met, the incentive value of the goals at the next higher level is invoked. Maslow. (1954) suggested such a hierarchy of needs. In order of descending potency they are: physiological needs, safety needs, belonging and love needs, esteem needs, and a need for self-actualization.

If a person's physical survival is endangered, all other needs are subordinate to this need. In societies where the struggle for physical survival is important, aggression is more easily elicited by frustrating this need. However, in societies where physiological and safety needs are met, the primary incentive goal becomes social approval (belongingness and esteem). Frustration of approval needs may produce both sadness and aggression (Larsen, 1974). At the peak of the need structure is self-actualization. According to Maslow, it is not possible to achieve self-actualization unless all other needs are met also. There is great confusion and ambiguity in the term "self-actualization."

Part of its meaning must lie in the transcendence of the individual's dependence on social approval. It is therefore a paradox to say that an individual must have social approval needs satisfied before he can be independent of them. Most modern societies suffer from alienation, which in turn elicits the need for approval. In the frustration of these approval needs is found the basis of interpersonal and international hostility.

SOME EARLY EXPERIMENTS

Demonstrating frustration of physical needs, Dollard et al. interrupted the feeding of a five-month-old baby at various times prior to satiation. The more milk the baby had drunk, the longer it took for the baby to start crying. The duration between bottle removal and crying was taken as an index of the strength of frustration. The more the drive was satiated, the less intense the response which followed frustration.

Other classical studies on the frustration-aggression hypothesis include Barker, Dembo, and Levin's (1941) experiment. They led children to a playroom containing various attractive toys. One group was permitted only to look and not to play; another group was permitted to play with the toys. Later both groups were permitted to play. The frustrated group of children frequently smashed the toys and, in general, exhibited more destructive behavior than the non-frustrated group.

Miller and Bugelski (1948) frustrated a group of young men working in a camp. The participants were induced by the camp administrator to look forward to a big time in town. Instead they were forced to take a difficult test. A scale measuring attitudes toward Japanese and Mexicans was administered both before and after the frustration. The results showed greater prejudice toward Japanese and Mexicans after the frustration. This lends support to the displacement idea; anger which might have been directed toward the camp administrator was displaced to innocent targets.

Miller (1948, 1951) suggested that the closer an organism is to its goal, the stronger the tendency to approach the goal, and the more intense the frustration if failure occurs *(and* the more intense the aggression). Haner and Brown (1955) did an experiment with children in which the participants were promised prizes for pushing marbles through holes in a board within specified time limits. If they failed, they had to push a plunger and start over again. The strength of the plunger push increased with failure. Haner and Brown found that the closer their participants came to finishing before failing, the stronger the plunger push (aggression).

These studies demonstrate some of the basic parameters of the relationships between frustration and aggression. Frustrated people will displace anger away from the most logical target if that target is too threatening. The intensity of the experienced frustration depends on the intensity of the drive toward the goal, the extent to which the need is satisfied, and how close the approach was made to the goal prior to failure.

RECENT SUPPORT FOR THE FRUSTRATION-AGGRESSION HYPOTHESIS

Franus (1957) studied the effect of restraining the child in many activities. Restraints frequently led to anger as manifested in crying, hitting, etc. Frustrations summate over time and produce extremely violent behavior. Palmer (1960) investigated a group of male murderers and their nearest-age brothers. The results showed that the murderers scored higher than their brothers on various indexes of frustration. Gillespie (1962) investigated the potency of three antecedents of aggression: (1) frustration, (2) attack, and (3) frustration plus attack. The three conditions, ranked from most to least potent, are: attack, frustration-plus-attack, and frustration. Keep in mind that whether attack will result in counter-aggression depends on the potential threat of the attacker to the person attacked. If the attacker is very threatening, the aggression elicited may be displaced toward less threatening persons. Buss (1963) studied the effect of interference in winning money and in attaining a better grade. Both types of frustration produced aggression. These various studies all confirm that frustration leads to aggression in a variety of settings.

PARAMETERS OF FRUSTRATION

Broadly speaking, parameters of frustration are those factors which determine the impact frustration has on an individual. Type of frustration is one important factor; some frustrations touch central needs in the individual, others are more peripheral. Other parameters of frustration include individual susceptibility, the arbitrariness and expectation of frustration, membership in socio-economic groups, and social cost motivation.

Types of frustration. Frustrations are moderated by many dimensions, and only by understanding these can we improve our prediction of the relationship of frustration to aggression. Brown and Farber (1951) speak of four types of frustration: physical barriers, delays between the initiation and completion of a response sequence, omission or reduction of customary reward, and the eliciting of a response tendency incompatible with the ongoing one. Obviously it makes a difference what kinds of frustration a person encounters. Physical barriers can be circumvented in many cases, and delays can be tolerated. Omission or reduction of reward, however, represents a loss of some potential incentive. The eliciting of a response tendency incompatible with the ongoing one results in an internal conflict resolved by movement toward the stronger response tendency. However, in making a choice some other goal may be lost. The first two types of frustration deal more with delays, the latter two represent losses of some kind.

A somewhat similar dichotomy is offered by Rosenzweig's (1939) primary and secondary frustrations. A primary frustration refers to the frustration of an active need, whereas a secondary frustration involves obstructions in the path to a goal. Maslow (1941, 1943) developed a typology similar to Rosenzweig's. The individual is confronted with both deprivations (primary frustrations) and threats (potential frustrations of basic needs). All the above types tend to fall into two classes depending on whether the frustration is actual (occurring at the moment) or expected (involving some threat of obstruction or delay in goal achievement). It is difficult to postulate which type is experienced as more frustrating. Man's imagination often makes the expected seem more ominous than the actual. For other people it is easier to deal with actual losses than with the uncertainties or delays of expected losses.

Individual susceptibility-frustration tolerance. Many people have advanced the concept of frustration tolerance to account for the obvious differences in individual responses to frustration. This is a threshold concept, above which the summated frustrations produce aggression. However, some individuals may experience a great deal of frustration without observable changes in behavior; others may "crack up" under the slightest provocation. Perhaps the chief difference between behavior above and below thresholds is the ability of the individual to engage in constructive problem solving. Whereas instrumental behavior is possible below threshold, only agitated and emotional solutions are possible above threshold. These emotional solutions include aggression, escape, and/or disorganization of behavior (Krech and Crutchfield, 1958, p. 315).

Since the aggressive behavior above threshold is primarily an emotional reaction, it could be suggested that anxiety is related to the frustration tolerance level. Wurtz (1960) has shown that, under appropriate conditions, anxiety may serve both as an inhibitor and as a stimulus for aggression. An anxious person may be afraid to attack the target of his aggression. However, the tensions may also summate until the individual loses rational control and "strikes out blindly." A person with a high level of anxiety may lose social judgment and fail to realize the impact of his actions.

A person low in self-esteem may experience higher anxiety than an individual who is satisfied with his self-concept. Rothaus and Worchel (1960) found that subjects with high self-ideal discrepancies (and therefore low self-esteem) were more hostile than those with low discrepancies.

Anxiety may also be deduced from physiological measures. Hokanson (1961) investigated the relationship between systolic blood pressure and hostility. The results showed that highly hostile participants had greater systolic pressure after frustration, than subjects low in hostility. Larsen and Schwendiman (1969) have shown that authoritarians are low in self-esteem, and Epstein (1966) indicated that high authoritarians are more aggressive than low authoritarians.

Anxiety may be thought of as an intervening variable between tension-producing stimuli and frustration tolerance. As tension-producing stimuli continue, anxiety increases to a point where rational and problem solving behavior is abandoned. Apparently passive individuals with high frustration tolerance (see Megargee and Hokanson, 1970) may explode in a fury of violence.

The arbitrariness and expectation of frustration. Pastore (1952) suggested that arbitrary frustration is experienced as more frustrating than frustrations involving some justification. It is easier to tolerate a frustrating situation if the goal interference appears reasonable and/or just. It is also easier to tolerate the frustration if the individual is psychologically prepared. Being prepared for frustration may enable the individual to bolster his defenses and build up his personal resources to raise frustration tolerance.

Arbitrary and nonarbitrary frustrations have been dealt with in several studies. Rothaus and Worchel (1960) studied the effect of these conditions and reported more hostile feelings and actions under arbitrary frustration. If the frustration appears reasonable, people may attempt to inhibit their aggressive feelings to a greater extent. Burnstein and Worchel (1962) reported results which pointed to response inhibition as the reason for the lower levels of aggression under nonarbitrary conditions. Kregarman (1961) and Kregarman and Worchel (1961) have shown that the expectation of frustration alone, or along with apparent reasonableness of frustration, reduced the number of potentially aggressive responses.

Haner and Brown (1955) did a study with children in which a buzzer interrupted a game they were playing. The children had to push the buzzer to start the game again. The results showed that the closer the children were to completing the game, the harder the buzzer was pushed. In short, it is more frustrating to be interrupted close to a goal than far away from it. Berkowitz (1961) suggested that there is a greater expectation of completion the closer one is to completion. The frustration experienced is the frustration of this expectation.

It is important to warn people of potential failure, enabling individuals to prepare and cope with the resulting frustrations. Part of this preparation may be in not raising hopes too high. If one expects to take six months to conclude an agreement, one should plan on twelve months. If the agreement is completed in a shorter time, it will be a pleasant surprise; if it takes longer than six months, there will be less hostility as the delay is expected. Frustrations which appear reasonable or are expected produce lower levels of aggression than arbitrarily imposed frustrations.

Group membership and the revolution of rising expectations. Different sections of society experience different types and levels of frustration. The upper classes probably experience fewer frustrations of the physical, or survival, needs, but perhaps experience frustration of other needs, such as needs for identity or for actualizing potentials. Since material goals are high on the list of values of the middle class, frustration of these achievement goals are intensely felt. The principal concern of the lower classes is the maintenance of a decent minimum standard of living. Survival is a real issue for large sections of the American population and, indeed, for the world. The intensity of the frustration experienced depends upon whether the goal frustrated is important to a person's need or value system. The importance of these needs, in turn, varies in different socio-economic groups.

Responses to frustration are moderated by group membership. These responses are taught by parents through child-rearing procedures. Certain socio-economic classes may emphasize "tough mindedness" in dealing with environment, whereas other groups may emphasize mediation or negotiation. In slums and ghettos the social environment may "demand" aggressive behavior, or the individual may simply not function. Thorpe and Johnson (1958) note that aggressive behavior and delinquency are related principally to socioeconomic and cultural factors. Social class memberships offer different opportunities for expressing and learning aggressive behavior.

The preponderance of physical violence in the lower classes is related to these learning opportunities (Falk, 1959). Violence by ghetto inhabitants is partially a result of their awareness of the discrepancy between their lives and those of other socio-economic classes. Before the advent of television this discrepancy was not so glaringly displayed. With mass media touching the lives of even the very poor, the observed differences have created desires for a better life. This desire has become known as the "revolution of rising expectations."

Combined with a rising consciousness of racial and class exploitation, the revolution of rising expectations has created a continuous basis for inter-group violence. Partial evidence is found in the Post (1959) study; sensitivity to discrepancies in social status was found to be a pre-condition for inter-class hostility.

The optimal condition for class violence is contact under obvious unequal conditions. Post found that, although hostility of lower-class children toward middle-class children is based largely on contact, the reverse is not true. On the contrary, hostility of middle-class children toward lower-class children primarily occurs prior to contact (perhaps in response to negative stereotypes). The important-ance of contact under unequal conditions cannot be overemphasized. To be frustrated, a person must be aware that he is missing something.

In groups or nations where there is a rising awareness of exploitation and a rising level of education, autocratic leadership will be experienced as frustrating. Rule by arbitrary decree is only acceptable in situations where other options are not obvious. The ready availability of information about the status of other classes or nations via mass media and direct contact often make traditional leadership frustrating to people concerned with social progress. In many parts of the world, rising levels of education and awareness of the status of other classes or nations are combined with little or no material progress.

In their classic study, White and Lippitt (1960) showed that autocratic leadership created more feelings of discontent, loss of individuality, and hostility than did democratic or laissez-faire leadership. In a study carried out in Uganda and Kenya, Ainsworth and Ainsworth (1962) found that the more acculturated segments of people were more frequently frustrated by authority and were more frequently aggressive. This relationship of awareness, frustration, and aggression was also found in a study by Feierabend and Feiera-bend (1968). Government coercion and the modernity of a nation were related to social frustration and external aggression.

Feierabend and Feierabend (1966) did a pioneer study of the relationship of the frustration-aggression hypothesis to international behavior. They studied systematic frustration in eighty-four nations. Systematic frustration is defined by the ratio: "social want satisfaction" divided by "social want formation." A state of "no frustration" would be defined by unity, that is, satisfaction of desires for goods or services equaling formation. The revolution of rising expectation, however, produces desires which frequently outstrip satisfactions. A condition of high frustration is defined by the ratio: low social want satisfaction/high social want formation. Satisfaction in the Feierabend and Feierabend study was measured by factors such as gross national product and calorie intake per capita; want was measured by literacy rate and degree of urbanization.

According to the frustration-aggression hypothesis, high frustration should lead to a condition of political instability. The authors obtained data about political instability based on the internal conflict behavior of the nations. For example, a general election would be given a weight of zero, an assassination of a political figure a score of 3, and civil war, 5. Political instability is defined as the aggressive behavior which results from a situation of unrelieved, socially experienced frustration. The study showed the higher the level of systematic frustration, the higher the level of political instability.

The authors made another interesting prediction based on the frustration-aggression hypothesis. Since social want formation is based, in part, on the modernity of a nation (and hence its literacy rate, etc.), greatest frustrations should be experienced by the nations intermediate on a modernity scale, that is, the nations which combine a high awareness of social want with relatively low satisfaction. Maximum political instability was, in fact, found for these intermediately modern nations, followed by those low on the modernity scale. The greater political stability of the nations which produce the lowest levels of goods and services may be attributed to lower want based on lower literacy and, therefore, lower levels of systematic frustration.

There is a lesson in this for both progressive and reactionary leaders of developing nations. It is possible to avoid political instability by keeping the people unaware of socio-economic achievements in other nations. However, considering the progress of international mass communication and transport, isolation is, at best, a temporary solution.

For progressive leaders there are two alternatives. One solution would be to match the modernity of a nation with consumer satisfaction. This, however, is extremely difficult in developing nations where a large portion of the gross national product has to be invested in heavy industry to assure the future prosperity of the country. Therefore, the only realistic alternative which would moderate want formation is the unifying effect of a militant ideology. Only through the support of ideology are people willing to postpone today's pleasure for tomorrow's achievements. The formula "low social want satisfaction/high social want formation" may be neutralized by a strong centralizing ideology. When the political instability of South Vietnam is compared to the relative political stability of North Vietnam, the only apparent difference is a unifying ideology in the North. The hardships suffered by all the people, North and South, cannot be questioned. Ideology has the advantage over military dictatorship: social behavior does not depend on coercion — and therefore surveillance. This makes the plots, assassinations, and other forms of violence characterizing political instability in dictatorships less likely.

Social cost. Widespread conformity is a phenomenon of nearly every society. While it may represent the uncritical acceptance of every norm of policy advocated by authority, conformity may also be the intelligent acquiescence to the rules of the social contract. Conformity is good or bad, depending on the awareness accompanying it and the objectives it serves. Unfortunately, slavish conformity characterizes large segments of the populations of all nations. Conformity is defined as the fear of or reluctance to be deviant. This fear in turn is based on a more generic fear — the fear of being rejected by one's group and thereby losing approval. It clearly follows that those highly desirous of social approval are more apt to conform than those less concerned. While deviation and social disapproval are threatening to many people, they are more threatening to some than to others.

Conn and Crowne (see Lazarus, 1969, p. 43, or Crowne and Marlowe, 1964) did a study on the relationship of approval-seeking to aggression. Their subjects were administered a scale which measured variations in motivation for approval. The subject and a collaborator of the experimenter (unknown to the subject) colluded to cheat in order to maximize winnings in a game they were playing. However, the collaborator violated the agreement in such a fashion that maximum payments were made to him, while minimum payments were made to the subject. Such a situation would frustrate and probably infuriate many people.

In the next phase of the experiment, the collaborator began to act exuberant and enthusiastic and tried to put social pressure on the subject to act likewise. The experimenters rated the subject's euphoria and found that approval-oriented subjects exhibited more euphoria than subjects low in approval-seeking. Rather than being angry or furious as might be expected after this type of outrageous frustration, the "high approval" subjects still tried to please. "After being treated in a dastardly manner by the experimental accomplice, approval striving subjects endorsed by word or action the simulated jubilation of the accomplice . . . ; low need for approval subjects . . . became sullen and resentful in facial expression and communication" (p. 177).

Fishman (1965) also found that high need approval subjects expressed less aggression against the frustrator than low need approval subjects. People who strongly need approval from others will evidently tolerate considerable frustration without overt retaliation. Such individuals have a high, if unrealistic, frustration tolerance.

There is a two-fold reason for this tolerance in high need for approval persons (and a general explanation for high frustration tolerance). Perhaps high need for approval subjects do experience considerable anger, but inhibit their responses for fear of alienating the people who make them angry. If response inhibition is the correct explanation, then such people carry a silent rage within them, which may readily be displaced to out-groups. For people low in need for approval, the relationship between frustration-anger and hostile behavior is more immediate.

The other possibility is that high need for approval people may misinterpret cues as a defense against frustration. I have frequently experienced in very passive people an unawareness of anything disparaging said about or to them. This unawareness borders on the ludicrous; pointed remarks are seemingly ignored or assigned to the realm of the benign. This is more than feigned ignorance, naivete, or stupidity and represents a very self-alienating defense wherein cues from the outside are dismissed unless they fit some attractive or benign category. The misinterpretation is caused by sorting the unpleasant cues out and/or by an inability to evaluate unpleasant cues the way they were intended. The result is a rather enduring case of self-alienation. Since frustrating cues are not admitted into consciousness, there is little chance for anger or aggression to occur.

Perhaps social cost can be considered a personality variable; that is, there are individual differences in the need for approval. It is the postulate of this volume that nearly all people spend a major portion of their lives seeking approval from others. This, if true, supports the high priority of this need, which appears difficult, if not impossible, to satiate. If the primary needs for love or affection are met, individuals seek wider audiences for approval. This certainly must be part of the story behind aspiring politicians, writers, and scientists. Social cost is a personality variable in the sense that the degree of internalized approval-seeking differs between individuals. Social cost is also a general social motivator for the vast majority of mankind. The thwarting of approval-seeking goals will be experienced as more frustrating than interference with other goal responses for high approval-seeking people.

Larsen (1974) suggested that at least two emotional responses are possible to frustration. In traditional frustration-aggression theory the role of anger as an intervening variable has been emphasized. In general, anger is directed outward toward the frustrating agent or some substitute target. An alternate response is sadness, directed internally and expressed in regret and sorrow at lost opportunities.

Frustration may also be divided into two broad categories, depending on the predominant needs of the individual. For the majority, the predominant need is social approval. While needs are not necessarily mutually exclusive, a smaller group of people seek personal identity and meaning in life. These latter needs may find expression in the search for tranquility or in contributing to human knowledge. It stands to reason that an individual will only experience frustration if some important need is interfered with.

The above discussion suggests two hypotheses. More people will be oriented toward approval-seeking goals than toward personal identity goals; since anger might lead to direct aggression and thereby the loss of approval, high approval subjects will give more "sad" responses than will high personal identity subjects. A corollary is that high approval subjects will displace more aggression toward minority groups. This follows from the fear of direct aggression on the part of high approval subjects, which may inhibit but not remove aggression.

To test these hypotheses, the literature on values research was searched for values which reflected either approval-seeking or personal identity goals. Through inter-judge agreement, 14 statements were retained, 7 approval seeking and 7 personal identity. These were presented to 70 undergraduates at Oregon State University, 32 males and 38 females. In addition, the Bogardus (1925) social distance scale was administered as an instrument of potential prejudice toward outgroups. The subjects were divided into 4 groups. Group 1 consisted of 24 participants who had chosen 5 or more of the 7 approval statements; Group 2 (N = 19) chose 4; Group 3 (N = 17) chose 3; and Group 4 (N = 10) chose 2 or less. Consequently, Group 1 was highly approval seeking; Group 2, mildly approval seeking; Group 3, mildly personal identity seeking; and Group 4, highly personal identity seeking.

In accordance with our hypothesis, more of the participants are oriented toward approval-seeking goals (43 versus 27, or in the case of the two extreme groups, 24 versus 10). These differences are statistically significant and lend support to the importance of social cost over other types of incentives. What is the most predominant response to approval frustration? It is *sadness*, not anger! The findings suggest that frustration does not always lead to anger; in the numerically larger group oriented toward approval, it leads, more frequently, to sadness. Perhaps approval-seeking people repress a considerable amount of anger, which in turn may be displaced toward out-groups who are not sources of approval.

Analysis of differences between Groups 1 and 4 on the Bogardus social distance scale indicates that the approval-seeking group is more rejecting of the out-groups listed. One possible explanation is that approval-seeking subjects are afraid to retaliate against significant others and, consequently, displace their anger to potentially safer targets. This could explain a considerable portion of stereotypic prejudice and aggression in our society.

The traditional frustration-aggression hypothesis should be modified to take into account the inhibiting effect of social cost. The inhibition of direct aggression may result in displacing anger toward minorities or other out-groups. Since seeking social approval may frequently be the major response even to frustration, the importance of other emotional reactions (sadness) as intervening variables between stimuli and behavior must be recognized. Apathy may be as frequent a response to frustration as is aggression. Whereas anger is the intervening variable for aggression, sadness may be the intervening variable for apathy. Understanding the relationship between frustration and aggression must take these modifying factors into account.

Criticism of the frustration-aggression hypothesis. The frustration-aggression hypothesis may be criticized for overlooking the possibility that factors other than frustration may affect aggression. For example, Buss (1961) suggested that attack (and pain) may also elicit aggression, and Durbin and Bowlby (1939) discussed two non-frustration causes for aggression: disputes over possession of external objects and resentment at the intrusion of a stranger into the group. Whiting (1944) suggested that there were several reactions to frustration other than aggression — for example, submission, dependence, and avoidance. The importance of dominance strivings was emphasized by Seward (1945). It is clear, if factors other than frustration may predict aggression, other responses than aggression may follow frustration. The theory does not cover all possible cases. In addition, a serious logical problem is found in the definition of the frustration-aggression hypothesis itself. Each of the two terms tends to be cited as evidence of the other; hence the definition is circular.

Whether aggression follows frustration is determined by a number of factors. The cultural norms which define appropriateness of behavior may either facilitate or inhibit hostility. In some cultures (and homes) aggression is encouraged, in others it is severely inhibited. Aggression is partially determined by the arbitrariness of the frustration. If the goal blockage appears reasonable to the individual, he is less likely to be frustrated. It is therefore impossible to have an objective measure of frustration; different reactions may be elicited by the same event.

Whether frustration is followed with aggression is also affected by the opportunity to retaliate. The opportunity may be missing if the potential target is not appropriate. For example, if the target is a child, moral compunctions enter. Or the target may be a more powerful figure. Thus, frustration is not always followed by aggression, as posited by Dollard. Perhaps it is better to follow Berkowitz's advice (Kaufmann, 1970, p. 29) that frustration and pain both belong to a more general class of aversive stimuli which are followed by aggression. While this is acceptable, it should be emphasized that aversive stimuli often, but not always, produce aggression.

The frustration-aggression hypothesis has stimulated a great deal of research, and the basic propositions are sound. The theory, however, attempts to be a global explanation for aggression but, by doing so, is caught in a difficult paradox. The frustration-aggression hypothesis does not cover all cases, as required. Consequently, rigor is lost, if the theory concedes to these exceptions. Or it is made meaningless by trying to make the concept of frustration broad enough to include all cases.

There are two alternatives for dealing with the weaknesses of the frustration-aggression hypothesis. One would be to seek for a higher level principle, for example, the aversive stimulus category. The second alternative is to search the experimental literature for lower level categories and to develop an inductive theory of aggression. A combination of these alternatives was used in Chapter 1.

SUMMARY

This chapter is concerned with the classical frustration-aggression hypothesis. Propositions developed from the hypothesis include the factors which determine the strength of the instigation to aggression, the function of intervening variables, and the evidence concerning catharsis.

Frustration is some form of interference with a goal oriented response. The stronger the incentive value of the goal, the more intense the frustration and aggression elicited. Frustrations, however, are related to needs. Where no needs are present, frustration, by definition, will be absent. A primary incentive goal is the need for approval. The relationship of frustration to aggression has been demonstrated in both early and recent experiments.

Parameters of frustration include types of frustration stimulus, individual susceptibility to frustration or frustration tolerance, the arbitrariness of frustration, membership in socio-economic groups, and social cost. Criticisms of the frustration-aggression hypothesis may be summarized by saying that factors other than frustration predict aggression, and responses other than aggression follow frustration.

5.

Aggression as a Personality Construct

A great deal of effort in psychology has been directed toward understanding individual differences. In the same situation, some individuals display more hostility than others. We also observe that an individual's hostility varies depending upon the situation. Thus, both personality and situation are important in understanding aggression. What accounts for the individual differences or personality factors in aggression? Before attempting to answer this question, let us briefly review some common sense and theoretical conceptions of the term personality.

SOME DEFINITIONS OF PERSONALITY

A popular notion equates personality with the social impression value of a person. We say a person has a "strong" personality or is "attractive." By these terms, we indicate the effect an individual has on people around him, that is, the qualities a person projects and impresses other people with. Social impressions are important to people's reaction toward each other. Allport (1937) extracted more than fifty definitions of personality from the literature.

Hall and Lindzey (1957) discuss several definitions of personality. A bisocial approach defines personality as the reaction of other people to the subject (social stimulus). This notion implies that the individual possesses no personality apart from the reactions of others. As the individual becomes aware of these reactions, he begins to define himself in terms of others. Personality may also be defined as what man really is, that is, what is typical and characteristic (the essence) of the individual. In this sense personality has both an organic and a perceived side. Individuals do not act haphazardly, but often show directive behavior. Some theorists place a great deal of importance on this organizational function which helps to integrate and direct behavior. Without some organization in a person's life, behavior would be dysfunctional. Personality is the structure which assists the individual in adjusting to his social world (functional value).

A composite definition of aggressive personality, using the above three functions, may be expressed as follows. If people react to a person with fear and/or resentment (social stimulus function), if hostility is typical and predominant (essence of the person), and if the subject's adjustment to problems of life and people (functional value) frequently involves hostility, the subject may be said to be aggressive. This eclectic definition involves the three main functions of personality: describing the social stimulus, essence, and functional value of a person's behavior.

CURRENT CONTROVERSIES IN PERSONALITY THEORY

Is aggression a drive which must be expressed, or is it dependent on an appropriate stimulus in the environment? In short, do aggressive personalities automatically express aggressive behavior, or is such behavior a function of an appropriate stimulus (e.g., frustration)? A related issue is the relative importance of the personality trait versus the pressure of the situation in which a person finds himself. The outcome of these issues affects the importance of personality as a variable in human aggression.

Immovable drive or appropriate stimulus. Some theorists think that all behavior is motivated by "drive." Drive behavior must be expressed in some fashion, either directly or indirectly. One variety of the drive position is that drive behavior will be expressed independent of any stimulus in the external environment. In an extreme sense (all other things being equal) this means that aggressive drive may find its expression equally in the serenity of a church or in a New York subway during rush hour. Common sense, however, tells us that these two situations elicit drastically different behavior from most people.

Another view is to consider aggression as a predisposition to be aroused. A predisposition to engage in certain types of behavior refers to a low threshold for engaging in this behavior or, to put it more succinctly, sensitivity to aggression cues. This implies both a heightened sensitivity to specific stimuli and also a sensitivity to an increased range of stimuli. Kagan's (1956) study lends support to the importance of stimuli. He presented cards, some of which contained aggression cues, to two groups of boys. One group was rated high in aggression, the other was rated low. The results showed that both groups gave about the same number of aggressive responses to the cards with low aggression cues, but the highly aggressive group gave more aggressive responses to the cards with high aggression content. If stimuli are not important in eliciting aggression, there should be no differences in the responses of the two groups to the high cue cards. Therefore the differences observed lend support to the importance of appropriate stimuli for aggressive behavior.

Berkowitz (1962) suggested: "The habitually hostile person is someone who has developed a particular attitude toward large segments of the world about him . . ." (p. 258). A large number of categories of stimuli are seen as threatening or frustrating and therefore capable of eliciting hostility.

Traits versus the situation. Another controversy concerns whether behavior is determined by personality traits (aggression, dependency, etc.) or by the situation. If behavior is determined by personality consisting of interrelated traits, one would expect considerable consistency in behavior across varying situations. If the situation determines behavior, little overlap in behavior should be expected between situations. Although certain conclusions may be drawn from the literature at this point, it is important to note that the two positions are not mutually exclusive. Traits and situation both account for behavior.

The importance of the situation in comparison with traits is suggested in several studies. Endler, Hunt, and Rosenstein (1962) studied responses to an anxiety questionnaire and found that situation accounted for eleven times the amount of effect as could be accounted for by individual traits. Mischel (1968, 1969) goes so far as to say that trans-situational consistencies of behavior are rarely found or supported by empirical data. In fact, the data indicate that the same person typically makes different responses in different situations. Correlations between responses in different situations are typically low (.20 to .30), and often reflect similar measurement methods. These are potent comments about the relative importance of situation versus traits. However, they do not convincingly suggest behavior cannot also be attributed to personality organization.

Two arguments suggest that personality organization is important. First, the situational dependent responses may be viewed as a personality variable. Individuals vary in the extent to which they conform to the demands of the situation. For example, a cluster of traits including authoritarianism, low self-esteem, and cognitive simplicity are probably all related to situational conformity. Due to man's lengthy dependency period in childhood, most people are vulnerable to social disapproval. This is probably the basic motivating variable for explaining situational conformity. If researchers understand the demands (expectancies of reward and/or punishment) made in a situation, they will observe a remarkable consistency across the situations in responding to these demands. Not understanding these demands is not an argument against personality organization as a predictor of aggression. The lack of correlations between responses may be attributed to the different demands made in these situations and conformity to these demands. To put it differently, there is a consistency in the inconsistency! People who are conformist believe they must acquiesce to the demands of a situation and are consistent in responding to these demands.

The second argument grew out of a re-analysis of the Endler, Hunt, and Rosenstein study (Endler and Hunt, 1966, 1968). The results showed interactions between individuals and situations account for more variance than either variable alone. Moos (1969) also found support for the importance of the personality-situation interaction. Since this combination explains more behavior than either variable alone, it is clear that we cannot disregard personality organization.

APPROACHES TO PERSONALITY TRAIT MODELS OF AGGRESSION

Various investigators have emphasized the importance of traits in predicting aggression. Some people's aggression seems constant — as if they constantly bear a "chip on the shoulder." Others appear passive for a good part of their lives, then explode in a violent episode. The consequences are quite different in the two cases. A chip-on-the-shoulder attitude may be expressed in constant verbal battering of others; but apparently passive people may commit murder as we shall see. In this section, we will also discuss the traits of the authoritarian personality which appear directly related to hostility. A brief consideration of history should indicate the important role played by submission to authority in working chaos and destruction upon humanity. Aggressive personality may also be viewed as actively striving for independence. An aggressive attitude is functional in certain societies and has helped men to cope with the vicissitudes of nature.

Under-control versus over-control. Appropriate self-control refers to the balance between assertiveness and inhibition of aggression. This means that individuals will usually inhibit themselves, except when provoked beyond endurance. Megargee (1966) suggested two types of aggressive personalities. He noted that criminal records often show the extremely assaultive person as a fairly mild-mannered, long-suffering individual. The resentment the assaultive person feels accumulates underneath rigid but brittle controls. This chronically over-controlled person is more dangerous than the under-controlled, because once the dam breaks, the result is an explosion of violence. The chronically over-controlled are the people who commit murders and other violent crimes, who release their pent-up anger in one disastrous act. The under-controlled may have a constant level of generalized hostility which is released in some manner. If the target of his hostility is too powerful, the under-controlled manages to displace the anger, or generalize the anger, to some less threatening target. The instigation to aggression therefore dissipates over time. The over-controlled, on the other hand, will rarely, if ever, respond to provocation. Whereas the under-controlled is only inhibited against a few targets, the inhibitions of the over-controlled are more general. This prevents the over-controlled from generalizing the hostility, and permits it to build up to the breaking point.

Megargee's (1966) typology of over-controlled and under-controlled persons was derived from a study of juvenile delinquents. The extremely assaultive boys tended, on the average, to be less aggressive and more controlled. In this typology one factor may have been overlooked. It would appear that the potentially explosive character of the over-controlled implies a sensitivity to frustration which accumulates within a limited time period. What of the passive people who never explode? One reason may be that they are relatively insensitive to frustrations. On the other hand, perhaps frustrations are infrequently received, permitting their effects to dissipate over time or permitting the individual to build up resistance. Only if over-controlled persons develop emotional reactions to frustrations (become angry) and these summate rapidly enough to reach and surpass some threshold are such individuals potentially explosive. Defining these parameters of over-controlled aggression becomes an important task of the future.

Authoritarianism. Adorno, Frenkel-Brunswik, Levinson, and Sanford (1950) outlined the traits characteristic of the authoritarian personality. These traits include an intense involvement with and acceptance of the conventional values in society, rejection of those who violate them, a compulsive submissiveness and fear of authority figures coupled with resentment easily displaced toward out-groups. There are three specific traits related to aggression. Authoritarian aggression refers to the tendency of being on the lookout for those who violate moral conventions and to condemn, reject, and punish these people. Another trait involves power and toughness. Authoritarian people are concerned with dominance, strength, and the glory of leadership and identify strongly with power figures. Vicarious satisfaction is obtained by means of this identification process; the authoritarian follower rarely has the power to achieve satisfaction by himself. The third trait is destructiveness and cynicism. A cynical attitude reflects disregard of moral considerations which might otherwise inhibit hostile responses.

The authoritarian personality is a constellation of these traits which mediate his responses to other people and direct his hostility. The target for authoritarian aggression is any group of people who are placed, or place themselves, outside conventional society; in the United States this broadly includes those outside establishment society. Blacks, communists, Jews, Arabs or others may become targets of authoritarian aggression at various times. Any cue which implies intended subversion of the existing order or changing of the status quo particularly inflames the passion of the authoritarian personality. The havoc against the Jews in Europe was facilitated by authoritarian aggression. It is also doubtful that the Viet Nam war could have been maintained for its duration had it not been for the willingness of the American people cynically to disregard the welfare of Viet Nam. This cynicism likely includes viewing Viet Nam's people as belonging to a lower category of humans (or as "communists") and being preoccupied with the idea that the power of the United States must be upheld no matter what the cost in human lives.

For many people who live alienated and powerless lives, the nation and its policy become a means of obtaining power vicariously and permits them status by ranking out-groups low in esteem. The poor white of the South has long been a bulwark of segregation and racial attitudes for that very reason. The essence of authoritarian aggression is found in giving high value and rank to the in-group, its leaders, and symbols, and low value to membership in out-groups. When members of other groups or categories (e.g., other nationalities) are seen as possessing fewer "human" qualities, it is considerably easier to act aggressively or condone aggression against them.

People with authoritarian personalities are especially responsive to in-group propaganda which advocates hostility toward other social, ethnic, or national groupings. As expected, Levinson (1957) found a correlation between authoritarian attitudes and a chauvinistic outlook. Smith and Rosen (1958) showed that high authoritarians were less "world-minded" than low authoritarians. This lends support to the idea that authoritarians display more hostility toward outgroups. The alienated position of many authoritarians may be the reservoir of frustrations, which eventually are displaced to outsiders. Christiansen (1959) found that latent hostilities, as measured by projective tests, were related to hostile foreign attitudes. Adhering to an ideology of nationalism was, in turn, an important factor in channeling personal aggression into international hostility.

Pettigrew (1958), in his study of racial prejudice in the North and the South, also found support for out-group rejection. In both regions, authoritarian attitudes tended to correlate with anti-black attitudes. However, he clearly demonstrated the importance of socio-cultural factors. The regional differences between the North and the South could not be explained in terms of personality differences — there was roughly an equal amount of authoritarianism in the North and in the South. The critical regional difference was that Southerners conformed to social norms supporting prejudice.

Since needs for approval are satisfied by means of identification with powerful others, authoritarian out-group hostility is extremely difficult to change. Mischel and Schopler (1959) found authoritarians highly resistant to attitude change. This rigidity may be partially attributed to the black-and-white world view which is characteristic of authoritarians and their refusal to compromise this view. Lane (1955) found that authoritarians preferred either all-out bombing or pulling out of Korea to continuing peace negotiations. In a study of game behavior, Deutsch (1960) found a similar unwillingness to compromise among authoritarians. It is easy to understand the unwillingness to compromise as the world view of the authoritarian provides him with meaning and continuity, and a threat to these is worse than a threat to life itself. This may also explain the authoritarian's willingness to sacrifice much in the defense of the status quo in his society.

Aggression as an active-independent dimension. Throughout man's evolutionary history, certain characteristics have proved functional; people in possession of these characteristics have survived. Since man has always lived in a world of scarce resources, survival has meant aggression in pursuit of goals competed for by many. Those who won in the pursuit of food and land (our ancestors) survived and reinforced this active-independent attitude in others.

In the United States, this attitude is best summed up by the term "rugged individualism." The John Wayne model from the movies displays this characteristic, and his continual popularity indicates the enduring nature of this attitude. The biblical injunction to subdue the earth is a facet of the same ideology, necessary to both the feudal and the modern capitalist systems.

Hostility on the part of upward moving middle classes toward the poor is the outward expression of rugged individualism. "Stand on your own feet," be "self-reliant," and "refuse hand-outs" are vestigial remains of attitudes very proper throughout the nineteenth century world. Unfortunately self-reliance was often achieved by competing with others and making other people dependent. The modern big business man, whether in agriculture or industry, has achieved self-reliance by making thousands dependent upon his decisions. This remains a major paradox of our society.

Today, self-reliance often takes the form of resistance to cooperation. This may obstruct relationships among people in groups and nations. Yet the nature of our economy, the critical problems of the world, and the very interdependency of our society require cooperation as a functional attitude for survival. Active-independent attitudes, once functional for survival, may now threaten stability and peace. People have been preoccupied with the East-West conflict centering around ideology; many have overlooked the potentially disastrous North-South conflict between the "have" and "have-not" nations. Poverty creates desperate conditions and desperate answers; preaching self-reliance for those who haven't the tools to improve life may only produce conflict.

The early studies on pecking orders in hens (Collias, 1944, 1951; Scott, 1958) suggest that aggression may have the active function of improving the lot of the strong members of a species. Superior status implies greater freedom of movement and more food. Allport (1958) discussed the hostility of established Yankee New Englanders toward incoming Italian and Greek settlers. The new settlers were seen as unwelcome competitors for available jobs. This suggests that aggression may become an acquired motive having functional value.

Sears, Maccoby, and Levin (1957) suggested that behavior producing satisfaction of needs may eventually become valued in its own right. People may learn to be aggressive because they learn to satisfy their needs thereby.

Millon (1969) discussed aggressive personality as part of an active-independent dimension. He suggests a real discrepancy between the self-image of the active-independent aggressor (which is an extension of rugged individual virtues) and how he is viewed by others. His self-image is expressed by the adjectives assertive, energetic, self-reliant, strong, honest, and realistic; on the other hand, others often see him as brusque, argumentative, abusive, dogmatic, having a low frustration tolerance, quick to be provoked, insensitive, and coarse. If these traits validly characterize the active-independent aggressor, it would tend to indicate that self-reliance is often associated with disregard (and not just neutrality) for others.

Types of aggression. Buss and Durkee (1957) developed a scale measuring seven types of aggression. In cases where a given type of aggression is predominant in a person's life, he may be thought of as an aggressive personality type. For example, some people have a predisposition for direct physical violence. Females, or physically weak males, may adopt an indirect style. Indirect aggression consists of such aggression as malicious gossip and undirected hostility (e.g., slamming of doors). Irritability is a combination of persistent frustration and lack of ego control. All of us have met people who appear ready to explode at the slightest provocation. Being under the arbitrary control of authority may result in negativism, defined as oppositional behavior directed against authority. Since we live in a competitive world, the advantages of others frequently result in jealousy and hatred; Buss and Durkee call this form of hostility resentment. Being hostile toward others and reluctance to recognize this hostility in oneself may lead to attributing the hostility to others, which is called suspicion. Verbal aggression is the expression of negative feelings in the style and content of speech. It is clear that these types of hostility are not mutually exclusive and several, or perhaps all, may be found in any given person at any given time.

Hartmann, Kris, and Lowenstein (1949) suggested nine types of aggressive personalities: reputation defenders, norm enforcers, self-image compensators, self defenders, pressure removers, bullies, exploiters, self-indulgers, and catharters. From the labels alone, one would expect a certain amount of overlap between the various types. It is difficult to think of substantive differences between "reputation defenders" and "self-image compensators," or between "bullies" and "catharters."

The following summary outlines the aforementioned personality trait models of aggression:

APPROACHES TO PERSONALITY TRAIT MODELS OF AGGRESSION

Megargee: Under-controlled versus over-controlled
Under-controlled — Constant, but low levels of violence.
Over-controlled — Passive, but potentially explosive.
Adorno et al.: Authoritarianism
Authoritarian aggression — Tendency to be on the outlook for, and to condemn, reject, and punish people who violate conventional values.

Power and toughness — Preoccupation with the dominance-submission, strong-weak, leader-follower dimension, exaggerated assertion of strength and toughness.

Destructiveness and cynicism — Generalized hostility, vilification of the human.
Millon: Active-independent strivings
Aggressive personality as part of an active-independent dimension: brusque, argumentative, abusive, dogmatic, low frustration tolerance, quick to be provoked, insensitive, coarse.

Self image — Assertive, energetic, self-reliant, strong, honest, and realistic.
Buss and Durkee: Types of aggression
Indirect, irritability, negativism, resentment, suspicion, verbal aggression.
Hartmann, Kris, and Lowenstein: Types of aggression
Reputation defenders, norm enforcers, self image compensators, self defenders, pressure removers, bullies, exploiters, self indulgers, catharters.

AGGRESSION AS A TRAIT

The literature lends support to aggression as a trait. Possessing an aggressive trait implies that aggression is typical of a person. A wide range of stimuli is perceived as functionally equivalent and, consequently, capable of eliciting aggression in aggressive people.

Consistency in aggressive behavior across situations is found in the Dittman and Goodrich (1961) study of hyper-aggressive boys. These boys exhibited a smaller variety of behaviors in different situations than normal boys. Levin and Sears (1956) also found evidence of consistency in hostility in various situations, as did Mussen and Naylor (1954). Our task now is to outline the personality traits which are related to hostility.

Physique. Personality may be rooted in a person's physique and sexual identification. Sheldon (1940, 1942) developed a typology of physiques and related these to different personality traits. His mesomorphic type, characterized by a predominance of muscle, tends to be assertive and competitively aggressive (Sheldon and Stevens, 1942). There are several explanations for this relationship (see Hall and Lindzey, 1957). Persons with certain physiques may find some responses more rewarding than others. Typically the muscular boy who achieves goals by means of aggression is rewarded for his efforts, whereas the physically frail boy would be more apt to use his intellect.

Another explanation for the relationship between physique and temperament is that certain physiques elicit social stereotypes. Society *expects* the muscular boy to be aggressive and the boy responds to these expectations. Certain environments may also affect physique and personality. Deprived neighborhoods may produce both physical toughness and aggression.

Sex differences. Sex differences in aggression have been thoroughly documented. Traditionally in our culture (and nearly universally) males and females are reared differently with different social expectations for their behavior. Irvine (1957), Buss and Durkee (1957), Hartup and Himeno (1959), Lansky, Crandall, Kagan, and Baker (1961), Jersild and Markey (1935), Sears (1961), Paolino (1964), and Wyer, Weatherby, and Ferrill (1965), all have demonstrated that males are more aggressive than females. These findings hold true for a variety of situations including measures of aggression, doll play, dreams, and direct expression.

Several explanations may be advanced for these sex differences. The Lansky et al. study indicated that, while boys were more aggressive, girls were more preoccupied with affiliation and sex anxiety. Women's stronger need for social approval and affiliation may be one reason for their lower expressed aggressiveness. Beeman (1947) explains the differences in terms of the higher level of the so-called "male" hormone, whereas Berkowitz (1961) suggests that men have learned stronger aggressive habits and women have learned stronger inhibitions against aggression. Janis and Field (1959) point to the stronger conformist tendencies of women; conforming to social conventions may reduce overt aggression. Sears, Maccoby, and Levin (1957) suggest that boys are encouraged to be aggressive, girls are not. Probably a combination of these reasons would provide the most adequate explanation for the differences between males and females in aggressive behavior.

One problem in the study of aggression is viewing it as a unidimensional variable. This simplistic interpretation overlooks the possibility of various forms of aggression. Perhaps females are more aggressive within certain types of aggression. Since conformity and social approval are found to a larger extent among females, it logically follows that females may be more likely to display aggression indirectly or displace their anger toward targets that are not significant sources of social approval.

However, these sex differences may be rapidly changing as a result of changes in sex roles, expectations, and norms of behavior. Brozan (1974) observed in a report:

> According to the FBI's Uniform Crime Reports, the rate of women arrested for serious crimes, such as homicide, aggravated assault, robbery, and burglary, went up by 246.2 percent from 1960 to 1972, compared to an increase of 81.7 percent for men. The female arrest figure for all offenses climbed by 85.6 percent, the total male arrest figure by 28.2 percent during the same period.
>
> "It's the dark side of the women's movement," said Gerald Caplan, director of the National Institute of Law Enforcement and Criminal Justice. "As women take on an enlarged and equal role in society as a whole it's not surprising that they show up more frequently on police rap sheets."

Ego control. The ability to control oneself is related indirectly to hostile behavior. There are at least two ways that ego control affects aggression. First, a self-controlled individual is less easily upset by (and more likely to minimize) emotional reactions to the inevitable frustrations which life brings. Since he is less likely to have uncontrolled emotional reactions, he is also more likely to divert energy to problem solving which may circumvent or overcome his frustrations. A controlled person is more likely to try again and to employ rational coping behavior. This may be reflected in altering approaches and goals and in other forms of constructive problem solving.

Redl and Wineman (1957) found in their study that highly aggressive youngsters are low in ego strength. Low ego strength is expressed by low frustration tolerance and an inability to cope with insecurity, anxiety, and fear. These youngsters were easily tempted by others to anti-social behavior. Tieson and Mussen (1957) likewise found a negative relationship between aggression and ego control.

Secondly, compared to individuals low in ego control, ego-controlled individuals can better withstand stress and pain. Torrance (1959) reported that subjects most confident of their ability to adhere to the military code of conduct (and thereby endure pain, degradation, and torture) were also less aggressive than those less confident. Lack of control in delaying gratification has also been related to aggression by Block and Martin (1955) and Livson and Mussen (1957). If a person demands immediate satisfaction in life, he will undoubtedly encounter many frustrations and possess many hostile feelings.

Paranoid thinking. Paranoid thinking is characterized by exaggerated and socially unrealistic estimations of self-worth, combined with perceived threats of persecution. The paranoid view of the world as a basically hostile place, in which one should be on guard against seen and unseen enemies, facilitates hostility. A paranoid person has the capacity of generalizing his hostility to nearly all people. "The only people I trust in this world are you and I, and sometimes I doubt you," may express the extreme paranoid position. Attributing hostile intentions to others justifies aggressiveness in the paranoid. The paranoid is especially adept at picking up cues of subtle deviations in people. The aggression is therefore not totally random, but is usually based on some minimal justification (though the target may be unaware of these deviations).

Paranoid thoughts of grandeur and persecution are a compensation for personal inadequacies rooted in the experiences of the individual. An inadequate self-concept may lead to a predisposition to act certain ways in expressing hostility. A person who feels hostile and persecuted, but without the realistic social or personal power to confront the sources of his frustrations, can be expected to displace or generalize his aggression. Hostility is displaced especially against targets less powerful than himself. Hostile feelings can also summate until they reach an explosive threshold, at which time the paranoid may take extreme action. It is unnecessary to point to a Hitler as an example of this pattern; everyday life is filled with violent examples. A paranoid may be passive for a time; but, since his world view is self-reinforcing, requiring no objective proof, the frustrations are never solved. This condition has the potential of accumulating frustrations until they result in an explosive, violent act.

Self-esteem. Low self-esteem is a frustration in itself; and, as we have noted, frustration is one condition leading to aggression. Coopersmith (1967) has investigated the relationship between child-rearing procedures and self-esteem. The antecedents of high self-esteem can be outlined in three general principles: "total or near total acceptance of the children by their parents, clearly defined and enforced limits, and the respect and latitude for individual action that exists within the defined limits" (p. 236). In other words, high self-esteem is related to tolerant and moderate child-rearing procedures and the absence of drastic and extreme punishment.

Individuals who are raised with extreme punitiveness within an ambiguous framework of permissible behavior, with little tolerance for individual deviations, will probably be low in self-esteem. Several investigators have shown that low self-esteem may lead to more covert, but not necessarily more overt aggression (Berkowitz, 1962; Block and Martin, 1955; Livson and Mussen, 1957). Less overt aggression is related to the perceived lack of power in achieving goals by direct means.

Achievement orientation. In our western civilization, there is a great deal of emphasis on competition and material achievement. It is not a novel idea that the psychology of people is a direct outcome of the forms of economic relations in their society. If the economic relations are fundamentally competitive (as they are under both capitalism and the incentive systems of the Eastern bloc), people's attitudes will also be competitive. As long as there is a scarcity of goods — as long as we live in a scarce resource society — the achievement of one individual generally results from another individual's loss.

This condition is directly related to social status, also. One achieves rank, status, and esteem by placing higher than others in some dimension which is considered socially important. Nearly all members of modern, industrialized societies have adopted this achievement value. Achievement motivation may be defined as a tendency to define one's goal according to some standard of excellence, below which a minimum number of other people fall, to ensure no impairment to self-esteem.

SOCIAL COST AND PERSONALITY

The evidence on two issues in personality theory suggests the importance of social cost as an intervening variable. Aggression is not elicited in the absence of an appropriate stimulus. This stimulus is most frequently a combination of aversive stimuli and approval. The relative importance of the situation over traits may be directly attributed to social cost. Social cost is the intervening variable between traits and aggression. For example, the relationship of physique to aggression is explained by the social expectations and approval of the aggressive role on the part of the muscular individual. Personality is a function in learning models of aggression, however, individual factors are easily overruled by the pressures of the situation. The remainder of the formulas in the learning models discussed in this chapter may be attributed to the effect of social cost.

Contrary to common practice, we do not define achievement in terms of some objective criterion, but rather as the point in rank below which an individual would suffer impairment of his self-esteem. Therefore achievement always refers to other people and to the expected social approval derived from surpassing a certain number of them. Achievement orientation is a form of approval seeking.

Atkinson (1964) noted that achievement motivation often took two forms; pleasure in success, and fear of failure. However, to understand why these elements possess motivating power, it is necessary to ask why there *is* pleasure in success and fear in failure. The criterion for both lies in some standard of excellence defined as the minimum number of people ranked below the individual, above which there would be no impairment of self-esteem.

Individuals differ in achievement motivation. Segments of society for whom upward mobility is possible (e.g., the middle class) experience more achievement motivation than segments for whom the objective conditions do not permit upward mobility. Since other people are a threat to relative rank position in society, achievement orientation may be related to aggressive behavior. Phillips (1960) showed in his study that hostile students were especially concerned with various aspects of grading and testing. Other evidence comes from the study of Wyer, Weatherby, and Ferrill (1965), who showed that males placing highest in academic effectiveness were also highest in aggressive expression. Roth and Puri (1967) also found that male achievers were more punitive than male under-achievers.

We know from another line of evidence (Adorno, Frenkel-Brunswik, Levinson, and Sanford, 1950) that authoritarian individuals are particularly concerned with status and middle-class values which emphasize achievement. Abrams (1965) demonstrated that high authoritarians had greater tendencies toward overtly hostile and aggressive behavior and that they were more concerned with themselves and less concerned with others than were low authoritarians. The research tends to indicate that the adoption of achievement values in a scarce resource and competitive society may lead to aggressive behavior.

Authoritarianism. The authoritarian personality consists of several traits previously discussed. Among these are elements of hostility expressed in a punitive attitude toward those who violate conventional values, a constant concern with power and toughness, and a cynical attitude toward things human. This preoccupation with status and power may be a compensation for feelings of weakness and low self-esteem (Larsen, 1969). It is logical to expect that highly authoritarian persons will be aggressive, especially in situations where the target cannot retaliate and/or in situations which have the appearance of legitimacy (approval of respected authority).

Such a situation is found in the learning-paradigm shock experiment used by several investigators, including Milgram (1963) and Larsen, Coleman, Forbes, and Johnson (1972). The essence of the experiment is: if X tells Y to hurt Z (by means of electric shock), under what conditions will Y obey or refuse? The person being shocked is really a confederate of the researcher, enacting the role of a learner in a learning experiment. Epstein (1966) found that authoritarian participants delivered more shock to a victim than persons low in authoritarianism. Larsen, Lesh, and White (1971) found that dogmatic subjects shocked more than low dogmatic subjects under certain experimental conditions.

The importance of the status of the potential victim was shown in a study by Thibaut and Riecken (1955). They asked the participants in their experiment to engage in a two-person task, where the second person (a confederate of the experimenter) frustrated the participant. The participant evaluated the confederate before and after the task; all were ROTC students. Authoritarian participants tended to be less rejecting when facing high status frustrators (ROTC officers), but increased in the intensity of rejection when facing low status frustrators. This indicates that authoritarian rejection is directed downward in hierarchal relationships.

PERSONALITY TRAITS AND AGGRESSION: A SOCIAL COST MODEL

The aforementioned variables may be integrated within a social cost model. Whether or not aggression occurs depends partly on the social reinforcement or punishment expected from a given interaction with another person. The traits just discussed cannot be understood apart from their relationship to approval-seeking, which is a fundamental aspect of social cost. A muscular physique leads to the social expectation (and reward) of physical prowess. Whether on the football field or in a fistfight, the muscular boy seeks approval in ways for which he is best adapted.

One of the most potent reasons for the differences in aggression between males and females is the more predominant conformity behavior on the part of females. Conformity to different social norms explains to a great extent the differences between males and females in direct aggression. Males are less concerned and restricted by social conventions and indeed are often rewarded if they perform in an aggressive manner. Both styles of behavior (and the rapid changes which are occurring in the behavior of males and females) can be understood as responses to social expectations and needs for social approval. Similarly, aggression may be functionally linked to drives and needs within an individual. Deprived of attention, some individuals may learn that hostility draws attention and find it rewarding for that reason.

Aggression may occur not because there is no need for social approval, but rather in spite of such a need. Low ego control may be thought of as impulsive disregard of sources of approval. The person low in ego control is saying, "I disregard the need for approval for my behavior." A person with a stronger ego would also be more cognizant of the potential social cost involved in attacking another person. Impulsiveness implies disregard of judgment — disregard for the need for approval.

Paranoid thinking can be described as a general distrust of sources of approval. "I would like to be approved, and I deserve to be approved, but instead I am unjustly persecuted." These feelings and perceptions lead to general hostility toward people and a low threshold for aggression. If the paranoid person trusted people in general as sources of approval (and not just high status leaders), the paranoid would not be a paranoid and the problems of paranoid aggression would be solved.

A person low in self-esteem has a more intense need for approval than one high in self-esteem. This condition leads the person low in self-esteem to avoid situations which might further impair his social approval. We may expect the low self-esteem person to be more timid and to seek indirect ways of expressing aggression. Since direct aggression may lead to retaliation (which an insecure and low self-esteem person fears) and possible disapproval by significant others, there may be less overt aggression, but not necessarily less covert aggression.

Achievement orientation is definitely linked to approval-seeking. The feeling of pleasure derived from ranking higher than someone else is a function of the expected approval of high social rank. In a society which values hierarchal relations, high rank is approved and gives pleasure. This facilitates ruthlessness and cynical disregard of other people, particularly those lower or potentially lower in rank.

Authoritarians have a high need for social approval from high status sources. Authoritarianism — submission to powerful others — is the grossest form of approval-seeking. This form of approval-seeking finds its expression in the rejection of minority and other out-groups.

The importance of the effect of social approval on aggression is indicated in several studies. There are studies which indicate the effect of direct punishment on aggression; the effect is often to "push" aggression into fantasy while displaying lower levels of overt aggression. Sears (1951) showed that severely punished children demonstrated higher levels of aggression in fantasy. Lesser (1957) showed that in children whose mothers discouraged aggression, the aggression was expressed more in jealousy and less in behavior. While punishment may lead to lower levels of actual aggression, it may also lead to higher levels of fantasy hostility.

Bandura, Lipsher, and Miller (1960) have shown that psychotherapists having strong needs for social approval were more prone to avoid dealing with hostility. Strong affiliation needs and needs for social approval lead people to avoid hostility. Allison and Hunt (1959) also found that those strongly oriented toward social approval tended to avoid aggression whether the aggression was justified or not. This social cost model of aggression is summarized as follows:

PERSONALITY TRAITS AND AGGRESSION — A SOCIAL COST MODEL

Trait	Function in Aggression
Muscular physique	Social approval of aggressive role.
Sex differences	Females more approval seeking, social approval for male aggressiveness, disapproval for female aggressiveness.

Ego control	Low ego control implies impulsive disregard of social approval.
Paranoid thinking	General distrust of sources of social approval leading to general hostility.
Self esteem	Fear of disapproval, therefore less overt aggression.
Achievement orientation	Achieving social approval by placing others below in rank. Aggression toward obstacles for higher rank.
Authoritarianism	Approval by high status sources especially important. Cynical disregard for those incapable of extending approval. Aggression directed toward powerless outgroup, minorities or sources threatening approved high status people or ingroup symbols.

PERSONALITY AS A FUNCTION IN LEARNING MODELS OF AGGRESSION

Human behavior is largely a function of experience of the past. To assess whether a given person will aggress, it is necessary to know the parameters of these past experiences, which predict the likelihood of hostility. Buss (1961) and Kaufmann (1970) have both developed learning models of aggression. Buss is concerned about the habit strength of aggression. Hull (see Hilgard, 1956) defines habit strength as "the tendency for a stimulus trace to evoke an associated response" (p. 131).

Ignoring the formal properties of learning theory, it would appear that habit strength refers to the ease by which behavior is elicited by appropriate stimuli. Habit strength is a function of the number of previous fights, the frequency and intensity of reward and punishment, and the norms for the expression of hostility and personality. The variables are apparently all interrelated; that is, the number of previous fights is related to the frequency of reward for aggression. Likewise, frequency of reward is a function of social facilitation. Social facilitation means pretty much what Pettigrew

(1958) calls "conformity to socio-cultural norms" and what has been referred to as "social cost" in this book.

Buss makes no attempt at assessing relative weights of the variables. Logically social facilitation must be the most important variable for many forms of hostility. Without aggression-approving norms (norms may be defined as standards of behavior socially approved) there would be no antecedents for or history of reinforcement. Except for occasional violent outbursts, personality effects would also tend to be moderated by the cultural norms for the expression of hostility.

Kaufmann adds several other variables to habit strength. People have "ideal" attitudes as to what is considered proper behavior and a propensity to act in accordance with these attitudes. They evaluate the rewards and punishments which are likely to result; but, if the conditions are right (Milgram, 1963; Larsen, 1971), most people will act contrary to their conscience. Kaufmann's "utility expected plus habit strength of behavior" is basically a social cost model. The most important social utility is approval for behavior, and the most important factor of habit strength is the frequency by which the behavior has been rewarded (or approved). Utility and reward may refer to physical incentives; but, if aggression is not motivated solely by survival needs, the socio-cultural norms for expressing aggression are of crucial importance.

The key variables in both models are summarized below:

LEARNING MODELS OF AGGRESSION

Buss (1961): Habit strength of aggression is described in terms of:
a) Antecedents (e.g., number of previous fights).
b) History of reinforcement (e.g., frequency and intensity of reward and punishment).
c) Social facilitation (e.g., cultural norms for the expression of hostility).
d) Temperament or personality (e.g., permissiveness, frustration tolerance, impulsiveness).

Kaufmann (1970): Aggressive function of ideal attitude times propensity to act according to the attitude plus utility expected plus habit strength of the behavior.

SUMMARY

This chapter was concerned with aggression as a personality construct. An eclectic theory of aggressive personality is suggested, taking into account the social stimulus function of a person's behavior, whether hostility is typical or predominant (and represents the essence of a person), and whether a person uses aggression functionally to adjust to the problems of life.

Studies have supported the importance of the presence of appropriate stimuli for eliciting aggression. This is an argument against the more vulgar forms of drive theory, which assert that aggression builds up in an incremental fashion and must therefore find some "release." Situational effects are relatively more important than any aggressive trait, but studies have shown that the interaction between the two accounts for more of the behavior than either variable alone. Due to this interaction effect, it is important to study traits in their own right.

Trait models emphasize the importance of under- versus over-controlled individuals. An under-controlled person may have a constant "chip on the shoulder," but the apparently passive, over-controlled person may explode in violence if sensitive to frustrations and if frustrated frequently within a given time period. Authoritarianism is the trait constellation which places high value on the in-group, its leader and its symbols, while placing low value on groups outside "conventional" society.

The world which emerged into modern capitalism developed an ideology of rugged individualism expressed as an active-independent personality trait. At a certain point in history, this trait was functional for survival; but, in today's interrelated world, it may simply obstruct cooperation. Self-perceptions of active-independent aggressors emphasize aspects of rugged individualist ideology; perceptions of others are less flattering.

Traits such as physique, sex differences, ego control, paranoid thinking, self-esteem, achievement, and authoritarianism have all been related to aggression. A social cost model is advanced which views approval-seeking as an intervening variable between the traits and aggressive behavior. For example, females are more approval-seeking and tend to show lower levels of aggression; aggressive behavior is more approved for males. Studies have shown that approval-seeking behavior is related to lower levels of overt aggression.

The essence of the learning models of aggression demonstrates the importance of social cost for behavior. Other variables in these models are confounded by social cost, or their effects are subordinate to socio-cultural norms.

6.

The Social Psychology of Aggression

Social psychology is the area of psychology concerned with the behavior of an individual person as a member of a group and the behavior of groups toward each other. Frequently such behavior is hostile, and often the goals of individuals and groups include the destruction of other individuals and groups. This chapter is concerned with social psychological factors which produce aggression.

The mass media is coming under increased scrutiny by public officials, psychologists, and other professional people. The daily television diet of many children contains a considerable amount of aggression. Do children imitate the behavior of aggressive television heroes? The modeling of aggression is a major issue discussed in this chapter.

Social psychology is the field of study concerned with inter-group behavior. The conditions of inter-group conflict involve essentially a categorization process where in-group members are rated favorably and all others are evaluated negatively. However, there is a complex interaction between several variables which produces this evaluative categorization. The relationship between these variables is discussed in a general theory of prejudice.

Prejudice refers to biased perceptions, frequently unjustified, of members of other groups. Unfortunately, prejudice does not merely stay in the minds of people; it often has behavioral ramifications. Prejudice provides the basis for aggressive inter-group behavior.

EXPOSURE TO AGGRESSIVE MODELS

In the process of becoming an adult some are exposed more than others to aggressive behavior. Some are born into ghetto conditions where violence is a daily occurrence; others are raised by mentally ill parents who daily exhibit a lack of restraint or extreme punitiveness; still others are fortunate to have loving and warm-hearted parents. It is clear that parents may model aggressive behavior. The degree to which parents punish their children (especially arbitrary or perceived non-justified punishment) serves as a model for the child's behavior toward others, especially less powerful others. Severe punishment may also serve to make the child more callous, or less sensitive toward pain and, therefore, less empathetic toward the pain of others.

Lefkawitz, Walder, and Eron (1963) investigated the relationship between children's aggressive behavior and parental punishment. They found that a child's aggression was related to the degree of physical punishment administered by the parents. Larsen and Schwendiman (1969) noted the relationship between perceived severity of parental punishment and authoritarian attitudes on the part of their subjects. Authoritarian and extremely nationalistic attitudes have, in turn, been associated with rejection and hatred of minority groups. Severe parental punishment can be both a model for a child to imitate and can make the child more insensitive to pain.

Much of the psychological literature tends to support the importance of models in the aggressive behavior of children. Lovaas (1961) showed a group of children a cartoon containing a great deal of aggressive action. In this respect the cartoon differed only in relative degree from most cartoons seen on television or at the movies. After viewing the cartoon, the children were permitted to play with a doll which could be activated to strike another doll. The children who viewed the aggressive cartoon activated the aggressive doll more often than the children who did not view it. Siegel (1956) also showed an animated cartoon to pairs of same-sexed nursery-school children. This cartoon was likewise high in aggressive action. The children in this study also showed a trend toward more aggression after being exposed to the cartoon.

Eron (1963) asked mothers and fathers to rate the programs favored by their boys and found a relationship between the violence in these favored programs and the boys' aggressive behavior as rated in school. Emery (1959) showed adult western movies to a group of boys and subsequently tried to determine the boys' feelings. The boys felt more threatened after watching these movies, thus showing that aggressive mass media does affect the emotions of children. Bandura, Ross, and Ross (1961, 1963) demonstrated that participants in their studies readily imitated an adult's aggressive behavior, whether the model appeared in person or on the screen. It is natural for children (*and* adults) to consider aggression as morally right and legitimate when models of such behavior are favored cartoon characters, movie heroes, or powerful parents.

WHY MODELING IS EFFECTIVE

There are several explanations why the modeling of aggressive behavior produces aggression. The aggressive actions of the models are made to appear just, whereas targets for aggression are stereotyped as socially undesirable. Frequently models of aggression are made to seem powerful and are rewarded for their actions. The media are guilty of distorting the real pain involved in violence, thereby interfering with the empathy process. Thus, modeling may work through the imitation or identification process. The media may also affect aggressive behavior by desensitizing the viewer to pain.

Justified aggression. Aggressive models in the movies are depicted with all the virtues of power, moral authority, and legitimacy. When violence is glorified, made attractive and desirable, it is no wonder that children want to imitate such behavior. The most common aggressive models of the mass media (cartoons, westerns, war pictures) are made to appear just and brave while they maim or kill characters. Usually the latter are deserving of punishment, leaving little for the conscience to argue with. This is partially accomplished by symbols or by commonly understood references to bad and evil. The "bad" cowboys wear black hats; the "good" ones wear white. Movie villains are made to deviate from some aspect of majority culture. At one time handle bar mustaches or swarthy complexions identified bad guys. Stereotypes usually serve the purpose of dehumanizing the "enemy," thereby marking him as a justified victim of violence.

Aggression, power, and reward. Children and adults learn to imitate models because these powerful models succeed in achieving their objectives. Having imagined that he is "Superman," the child transfers to his own life the expectancies of outcomes similar to those Superman experienced. This does not imply perfect transference of reward, but enough of a transference to affect the individual so he behaves more aggressively.

If someone saw a daylight robbery with many witnesses present, and if the robber got away with a great deal of money and was never caught, that person might come to several important conclusions. First, someone showed him how to obtain something of value without threat of punishment. "If he could do it, I could too," a person might reason.

Often parents play similar roles with their children. A parent may give a severe thrashing to a child and "get away with it" without retribution. Of importance here is the perceived positive, or rewarding, outcomes which usually accompany the modeling of aggression. Aggression in the mass media is usually rewarded (the hero wins and the bad guy receives his just punishment).

Sears, Maccoby, and Levin (1957) and Bandura and Walters (1959) have suggested that the identification process finds its origin in the dependency relationship. The child wants to be rewarded; therefore, he imitates the behavior of his powerful models. The models who play these roles combine high status with power over the child. Lefcourt, Barnes, Parke, and Swartze (1966) showed that aggressive responses increased in the presence of a low expectancy of model censure. Walters (1966) came to a similar conclusion in his study. Observation of aggressive models increases the probability of aggressive behavior if the model is either rewarded or not punished.

Pain and perceptual distortion by mass media. Another factor which may explain why violence in mass media affects aggression is the relative distortion of pain by the media. People who die violently in movies usually die very anesthetically and apparently with little or no pain. This distortion is accomplished by means of several subtle techniques. One approach is to keep the dying person at a distance. An example would be the popular western scene in which the surrounded cowboys kill hundreds of attacking Indians. The killing is usually so far away that a person cannot see, hear, or otherwise empathize with pain or death.

SOCIAL COST AND SOCIAL PSYCHOLOGY

Social cost plays a predominant role in the social psychology of aggression. The imitation of models of aggression may be partially understood as a function of approval-seeking. Powerful models are, at the conceptual level, significant others; and the imitation of their aggressive actions is motivated by the desire to be approved or to participate in approved behavior. Imitation is more readily brought about in people with low self-esteem, who are more vulnerable to social cost.

The social cost of aggression shows the powerful role of this variable in producing deferential behavior. The approval-seeking from significant others predicts the displacement of aggression away from significant others toward weaker targets. The stereotypic hostility toward out-groups which characterizes so much of human behavior is probably the effect of the displacement process motivated by social cost. A theory of general prejudice is based on the generic nature of social cost. The rejection of others on the basis of belief and categorical differences is motivated by the desire to get along with significant others — to maintain low levels of social cost.

Distance reduces empathy. Can anyone be sure whose bullet killed who, or if anyone really died? On the other hand, people who do die in "close-ups" on the screen often die in a grotesque and unreal way — or serenely. This distorts the terror that pain can be. In Halloween thriller shows, for example, the whole scene is so unreal that people tend to laugh where they should be terrified. In movies which attempt to show death authentically, the pain of a violent death is reduced to an absolute minimum. In many cases, there is time for the actor to say a few serene words before expiring. Furthermore, it is doubtful that an actor's interpretation of a violent death can ever be accurately realistic. The net result of all these artificial factors is to reduce the empathetic processes; aggression seems less personal and therefore more acceptable. The illusion remains that no one really gets hurt.

Modeling: imitation or desensitization? Is aggression elicited as a result of imitating the model or is there another dynamic involved? Perhaps the individual becomes less sensitive to the pain of others (desensitized) as a result of repeated exposure to media violence.

Densensitizing is frequently used as a therapeutic technique to help people overcome fears and phobias. If a person has a fear of, say, furred animals, it is possible to overcome this fear by gradually exposing him to the feared object. The gradual exposure may be combined with something which has a positive reward value. Desensitization of a child's fear of furred objects might take the form of introduing such objects gradually, while he is eating ice cream. It may be assumed that the positive value of the ice cream would overcome the fear involved in each small gradual exposure, so eventually the fear is gone.

This is precisely the mechanism involved in the exposure of violence over television or other mass media. The spectators frequently view aggression models in connection with the chewing of popcorn, the drinking of beer, or the relaxation of being with friends. This situation contains the elements of desensitization experiments and would presumably reduce common fears or anxiety about violence.

Larsen and Schwendiman (1968) found a relationship between self-reported preference for programs containing violence and "hawkish" attitudes toward the war in Vietnam. While the study had no bearing on cause or effect, perhaps the preference for violent programs might have been a result of gradual desensitization brought about by violence modeling.

This is not meant to minimize the result of imitating a model's behavior. The modeling of aggression creates behavioral changes in the viewer by both the desensitization and imitation processes.

GENERALIZING FROM THE MASS MEDIA TO REAL LIFE

How much of the violence modeling affects a person's behavior in real life? There is a difference between the imaginary world of the media and the world of real behavior. Nevertheless, there are several factors which argue against negating media influence. For children, especially, but also for many naive adults, the media world is a very real world. Many people have great difficulty in discriminating between the two.

Learning theory suggests a generalization effect which occurs between stimuli eliciting a given response and other stimuli eliciting a similar, if not the same, response. This is commonly known as classical conditioning and began with the work of Pavlov. He noted that dogs not only salivated to food, but also to any other stimulus which was experimentally associated with food. Thus one could expect, on the basis of learning theory, similar responses to similar stimuli.

The major generalizing effect which occurs from the mass media to real life is a reduction of the fear of violence and pain. To overcome this undesirable effect, the media could either stop producing violent shows or create shows with more vivid and explicit descriptions of pain.

PERSONALITY AND ACCEPTANCE OF AGGRESSIVE MODELS

People do not all imitate models of aggression in the same manner or to the same extent. It is apparent that both the personality of the model and the personality of the spectator may affect the acceptability of the model and, therefore, subsequent imitation. The model must possess some degree of status or power for the viewer. In studies of persuasion (Hovland, 1957; Hovland and Janis, 1959), the credibility of the communicator (model) in the role he is playing has been shown to be an important factor affecting the acceptance of the message. Status, power, and credibility, all are important social-psychological variables of the model.

The spectator who readily imitates a model's behavior probably has complementary personality traits, Hovland and Janis (1959) have shown that low self-esteem is a trait affecting persuasion in some cases. Authoritarianism is characterized by a number of traits, including subservience to authority figures. It might be expected that people who are subservient would more readily imitate behavior.

Larsen's study (1969) showed moderate relationships between measures of self-esteem and general authoritarianism (dogmatism). Those individuals who were low in self-esteem tended to be highly authoritarian. Epstein (1966) investigated the imitation of aggression toward out-groups as a function of the subjects' authoritarianism.

The results of the study showed that high authoritarians do not discriminate well between ethnic models but tend uncritically to imitate any model. Perhaps these findings could best be understood as a result of the simple cognitive style of high authoritarianism which prevents differentiation in judgment and leads to the uncritical acceptance of any model.

CRITICISMS OF MODELING THEORY

The basic argument behind modeling theory is that television, for example, may serve as a model by stimulating aggressive impulses and by reducing inhibitions to aggression. Although we have noted the conflicting evidence in the idea of catharsis (when aggressive energy is dissipated there is lower instigation to aggression), this is a second possible outcome of modeling. Television may act as a catharsis of hostile feelings and, in line with this, reduce the possibility of aggression.

Feshbach and Singer's (1971) study lends support to the catharsis hypothesis. They point to a complex series of variables which determine whether televised aggression serves as a model or as catharsis. These include: "the type and degree of violence depicted; the overall dramatic context; the outcome of the violence; the personal attractiveness of the aggressor; the justifiability of the aggressive acts depicted; the degree of prior exposure; the age, intelligence, aggressive predisposition, emotional state, and stability of audience; and the nature of the viewers' reaction" (p. XII). Feshbach and Singer studied the effect of a sustained diet of televised aggression on several groups and found evidence that exposure to such a diet produced reduced aggression in one group. This group (boys' homes) came from a lower socio-economic background. No effect was found in the private school group. Also, the design of the experiment was confounded by permitting the group exposed to a nonaggressive television diet to occasionally watch aggressive programs. The authors observed that aggressive shows are frequently followed by punishment which should decrease the level of imitation.

What the Feshbach and Singer study shows is that modeling learning is an extremely complex phenomenon. The points concerning modeling made in earlier sections of the chapter were not disproved by the Feshbach and Singer study. In many other studies the modeling effect has been demonstrated. However, the heightened aggression in these studies could, in part, be a result of the subtle "suggestions" of the experimenters that aggression was the appropriate response. Further controlled experiments are necessary to outline the complex interaction between variables which produce modeling and those which produce catharsis.

INTER-GROUP CONFLICT: THE CATEGORIZATION PROCESS

When groups come in conflict with each other, it is the result of certain factors. Conflict conditions tend to accentuate categorical differences between groups. This, combined with the dogmatic nature of most groups, is a sufficient cause for conflict. Inter-group conflict is largely the result of placing people with similar beliefs in the in-group and all others in rejected out-groups.

Conditions producing inter-group conflict. Williams (1947) advanced four conditions productive of group conflict. First, the groups must be visible to each other. There must be some way of identifying members of groups. Visibility is especially acute in the case of race where skin color and other categorical differences are immediately apparent. Secondly, there must be some contact between groups.

The third condition is competition between groups. The notion of competition implies scarce resources and what many social scientists would call a "zero-sum world." A zero-sum game is like poker; if you win, the other player loses. In zero-sum games there is a direct relationship between wins and losses. In a non-zero-sum game, there is no relationship between the one player's wins and another's losses — it is possible for all to win or all to lose. Our competitive society is best characterized by the zero-sum model, where the gain of one group is often at the expense of another group.

The fourth condition for conflict is that there are differences between groups in values and behavior patterns. Differences in social values help to stereotype and dehumanize members of other groups.

Ethnocentricism, the idea that what is human and good is defined by the values of one's own group, is the common human experience. It would reduce conflict if people would realize that differences in values often are not absolute differences, but rather differences in emphasis on a common hierarchy of values. One group might place primary value on equality and secondary value on freedom, whereas for another group the reverse might be true. Both groups, however, value both equality and freedom.

Ideological conflicts between groups are often based on subtle differences which are twisted and exaggerated until they appear absolute and not subject to negotiation. In fact, those with similar belief systems are often bitterly hostile toward each other. The hatred between Stalinists and Trotskyites was strong and bitter, despite the fact that the ideology which they had in common far outweighed their differences.

Why this hostility? Festinger (Berkowitz, 1962) advances three explanations why individuals with similar, but not identical, belief systems are often more hostile toward each other than toward members of groups which are obviously more different in beliefs. First, between closely similar groups there is direct competition for the allegiance of followers or potential followers. Examples from history are plentiful. Extermination of Protestants by Catholics (and vice versa) took place on numerous occasions. Recent Marxist history is dominated by the vicious struggle between those who followed Stalin and those who followed Trotsky after Lenin's death.

Another reason for hostility is perceived rejection. If someone is very close to you in beliefs, and then rejects yours, the rejection is felt much more acutely. Opposition is often interpreted as personal rejection. In this world of uncertainty, we need others to shore-up our beliefs. The need for support is especially great in areas of abstract values or ideologies. Such ideologies concern our view of what the world is or ought to be like and, therefore, get close to defining what "meaning" life has. It is obviously very threatening to have such views challenged, especially since there is always an element of uncertainty in any belief system. This uncertainty in belief systems is the third explanation advanced by Festinger for the rejection of groups or individuals with closely similar beliefs.

The hostility toward or rejection of people with similar beliefs can also be explained by the frustration of an expectancy of support. Apostasy blocks this expectance, producing feelings of belief uncertainty and hence, the need to shore-up this uncertainty by means of rejection. These four conditions, based on expectancy of outcomes of future interactions between people, appear to explain why belief-similar groups show intolerance and bitterness.

In short, we like people with similar beliefs. Numerous investigators (e.g., Fiedler, Warrington, and Blaisdell, 1952; Lundy, Katkovsky, Cromwell, and Shoemaker, 1955) have shown a relationship between perceived similarity of beliefs and sociometric preferences (liking). Acceptance or rejection of others is basically a categorization process by which we put people into two broad classes; those with different beliefs we reject. In fact, Rokeach (1960) suggested interpersonal congruence in belief systems was the most important kind of categorization — more important than race or ethnic groupings — and fundamental to the rejection of other people.

Adherence to dogmatic groups. Several groups in our society have aggression as an inherent part of their program. Groups which are dogmatic (i.e., closed-minded in doctrine or program) may perceive a greater threat from heresy and consequently condone aggressiveness to a greater extent than less dogmatic groups. Some groups are, by nature, combat groups and function largely to provide outlets to channel aggression and hostility. War, in some cases, is but the continuation of politics (or power struggles) started by other means.

Objective differences in interest often lie at the base of political differences and are one reason for joining a political party. There are other reasons also, including appeals to emotional socio-political symbols and tradition. These appeals may have little to do with objective interests. Nevertheless, membership in a political party implies favorability toward members of the party with which you have common interests and hostility toward parties which frustrate these interests. Hostility is particularly a part of the extreme left and right, where the objective differences are perceived most clearly.

Perceived enhancement of differences may in turn lead to greater dogmatism and closed-mindedness, having two possible consequences. First, under such conditions, communication is impossible and usually consists of slogan making. Primarily slogan making has the function of reinforcing, or making secure, the political position of party members. In addition, slogan making indicates to hostile forces and to the world in general that no compromise is possible. Compromise is looked upon as being morally wrong, because the conflict of interest is perceived as being unsolvable by means of negotiation or compromise, and only "party" victory will, in the long or short run, solve the underlying problems. The accentuated differences, as perceived by extremists of any sort, lead to the inevitable consequence — conflict. Whether the extremist is correct or not, accentuated differences lead to implacable hostility and aggression.

Extremist political parties also attract certain individuals who, being already frustrated, look for some way to channel their aggression. Groups may function both by reinforcing aggression and by directing aggression.

Different population subgroups handle frustration in different ways. Some people learn to handle feelings of aggression indirectly, by verbal rather than physical assault. The middle and upper classes have learned to channel aggression in non-physical ways or by having someone else carry out the assault. Middle- and upper-class people use the courts to arbitrate conflicts and rely on the police for force. It is less common for lower-class people to rely on indirect means; they have greater preference for solving problems directly. Pittman and Handy (1966) in their survey of homicide and aggravated assault found that both of these types of crime reflect the culture of population subgroups whose members learn to confront others with physical assault when faced with a conflict situation. Aggression can be handled by direct confrontation, by punishing the aggressor, or by punishing oneself. Class membership is one factor which may affect the way in which aggression is handled.

Religious group membership can also be a factor in directing aggression, as demonstrated by Brown (1965). His study showed that Catholics tend to be more punitive toward others than members of other religious groups. Other religious groups tend to de-emphasize absolute claims to truth and infallibility, whereas the Catholic Church has made such claims. Any group which lays claim to dogmatic infallibility is likely to promote hostility toward members of groups which differ on points of doctrine.

The group categorization process isolates a person from other groups and viewpoints. Isolation can produce a sense of fear. Many people fear the unknown, and fear easily converts to hatred and aggression. We are aggressive toward objects we fear. Segregation, or isolation, ensures peaceful relations only to the extent that it is complete. Complete isolation, however, is impossible in our interdependent society. Membership in racial groups is still the most important condition ensuring isolation from other groups.

Thompson, Travis, and Bloom (1966) concluded from their study that racial isolation is strongly correlated to willingness to use violence. This was especially true when an individual felt strong dissatisfaction with life combined with powerlessness. Under conditions of isolation it is difficult to refute negative stereotypes of other races. When the maintenance of these negative images is made possible by such factors as severe frustration and poverty, with no hope for change (feeling impotent), violence often seems the only alternative. In such cases violence is cathartic and serves mainly as a release valve. Ghetto violence is often cathartic — in contrast to the goal-oriented violence of political parties.

THE SOCIAL COST OF AGGRESSION

In other chapters and sections of this book we have referred to social cost as an intervening and integrating variable relating aggressive stimuli to aggressive responses. Now it is time to focus on the parameters of social cost and aggression. Social cost produces deferential behavior resulting in approval-seeking and displacement of aggression. The outcome of social cost pressures is that people tend to comply with the social expectations of any situation in which they find themselves. When such situations have expectations of aggression, the individual usually conforms. This discussion leads directly to a comprehensive theory of prejudice to be discussed in the last section of this chapter.

Deferential behavior. Society has, over a period of time, developed expectations of behavior from individuals with certain characteristics. The big boy is expected to be tough, girls are expected to be emotional and tender, people with red hair are expected to have tempers, and so forth. By means of these expectancies, we help to define a person's self-concept, what he believes himself to be or thinks he ought to be.

In many cases, it is rewarding to fulfill the expectations of significant others. This is demonstrated in the situation where Mom and Dad show pride in their son who beats up other boys in the neighborhood and "handles himself well." In fact we learn at an early time to appreciate the power of significant others to reward and punish.

Mandel (1959) studied the aggressive behavior of boarding-school boys. The aggressive behavior of these boys was directed toward boys who were weaker than they. The individual lowest in the pecking order, unable to retaliate, becomes frustrated. Two possible emotions which may accompany frustration are fear and anger. The less powerful one feels, the more vulnerable one is to attack, and the more likely it is that fear will predominate over anger. The result is deferential behavior toward powerful individuals, and the frustration is passed on (displaced) toward persons lower in the pecking order.

Cantril (1941) has described lynch mobs as being composed of frustrated individuals who, nevertheless, felt strong enough to attack those lower in the pecking order. Lippitt, Polansky, Redl, and Rosen (1952) studied camp youngsters. On the average, these youngsters directed more deferential and approval-seeking behavior toward individuals deemed high in status. Support for this idea was also found in the Cohen (1955) study. Girls interviewed reported less overt aggression when the person who frustrated them was high in authority. Most people follow the pattern of showing deference to high power figures and seek substitute or "safe" targets upon which to vent their frustration. We tend to displace our anger from the frustrating agent to a relatively innocent target. Why?

Approval-seeking and displacement of anger. The typical scene which illustrates displacement may proceed somewhat as follows. A man has a hard day at the office. He is abused repeatedly by his boss, but fails to retaliate for fear of losing his job. His anger and frustration accumulate during the day; finally, when he goes home after work, his wife reaps the hurricane. Being afraid of the boss, the man vents his anger on his wife. What explanations exist for this behavior?

Freud, long ago, advanced his psychoanalytic theory based, fundamentally, on a closed energy system; energy does not escape, but may be displaced from one object to another. In the previous example of this displacement, energy is being built up but its discharge is delayed since the boss is not a suitable target.

Neal Miller (1948, 1951, 1959) advanced an explanation based on stimulus-response learning theory. People learn to respond to a frustrating agent (stimulus) with aggression (response). At times, however, because of the frustrating agent's power, the response is blocked. Basic to learning theory is the concept of generalization. Stimulus generalization occurs when another stimulus (wife) is able to elicit a response (aggression) similar to that of the original frustrating stimulus (boss). It is generally assumed that there is a gradient of generalization in which the magnitude of the aggressive response is dependent on the similarity of this second stimulus to the first.

Perhaps the most crucial similarity (despite obvious dissimilarities) is that, probably, both boss and wife have been frustrating agents to the man in the past. Worchel (1957) goes so far as to suggest that displacement occurs only if the object of displacement is also perceived as frustrating. Being an innocent victim may apply only to a particular situation, and displacement may represent "paying up" of a backlog of overdue anger. Perhaps the frustration felt at the hands of a more powerful agent is just that increment of general anger necessary to set off hostility toward another target which is also perceived as frustrating. If this is true, it is not necessary to assume any similarity between the boss and wife, except that they are both frustrating agents.

Such an explanation is more congruent with the cognitive-affective bias of this author. Psychoanalytic and learning theories both view aggression as a drive which impels a person to action. Displacement in such a model should be tension reducing. Hokanson and Shetler (1961) showed, however, that tension may also be reduced by other indirect behavior. Furthermore, Hokanson, Burgess, and

Cohen (1963) demonstrated that only aggression directed toward the aggressor would reduce blood pressure; aggression which was displaced toward substitute targets did not reduce blood pressure. This indicates that displacement does not reduce tension, as might be expected from drive theory. Is there an alternative explanation for the phenomenon known as displacement?

To discuss this question, it is important to state some basic assumptions. It is assumed that (at least in the Western World) there are learned sets to compete from which an individual learns to value himself as he is ranked in the opinion of significant others on some important attribute. Self-esteem is therefore derived from significant-other esteem. We also learn quickly that competitive situations could have negative outcomes for us; that is, the possibility that we may "lose" always exists. Anticipation of the outcome of interaction is a critical variable in understanding displacement.

We have already noted that such displacement occurs when the frustrating agent is perceived as being too powerful to be dealt with directly. In essence, the individual looks upon the situation and makes a fair estimate as to what the outcome would be (for example, losing the job) if he attacks the frustrator directly. In general, direct counter-aggression will only occur if the perceived outcome is positive or if alternative outcomes are more negative. This seems a more reasonable explanation for displacement at the human level than the drive-generalization ideas of psychoanalytic and learning theories. The basic motivational variable is the maintenance of self-esteem by having winning outcomes, or at least avoiding losing outcomes. It is the fear of a negative outcome which prevents an individual from confronting the frustrator directly. Perceived high power in the frustrator results in fear and insecurity.

Pepitone and Reichling (1955) found that frustrated individuals were willing to direct verbal hostility toward experimenters only when the experimenters were absent. Magaziner (1961) showed that insecure individuals who had been attacked displayed more displacement of aggression than other groups. In Bandura and Walters (1959), children high in aggression were covertly or indirectly aggressive toward powerful figures (parents and teachers), while more directly aggressive toward peers.

Situational conformity. People are rewarded by behaving appropriately and according to the expectations of their significant others. Punishment and ostracism result for those who do not. Aggression, as well as altruism, is best understood in terms of conformity to expectations of a social situation and, within that context, the expectations of significant others. Powell (1966) suggested that general personality traits are not useful predictors of aggression unless they are considered within the demands of the specific situation. Simpson (1967) went further and interpreted his results as supporting the position that aggression is the response to specific situational cues. Larsen et al. (1970, 1974) found strong support for situational conformity. Social cost produces deferential behavior characterized by approval-seeking from significant others, the displacement of aggression away from significant others, and conformity to the aggressive demands of a situation.

A THEORY OF GENERAL PREJUDICE

The problem of prejudice involves the development and maintenance of biased perceptions of members of other groups prior to interaction. Why are people prejudiced in their perceptions? In this section a general theory of group prejudice will be outlined. The variables which predict prejudice include social cost, belief incongruence, and social categorization, that is, varying characteristics in individuals toward whom prejudice is directed. Two additional variables are the nature and importance of the anticipated interaction with members of other groups. If the nature of the interaction is competitive and the issue important, negative bias will result.

Norm conformity. Pettigrew (1958) noted that attempts to understand bigoted behavior have generally taken one of two forms. Either the theory has emphasized the psychological aspects of the individual bigot, that is, his personality (authoritarianism, relative hostility or aggression, frustration experienced, etc.); or it has emphasized the socio-cultural correlates of bigotry, such as the local community norms on racial tolerance and conformity to these norms. While both psychological and socio-cultural variables explain racial prejudice somewhat, Pettigrew noted that the latter variables are particularly crucial: "The problem is clear! Conformity . . . is associated with racial intolerance, while deviance from these mores is associated with racial tolerance" (1958, p. 40).

Another way of making this point is to say that people reject members of other groups mainly because they want to get along with members of their own groups. If the psychological variables were of chief importance, each bigot might be considered mentally disturbed and in need of treatment. It should be clear that such an approach would make the eradication of racial bigotry impossible. There are too many bigots and too few therapists.

Looking at bigotry from the social-cultural point of view changes the picture considerably. If "getting along" is a major concern, then the social conditions must be changed — changed in such a manner that getting along with a minority or out-group does not imply rejection by one's own reference group. The focus must be on the social conditions defining the acceptability of interracial behavior, not on the individual bigot.

Belief incongruence. Rokeach (1960) approached the problem of prejudice through the belief system of the individual and the perceived belief system of others. He suggested that perceived difference in beliefs is the critical variable determining racial prejudice. Rokeach reached the conclusion that belief congruence overrides racial or ethnic congruence except when the perceived cost is too great. Rokeach and Mezei (1966), in surveying the relative importance of beliefs versus race in several laboratory studies, stated:

> If society's constraints were altogether removed . . . man would still discriminate, if discriminate he must, not in terms of race or ethnic grouping, but in accord with his basic psychological predisposition, characteristic of all human beings, to organize the world of human beings in terms of the principle of belief congruence. (Pp. 171-72)

Social Categorization. Triandis (1961) taking issue with Rokeach's position, stated, "People do not exclude other people from their neighborhood, for instance, because other people have different belief systems, but they do exclude them because they are Negroes" (p. 186). He obtained a "race effect" which accounted for four times as much variance as did any of the other predictors employed in the study.

Stein, Hardyck, and Brewster-Smith (1965), in trying to integrate the discrepant findings of Rokeach and Triandis, found strong support for belief congruence. They maintained that if people encounter each other under conditions which favor the perception of belief congruence, racial prejudice is substantially reduced. Triandis and Davis (1965) did another study which showed intimacy to be an important variable — the more intimate the behavior, the larger the weight given to the race component.

Tajfel (1969) has proposed a three-factor theory. Three cognitive processes are considered important in the genesis of prejudice: categorization, assimilation, and search for conceptual coherence. Categorization is perceiving a difference so that, on the basis of that difference, people are assigned to groups (for example, black and white). Assimilation is learning the preference for one's own group. Tajfel explained the search for conceptual coherence as an attempt on the part of the individual to adjust to social change, so that his behavior appears consistent to himself.

Social cost and prejudice — an integrative approach. A careful consideration of these theories indicates an overlap between concepts. Since society's constraints are not "altogether removed," but are vividly present in community norms, media, and literature, the importance of social cost as a potential integrative variable is apparent (Larsen, 1972). One definition of social cost is the extent to which a person would receive punishment from his significant others (parents, employers, etc.) if he entered into a relationship with a person of a different category.

Pettigrew's concept of social conformity and Tajfel's concept of assimilation both explain the individual's desire to "get along" with his fellow man. It seems reasonable that the motivation for "getting along" is the threat of punishment from significant others. Tajfel's search for conceptual coherence and Rokeach's idea of belief incongruence also overlap. The dogmatic (closed-minded) individual has a greater need for cognitive consistency and, therefore, reacts more strongly with rejection toward groups, or persons, perceived incongruent in belief systems. It could also be reasoned that the exaggerated need for congruence is motivated by a desire to "get along" and to avoid social punishment — to maintain low levels of social cost.

Finally it could be argued that the categorization process is developed for similar reasons. Categorization permits a person to maintain a clear distinction between the sources of social reward and the sources of social cost and may be motivated by the necessity to make such distinctions to survive. The Triandis and Davis (1965) findings, which indicated the importance of intimacy in the race-versus-belief incongruence controversy, lend similar support to the importance of social cost. The reason that race is more important than belief incongruence for the most intimate relationships such as marriage is probably that race, for these relationships, contains greater possibilities of social ostracism, that is, high levels of social cost.

This review should indicate the importance of considering social cost as a predictor of preference for and rejection of others. While there is overlap between these concepts, and social cost may serve as an integrating variable, there may also be unique nuances. Keeping this in mind, a three-factor theory is proposed. The avoidance of social punishment involved in the idea of "getting along" in social conformity and assimilation may best be termed social cost. Belief incongruence and search for conceptual coherence have the property of cognitive consistency in common. Finally, there is the process of categorization, the maintenance of perceptual distinctions between objects. These three factors seem to explain the literature as we now understand it.

Relative importance of social cost, belief incongruence, and race. Assuming that there is interdependence, as well as peculiar nuances, between the processes, the relevant question at this stage of theory building becomes, what is the relative importance of these predictors of prejudice? This question was investigated by determining the relative importance of these factors in predicting preference for "types" of people in specific relationships (Larsen, 1974). "Types" mean people who vary on these factors, so that they represent either high or low social cost, or are either congruent or incongruent in beliefs (cognitive consistency), and race (categorization).

Subjects in five studies completed a "Person Preference Test," requiring the subjects to state their preferences among eight person types composed of all possible variations of the three variables across six relationships varying in intimacy. The subjects ranked, in order of preference, the eight person types. One study asked the subjects' preference for each of all possible pairs. The results showed that complete congruency (same beliefs, race, and low social cost) is most preferred. Congruent race is particularly important for the most intimate relationship, marriage. Excluding consideration of complete congruence, the relative preference of the person types were incongruent race, belief incongruence, and high social cost.

The data supports the relative importance of social cost over belief incongruence and race, and the relative importance of belief incongruence over race. It should be clearly understood that we are dealing with the question of the *relative* importance of these variables. Although social cost as operationalized here is the most important of the three, this does not imply the lack of importance of belief incongruence and race. This would be especially true in situations where these variables are confounded by social cost.

Triandis's and Davis's (1965) findings showed, as did these other studies, that race was particularly important for intimate relationships. They offered no theoretical explanation for why this was so. However, it seems likely that social pressures and cost, regarding race, would be especially intense in intimate relationships like marriage.

In addition, Larsen reported on two laboratory experiments which also required subjects to make choices between confederates who differed in social cost, belief incongruence, and race. On the whole, these studies supported the relative importance of social cost over belief incongruence and race.

Table 6.1 shows a summary of the results of the Larsen research program. There are minor variations, but since these results summarize seven different samples obtained at different times and employing four different methods, the relative consistency cannot be overlooked.

Social cost is not once chosen as the most preferred; and, in the two cases where it changes place with belief incongruence, all differences are statistically insignificant. It is therefore possible to offer the tentative proposition that social cost is the relatively most important variable in predicting preference or rejection as compared to belief incongruence or race. The pressure of the social environment, the status attributed by the group, the need to be socially accepted, and the fear of being rejected which are tied up with the

Table 6.1

Preference order for choices of types or stooges incongruent
in social cost, belief incongruence, and race for
the seven studies

Preference Order*

	Social Cost	Belief Incongruence	Race
Study 1	2	3	1
Study 2	3	2	1
Study 3	3	2	1
Study 4	3	2	1
Study 5	3	2	1
Study 6	3	1	2
Study 7	2	3	1

*1 is most preferred, 3 least preferred.

concept of social cost are variables which deserve closer scrutiny in the area of interpersonal and inter-group rejection.

The observed differences may even be deemed conservative, as social cost is confounded with belief incongruence and race and is therefore responsible for part of the variance in these two concepts, as well. Since social cost theory encompasses both belief incongruence and race, it is also more parsimonious. Social cost may also be the reason why perfect congruence on all three variables is preferred most for the intimate relationships and least for the less intimate relationships. For example, in marriage, a cost would undoubtedly accrue from significant others if the partner were belief incongruent or of a different race. In a recent cross-cultural and cross-national study (Larsen, Larsen, and Ommundsen, 1975), the generic nature and relative importance of social cost was affirmed.

Mezei (1971) has independently developed a program of research very similar to the ideas contained in the Larsen study. He found that race prejudice was significantly higher than belief prejudice for marriage. However, when perceived social pressure is held constant, belief similarity is more important, even for marriage. He notes:

> Whenever conformity to social pressure is a significant determinant of behavioral intentions, the balance model for

determining the acceptance or rejection of another person can be, and needs to be, expanded to take into account both the belief congruence and the social pressure variables. (P. 80)

Since human beings are gregarious and uniquely dependent on social approval for behavior, it is doubtful whether societal constraints will ever be removed or conformity to social pressure ever be found a non-significant factor. For those practically or theoretically concerned with the problem of racial prejudice, or the general rejection of other people, any remedy must begin with the social cost of the situation. If social cost were truly eliminated, and not statistically controlled, there is nothing in the literature to suggest that discrimination on the basis of either categorical or belief differences would exist.

If the social cost proposition is correct, the social policy leading to improvement of inter-group relations is also clear. To improve images of members of other groups and reduce the negative effect of social cost, society must improve the conditions of contact between members of groups. The conditions of contact which will reduce social cost are outlined by Allport (1958); they include equal status, common goals, and interdependence, only possible by means of the positive sanctions of government.

Anticipated outcome and importance of interaction. The three-factor theory of prejudice previously discussed is incomplete. In order for social cost, belief incongruence, and race to affect racial rejection there would have to be some anticipation of the outcome of interaction between the individual and these "types" of people. — May we anticipate such interaction to be pleasant or unpleasant? Would it be costly or rewarding? In addition, some interactions are more important than others.

At least two other variables are important in the rejection of or hostility toward members of other groups. The reason people react to race, belief, and social cost differences is that they anticipate some negative or positive outcome from interaction. Anticipated interaction or outcome is an important variable in producing rejection.

Rabbie and Horowitz (1969) have demonstrated that, when people experience a common fate as a result of belonging to a particular group, they tend to view members of their own group more favorably than members of other groups. Not only are images, or perceptions, of other people affected, but Tajfel, Flament, Billig, and Bundy (1971) have shown that belonging to groups also affects decisions made about members of one's own group and members of other groups. In particular, the in-group is treated more favorably than the out-group. This is true even if the groups consist only of people with a particular artistic preference and even if there is no relationship between this artistic preference and the decisions being made (the awarding of punishment or reward).

Doise (1969) has shown that these biases occur before any inter-group decision, suggesting that biased perceptions serve to justify the anticipated interaction. For example, if the nature of the interaction is expected to be competitive, negative images and decisions occur; if the interaction is expected to be cooperative, positive images or decisions result. A great deal of research indicates that the importance of an issue influences individuals' subsequent responses (for example, see Engley, 1967; Sherif and Sherif, 1967). Doise, Csepeli, Dietrich-Dann, Gouge, Larsen, and Ostell (1971) predicted: simple group membership would lead to more favorable images of the in-group (categorization), anticipated cooperation would lead to more favorable images and behavior toward the out-group than would competition, low common fate (low importance) would produce less biased images and behavior than would high common fate.

The results of the Doise et al. study showed, without exception, that in-group–out-group discrimination occurred consistently for all groups. On the basis of being told that they belonged to a group which had only an aesthetic preference for ambiguous photographs in common (the photographs were blown-up pictures of blood cells), the participants rated members of their own group more favorably than members of any other group. This was true before any decisions, and therefore interaction with the other group, occurred. We may, therefore, assume that simply being assigned to a group category is sufficient for producing out-group rejection. The participants systematically gave less money to members of the out-group in the anticipated competitive situation. This was true even if this strategy led to an objective loss for the in-group. There was a tendency for members of the competitive group to maximize the differences between themselves and the out-group. There was also a tendency for this to occur more often in the high common fate (high importance) group than in the low common fate group.

If categorization leads to discrimination in inter-group behavior (decision making) so that the in-group is more favorably treated than the out-group, is the opposite also true? Would the anticipation of inter-group behavior and actual decision making lead to categorization?

To investigate this question, Doise et al. included four "objective" traits in a task rating the "other" group members. These traits dealt with physical characteristics (blond/dark, tall/short, fat/thin, colorful/quiet). Comparing the experimental groups and the control groups showed that the experimental groups rated "own" and "other" groups differently on these traits. This indicates that the anticipation of behavior may lead to categorization.

The research discussed in this section indicates the importance of five variables in producing prejudice. Social cost is generic to belief and categorization prejudice. People are prejudiced because they want to get along with their significant others and avoid ostracism. The prejudice formula also includes the anticipated competitive nature of the interaction and the importance of the issue which brings the groups in contact with each other. The elimination of unsupported negative bias must utilize the information derived from these studies.

SUMMARY

In this chapter, topics broadly defined as social-psychological were considered. The literature shows that observation of aggressive social models may increase the likelihood of aggression. The role of the mass media was discussed; violent programs may induce aggression because models are justified in aggressive behavior, are frequently rewarded, and appear powerful, and because pain is distorted, thus possibly interfering with empathetic processes. Some people are more likely to imitate aggressive models than others. A combination of model credibility and persuadability of the spectator is essential for imitation. The variables producing modeling effects interact in a complex pattern which is only partially understood.

Being a member of any group creates negative images of and behavior toward other groups. This seems an inevitable result of the competition encouraged in the Western World. Each individual anticipates the outcome of any interaction; and, in competitive situations, there are always possibilities for loss and other negative outcomes. This is probably one very important reason why almost any group membership is productive of aggression and hostility.

The importance of social cost as a generic variable was emphasized. The individual seeks to maintain his self-esteem and, consequently, seeks to anticipate the outcome of any potential interaction. Social cost predicts deferential behavior toward powerful others, the displacement of anger, and situational conformity.

A theory of general prejudice was presented in outline form. The literature has shown the importance of norm conformity, belief incongruence, and social categorization in prejudicial perceptions and behavior. The results of several experiments show that social cost produces more rejection than belief incongruence and race. Social cost is basic to understanding the social psychology of aggression.

We began this section on human aggression with an evaluation of the major theoretical concepts and their mythological or model building components. It is time now to assess what we have learned and to formulate a comprehensive model of human aggression. The next chapter outlines a two-factor model which accounts for both the rational learning nature of man and the possibility of reflex aggression in response to noxious stimuli.

7.

Types of Aggression—Toward a
Comprehensive Theory of Human Aggression

The nature or nurture question of human aggression discussed in Chapter 3 is a "pseudo" question. As indicated, human aggression is not caused by either nature or nurture alone. Nature and nurture interact in producing behavior. The evidence indicates the predominant importance of learning in human aggression; however, as Berkowitz (1973) points out, "Innate determinants do enter into man's attacks on others, primarily in connection with impulsive reactions to noxious events and frustrations" (p. 40). This observation supports the theory, suggested in this chapter, that two types of aggression are evident in human behavior: stimulus equity aggression, provoked by pain and other forms of arbitrary-noxious stimuli; and situational conformity aggression, which will be discussed later.

STIMULUS EQUITY AGGRESSION

An example of stimulus equity aggression is the automatically hostile reaction to having one's feet stepped upon. A recipient of pain finds that it takes a great deal of personal and social inhibition to prevent the expression of verbal hostility toward the instigator of the pain. Pain, or arbitrary-noxious stimulus, elicits stimulus equity aggression, with rage and injury oriented responses the resulting behaviors. The aim of these responses is to injure, either verbally or overtly, the instigator of the stimulus. The predominant intervening variable is the emotional reaction of anger. Learned inhibitions of aggression are less effective with this type of response. Stimulus equity aggression is characterized by an efficient and immediate circuit between stimulus and response.

Although the organic and physiological factors are not clear, it is apparent that there may be some genetic basis for this more primitive form of behavior, as suggested in the innate formulations on aggression. Undoubtedly, a large proportion of the violent criminals belong to the stimulus equity category, but as a whole the theory applies only to a small amount of human aggressive behavior. After all, violent criminals are only a small part of the total criminal population, who in turn are only a small part of society. Perhaps the innate factor is the excessive presence of the so-called "male" hormones in the violent criminal population.

Stimulus equity theory suggests a balance between stimulus and response, at least for the limited class of aversive stimuli (pain and arbitrary-noxious stimuli) and the consequent rage reaction. This class of aversive stimuli sets off a reaction sequence which is difficult to inhibit through social and cognitive factors. Because of individual differences in genetic inheritance, arbitrary-noxious stimuli may set off stronger reactions in certain individuals than in others; but for all people, inhibitions are less effective for this class of stimuli.

The rage reaction establishes an equity between the intensity of the stimulus and the intensity of the response. Since stimulus equity aggression is affected more by the emotion of anger than by cognitive factors, the rage reaction is initially emotional in nature. Subsequent reactions may, however, be interpreted cognitively in terms of justice or equity. Perhaps our cognitive-social conceptions of justice are derived from these primitive stimulus-response reactions. The aforementioned relationship is diagrammed in Figure 7.1.

Stimulus equity aggression, then, is initiated by a class of aversive stimuli best termed arbitrary-noxious. This class in addition to pain contains other forms of arbitrary stimuli such as frustration instigated by people high in power who are unlikely targets for retaliation. Displacement and other forms of cathartic activities which frequently follow arbitrary frustration are characterized by anger and injury aims and may be delayed forms of this rage reaction.

The predominant intervening variable between the arbitrary-noxious stimuli and rage is anger. Cognitive factors are less effective in inhibiting the immediate response and often fail in preventing displacement in the long run.

SITUATIONAL CONFORMITY AGGRESSION

Humans are characterized by plasticity and modifiableness by the social environment. Therefore any comprehensive theory must begin with an analysis of the factors facilitating aggression in the social structure. Pettigrew (1958) came to the conclusion that conformity is a crucial variable underlying racial intolerance. Since racial intolerance is a form of aggressive behavior, the analogy is well applied here in a broader perspective. Situational conformity aggression is determined by the expectation of reward and punishment, that is, by the perceived social cost of an aggressive act.

Figure 7.1
Stimulus Equity Aggression

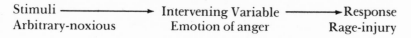

Stimuli ⟶ Intervening Variable ⟶ Response
Arbitrary-noxious   Emotion of anger   Rage-injury

Learning factors: low in importance
Cognitive-social inhibitors: low in effectiveness

In some cases, moral values of the individual may inhibit the aggressive expression, however, such qualms are easily overridden by coercive factors from sources which have been attributed high social power. Authoritarian persons attribute high power to significant others and are known to display excessive hostility toward out-groups (where the social cost is low). Larsen and Minton (1971) have related the high attribution of power to chauvinistic nationalism, dogmatism, and competitive behavior. Most people are affected by the perceived power of significant others and will weigh the potential social cost of an action before deciding on a response.

SOCIAL COST AND TYPES OF HUMAN AGGRESSION

Although emotions may distort the social cost of aggression, situational conformity aggression is characterized by evaluation of alternative courses of action following non-arbitrary goal blockage. The instrumental reaction to frustration depends on the expected social cost, which in turn is dependent on three parameters. These parameters include the strength and nature of aversive stimuli possessed by the frustrator, the potential threat to personal survival following the instrumental reaction, and significant-other support for aggression. While these factors are important, they do not always operate at a high level of consciousness. By trial and error we have developed rather accurate perceptions of what is expected in each situation, and the identification of the significant others. The social cost utility theory proposed here does not imply unduly long evaluations of courses of action. The situational conformity process works efficiently and, often, automatically. This is accounted for by the fact that most of us have developed positive attitudes toward significant others and have the ability to quickly identify these persons in any situation.

The mass murder of Jews during World War II is an example of instrumental aggression; the murderers themselves were in a coercive situation containing high attributed power (to officers, etc.) and unacceptable social cost (their own lives) if they would refuse to carry out an order. In this case, as in the case of most mass aggression, the coercive factors of the environment outweighed any moral or internalized inhibitions. The behavior of lynch mobs is characterized by similar factors.

Wheeler (1966) defines contagious behavior as the type of behavior the individual is normally motivated to engage in but prevented from by barriers and inhibitions. Whether individuals are normally motivated to commit murder is questionable. The lynching situation, however, is characterized by low (or nonexistent) social cost for participation and a probable high social cost for failure to participate.

It is proposed that the basic variable producing situational conformity aggression is social cost. Most frequently it is the perceived social cost which determines the course of action a person takes when faced with frustration.

The stimulus in situational conformity aggression is some form of goal blockage. This goal blockage sets in motion cognition of alternative courses of action and an evaluation of the possible social cost of these actions. The eventual instrumental response aimed at removing the goal blockage is based on the expectation of short-term and long-term social cost. In essence, as individuals, groups, or nations, we conform to the expectations of a situation (situational conformity). The demands of the situation involve choosing the course of action with the least long-term perceived social cost.

Situational conformity theory emphasizes the importance of both potential reward and potential punishment. The social cost concept explains the achievement of the maximum reward (goal achievement) at the least cost. It is, therefore, a utility theory at the perceptual level — not a rational theory. This means that, objectively, aggression may be totally irrational, while subjectively (i.e., at the perceptual level), the expectations of social cost have been duly evaluated and accepted.

Effect of perceptual distortions and motives on social cost. The importance of perception as influencing social judgment cannot be overlooked. Regardless of whether we speak of individual, group, or international aggression, people make decisions and their judgments are influenced by numerous factors.

Perception may be a most unreliable indicator of reality. We draw inferences about "real" events; but these inferences are colored by our emotions, our value system or ideology (Larsen, 1971c), and the intensity of our motivations. In a direct way, these factors influence what comes to our attention. Our brains simply cannot be attentive to all details and select only parts of reality for our evaluation. The data selected are, to a large extent, determined by our defenses and our need to seek the pleasant and avoid the unpleasant, that is, our need to reduce social cost to a minimum. Our defenses, designed to protect the ego, distort reality. Differences may be exaggerated and opponents with differences may be seen as enemies. The threat to oneself is exaggerated out of proportion to any objective criteria.

Motives may also affect perception and social judgement. Most motives are ambivalent in the sense that the same stimuli may arouse both negative and positive expectations (Hardy, 1964). The negative expectation is the social cost; the positive expectation is the desirability of achieving the goal in question. If the desirability is very high, for example, if the goal makes the achievement of intrinsic values possible, it may outweigh any cost and move the individual to action. At the same time desirability may also affect perception in such a manner as to reduce the perceived social cost of the action. In any event, motivation (the propensity to act) is determined by the relative strength of the avoidance movement, caused by the perceived social cost and the approach movement, caused by the desirability of the goal.

Desirability of the goal may also affect the perceived probability of achieving the goal. Underground armies and liberation forces in past and present wars often fight against what appear to be insurmountable odds. Yet the desirability of the goal, freedom or independence, may reduce the perceived strength of the occupiers; and, in the manner of the self-fulfilling prophecy (acting in accordance with self perceptions and thus fulfilling them), the objectively inferior forces often are equal or superior in strength to the objectively superior forces (who are low on goal desirability and ambiguous, or high, in perceived social cost).

Parameters of social cost. There are three parameters determining social cost. One is the avoidance properties of the aversive stimuli in the situation. How much capability for administering punishment is possessed by the instigator to frustration? What is the nature of the aversive stimulus which prevents goal achievement? Since there are qualitative, as well as quantitative, differences between goal blocking stimuli, the aversive stimulus in itself is a weighted factor in the expectancy of social cost. For example, it makes a big difference whether the goal blocking stimulus is a nuclear arsenal or a .22 single shot rifle.

The second property is the amount of threat in the situation which follows aggression. This is partially, but not completely, defined by the quantity and quality of aversive stimuli. In addition, there is the perceived intention of the instigator to frustration and the amount of risk to personal survival following the counter-aggression of the instigator. If the counter-aggression commits the frustrator to total war, to winner-take-all conflict, the counter-aggression may contain considerable threat.

Situational conformity aggression, then, is initiated by some goal blockage leading to a cognition of alternative courses of action associated with an evaluation of the social cost of each move in terms of both short- and long-term effects. In contrast to stimulus equity aggression, situational conformity aggression depends a great deal on previous learning. Cognitive-social inhibitors tend to be high in effectiveness and tend to make any reaction cautious. Emotional factors are not ruled out, but they probably affect behavior mainly by distorting the perceptual process. These points are summarized in Figure 7.2.

Figure 7.2
Situational Conformity Aggression

Stimuli	Intervening Variables	Response
Nonarbitrary goal blockage	Cognition of alternative courses of action and expected social cost (aversive stimuli, threat, significant-other support). Emotions may distort social cost.	Instrumental reaction

Learning factors: High in importance
Cognitive-social inhibitors: High in effectiveness

SOME APPLICATIONS OF THE TWO-FACTOR THEORY

Both stimulus equity aggression and situational conformity aggression represent extremes in behavior. At one end of a continuum is the purely emotional reactive aggression; at the other is the cooler, more cognitive and evaluative aggression. The discussion of these two types was not meant to imply the absence of intermediate forms of aggression, that is, forms which are partially stimulus equity and partially situational conformity. However, since the hypothesized sources are quite different (genetic inheritance in stimulus equity, social development in situational conformity), the overlap between the two forms may be minimal. Stimulus equity aggression is primarily the interest of therapists, police, and social work agencies; situational conformity aggression is the concern of social psychologists (inter-group conflict), political scientists, and international relations experts. The former requires individual treatment, unless the arbitrary stimulus is social. If a sufficiently large number of people find communication avenues closed to them (arbitrarily), rage may be expressed in riots or other demonstrations. The remedy for the latter lies in reformulation of the social structure, providing more incentives for dissent, and in social support, aimed at strengthening internal values against brutality.

COMPLIANT AGGRESSION—AN EXAMPLE OF SITUATIONAL CONFORMITY AGGRESSION

One paradigm for studying aggression under controlled conditions is to investigate the willingness of subjects to apply electrical shock to a victim within a learning study situation. Milgram (1963, 1964a, 1964b, 1965a, 1965b, 1967) reported on a comprehensive laboratory study of obedience. The basic model of his studies was: if X tells Y to hurt Z, under what conditions will Y obey the commands of X, and under what conditions will he refuse? The basic procedure involved commanding naive subjects to administer increasingly severe "shock" to a victim who was really the experimenter's collaborator. The victim acted the role of a learner in a learning experiment. Milgram found that subjects would "shock" victims at even highly dangerous levels on the command of the experimenter and suggested, but did not investigate, that both the social structure of the situation and the subject's personality were determining factors for this form of aggression.

Larsen, Coleman, Forbes, and Johnson (1972) proposed to investigate this question of the willingness to administer shocks as a function of personality and situational variables. A major difference in procedure from Milgram was that in no case did the experimenter order the subject to administer the punishment. Rather than obedience to commands, the experimenters permitted the situations to exert their influence; therefore, the basic variable studied was situational conformity. The term "subject" is used to denote the person whose behavior is being investigated. The "learner" was actually a collaborator of the experimenter, and no voltage was passed. This rationale was developed in order to investigate aggressive behavior without the subject's awareness, otherwise the behavior might have been influenced by this knowledge.

Prior to the experiment, the subjects had completed five indexes thought important to measuring personality dynamics relevant to aggression: the aggression scale (Larsen, 1971a); the attributed power scale (Larsen and Minton, 1971); the Buss hostility scale (Buss and Durkee, 1957); the parental aggression training (PAT) scale (Larsen and Schwendiman, 1970); and the machiavellianism scale (Christie and Geis, 1970). When the subject arrived for the experiment, he was told that the purpose of the research was to investigate the effects of punishment upon learning. The instructions for the experiment include: "[The learner] is asked a series of sixty paired-comparison questions. Whether his answers are right or wrong are indicated to you by the appropriate light flashing on this machine (the experimenter points to the machine). Your job, then, is to shock the learner after each wrong answer . . . be the most effective teacher you can be, using shock to punish the learner for wrong answers." The learner sat in one room separated by about 20 feet from another room in which was placed the shock apparatus. The apparatus consisted of a gray rectangular box, about 8 inches high and 12 inches wide. In the upper right-hand corner, there was an orange light labeled "right;" and in the upper left-hand corner, an orange light labeled "wrong." A meter indicated with a needle the amount of voltage used. Below this meter was a switch used by the subjects to control the length of time during which the shock was administered. A dial was located on the right side of the machine and calibrated from 9 to 390 volts; the 0-120 range was labeled in green as "Slight" shock, the 121-240 range was labeled in yellow as "Moderate," and the 241-390 range was labeled in red as

"Danger: Severe Shock." It was possible for the subject to select any voltage level, although every tenth voltage was clearly marked.

The room with the "learner" was equipped with an "electric chair" consisting of shock electrodes and a machine which communicated the learner's response to the subject. The learner's machine (unknown to the subject) also recorded the subject's choice of voltage levels. The experimenter introduced the subject to the learner and stated as a final instruction, "Although the shocks can be extremely painful, the learner does not suffer any permanent damage."

There were other experimental conditions in addition to the control condition already described. In the "model" condition, pretensions about the experiments being behind schedule were made. In order to speed things up, the subject was asked to watch the current "teacher," who was actually a collaborator and was administering shocks at very high levels. It was reasoned that the subjects would find it easier to administer punishment (find it more legitimate) if someone first modeled such behavior. In the "conformity" condition, a team of three made shock level decisions, but two, unknown to the subject, were collaborators. One always went 10 points ahead of the last shock level and the other always 20 points ahead, but the subject administered the shock composed of the average of the individual decisions. In the "high model" condition, the experimenter left the dial on 350 volts rather than turning it back to zero as in the control condition. The only variable here then was the "suggestion" that someone has previously shocked at this high level. Note that, in all these situations, the only coercive element was the demand of the situation itself, not unlike many real life conditions.

The results showed no relationship between the personality variables measuring aggression and the tendency to administer punishment. While this does not represent a critical test, it does suggest the need to reevaluate any study of social attitudes which does not take into account the situational context. Rokeach (1970) noted that the discrepancy between measured attitudes and actual behavior may be attributed to the fact that, in most experiments, only attitudes toward the attitudinal object are measured. By also measuring attitudes toward various elements in the situation, he demonstrated considerable increases in the amount of total variance accounted for.

This result suggests the need to understand the demands of the situational factors in order to understand aggression.

All the experimental conditions which contained pressures from the situation showed significantly higher levels of shocking than did the control condition. The shock levels were frequently at highly dangerous, and obviously painful, levels. It is clear that, even if the demands of the situation are comparatively mild, nearly one hundred percent of the people will engage in injurious behavior. Due to careful debriefing, there is no doubt that the experiment was accepted as realistic by the subjects. The subjects were obviously tense and most of the verbal comments made by them dealt with the conflict between their moral convictions and conforming to the demands of the experiment. Only 3 subjects out of the 213 refused to participate once the experiment was explained.

An idea of the high levels of shock administered can be gained from the average maximum voltage shocked; for control it was 157; for model 172; for conformity, 293; and for high model, 237. These voltage levels, if real, would produce excruciating pain. Whereas Milgram found that subjects would commit personally distasteful acts by command, Larsen et al. demonstrated that nearly all people sampled responded in a similar manner to apparent mildly compelling situations. One is tempted to suggest that situational conformity is the prime mover of all things human, and an evaluation of the parameters of situational conformity is a key prerequisite for a comprehensive theory of aggression.

SUMMARY

The chapter attempted to outline a comprehensive theory of human aggression. The theory suggests two types of aggression. One type, stimulus equity aggression, is conceived of as an emotional-reactive response to an arbitrary-noxious stimulus. An example of such a stimulus might be the pain derived from someone stepping on your toes, which in turn would lead to an emotion of anger and a rage and an injury oriented response which is expressed, depending on dominance or power factors, in the environment. As a whole, learning factors are lower in importance for this class of stimuli, and thus cognitive-social inhibitors are less effective against rage reactions.

The other type, situational conformity aggression, is a response to a stimulus of goal blockage not perceived as arbitrary, as there are alternatives for action. The intervening variable is the cognition of the alternative courses of action and the expected social cost of each. This is not a rational theory, as the literature testifies to the importance of motivational factors influencing perception. Goal desirability may reduce the perceived social cost of an action.

III.
INTERNATIONAL HOSTILITY

The final level of aggression considered in this book is international hostility. Throughout history warfare has been a human experience. With the advent of the nuclear age, the possibilities of destruction stagger the imagination. In this section, then, we focus first on the factors which lead to hostile international images in individuals. The objective reasons for war are always closely correlated with rationalizations for war based on hostile images. The second major purpose is to discuss the processes leading to conflict management and resolution. The self-fulfilling prophecy says that a person will act in the present according to what he believes will happen in the future. We shall discuss people's anticipation of the future with respect to war and peace.

The purpose of this section is to outline the causes of international hostility, to suggest remedies and solutions, and to examine what people in twelve nations expect of the future with respect to war and peace. Chapter 8 outlines two models for hostile international images based on the experimental literature. It is possible to prevent conflicts from becoming overt without resolving the underlying causes. Yet, in the dangerous world in which we live, the control of conflict is crucial. Conflict management is discussed in Chapter 9. However, a peace based on control alone is inherently unstable. A permanent peace must be based on the resolution of conflict. This requires a peace ideology as a guideline for conflict resolution; such an ideology is outlined in Chapter 10. The final chapter of the section, and of the book, is a report of an international study investigating people's anticipation of the future up to the year 2000. What do the world's people expect the future to hold with regard to the question of war and peace?

8.

The Development and Maintenance
of Hostile International Images

In this chapter we are concerned with international images, particularly hostile images, as mediators of international conflict. An image is a psychological construct representing all the current knowledge, beliefs, and emotions an individual possesses concerning a particular subject. Images are what people believe is true about the world around them. They function as anchor points in selective information gathering and processing; consequently, they reduce the complexity of information to manageable proportions. Images are dependent on experiences and may therefore vary in dimensional complexity. Some images are simple, as exemplified in extreme good/bad dichotomies ("the communist world is evil — the 'free' world is good"); and some are very complex. People's images generally fall at some point between these two extremes; that is, they may be characterized as being relatively simple or complex.

The set of beliefs and values known as ethnocentrism contributes to hostile intergroup images by accentuating the differences between a person's values and habits and those of people who belong to other groups. A number of variables contribute to this contrast effect. Based on the review of the literature, two models of hostile inter-group images are proposed in this chapter. One emphasizes the social psychological factors predicting hostile inter-group images. The second is a comprehensive socio-cultural model of levels of influence of preponderant importance. A key integrating concept in both models is social cost. This information is employed to illustrate the process of changing of images from predominantly negative to predominantly positive. Finally, we will discuss the relevance of this perceptual approach to national decision making.

ETHNOCENTRISM AND INTERNATIONAL IMAGES: A REVIEW OF THE LITERATURE

The psychological images held of other nations correspond more or less to reality. To the extent that such images are realistic, they prevent miscalculating the intentions of foreign "opposition" and therefore serve the cause of peace. This is especially true since misperceptions are rarely friendly and are more often biased toward paranoid images and hostility. Some individuals hold truthful

---

SOCIAL COST AND HOSTILE INTERGROUP IMAGES

The potential assimilation of foreign values is threatened by "significant other" rejection, because discrepant habits and values threaten the stability of the group. The effect of social cost on hostile images is that ethnocentric pressure produces high social cost for individuals who interact with "foreign" peoples. High social cost in turn contributes to the cognitive-perceptual contrast effect which accentuates the "foreignness" of other peoples' beliefs and habits. The contrast effect is the justification for ethnocentrism, that is, the syndrome of traits which produces out-group rejection and hostile images. The social psychological model for hostile images shows that the combined effect of personality traits and group pressure is to increase the social cost of foreign contacts as a function of the intimacy of the contact and the psychological and cultural distance between the groups. The socio-cultural model indicates levels of preponderant influence, starting with the competitive nature of our society and leading to approval-seeking and hostile images. The change of hostile international images must be based on this social cost interpretation. Change attempts must be directed primarily toward the opinion leaders who serve as significant others. These can be readily identified by means of the social position index developed by Galtung.

images of other groups part of the time; a few hold approximate realistic images of other nations all the time; but the majority rarely, if ever, have truthful images of other nations. The syndrome of traits known as ethnocentrism is the source of negative images of other peoples. Ethnocentrism produces a contrast effect, so the beliefs and habits of other people are viewed as discrepant, esoteric, and foreign. The property of "foreignness" falls along a dimension anchored by the very familiar at one end and by the very exotic, fearful, and incomprehensible at the other extreme.

Ethnocentrism is essentially the view that the very familiar culture and values of one's own group are morally "good." The values of this familiar group therefore become standards of comparison for all other groups, presenting a test which all other groups must necessarily fail. Behaviorally, ethnocentrism involves the rejection of members of other groups simply because they are outsiders; they do not belong to the in-group. At the perceptual level, ethnocentrism is basic to hostile images. Negative inter-group images are the result of perceiving a broad range of objects as foreign (contrast effect) and perceiving a narrow range of objects as familiar (assimilation effect). Contributing to the contrast effect are conditions of contact which make differences between groups salient: low levels and simple forms of information about the other group, paranoid values, conformity pressures, personal insecurity, personal belligerence, and threat. These factors all aid in making the values and habits of other peoples seem more foreign and psychologically distant and therefore contribute to ethnocentrism.

The contrast-assimilation effect. One need only observe the casual visitor to a foreign country to be cognizant of the contrast effect. A principle from psychophysics serves as an important aid to understanding the traveler's judgment of a foreign culture. Psychophysical experiments with weights have shown that if an individual compares a series of weights (say from 10 to 300 grams) with a standard weight (for example, 75 grams), an interesting perceptual distortion occurs. Those weights which are relatively close to the standard weight (75 grams) are experienced as being even closer than they really are, whereas those objectively much lighter or much heavier are perceived as being even lighter or heavier than they really are. This contraction and expansion of perception of subjectively experienced weights is known as the contrast-assimilation phenomenon.

The principle has been used outside of psychophysics to explain social judgment and, especially, the distortion which occurs when a person has a strong attitude and is very ego involved with the object he is trying to judge. See Sherif and Hovland (1965) for a discussion of contrast-assimilation as related to social judgment.

While all individuals evidently are subject to this principle, some persons are more apt to distort reality than are others. Larsen (1971c) found evidence that those individuals who are closed-minded (dogmatic) are more apt to be affected by the contrast-assimilation principle than are individuals who are open-minded. He asked a large sample of college students to place a series of attitude statements on three issues into one of eleven categories. Category 1 was very favorable toward the issue; Category 6, neutral, and Category 11, very unfavorable toward the issue. The instructions involved placing these statements into categories independent of the individual's own attitude — in other words, to make objective judgments as to where these statements belonged. The sample also completed Rokeach's (1960) dogmatism scale.

Results of the study showed, among other things, that highly dogmatic subjects placed more statements into the extreme categories (1, 2, 10, 11) than did subjects low in dogmatism. It would appear that dogmatic individuals, as a result of certain child-rearing procedures and cultural experiences (or lack of these), develop a primitive way of thinking about the world, characterized by more than average dependence on the contrast-assimilation principle.

When any traveler visits a foreign country, he is barraged by cues and stimuli which indicate the degree of "foreignness" of the exposure. If the differences are slight, the experience may be assimilated, and the foreign culture will be seen as being more like the native culture than it really is. At the other extreme, we may observe the phenomenon known as "cultural shock." This condition is characterized by fear, bewilderment, and disorientation, as the traveler is exposed to the foreign culture. Cultural shock is produced by the emphasis on the foreign aspects of the culture, producing the contrast phenomenon.

Exposure to that which is considered foreign is high in social cost. Whether the traveler experiences it directly, or the citizens at home experience it as mediated by the news media or official propaganda, foreignness threatens the established values and beliefs of the individual. These values and beliefs were developed from significant others; therefore, the assimilation of foreign values results in significant-other rejection. Since most national groups are ethnocentric, there is always the potential of significant-other rejection as a result of cross-national contacts and relations. In order to survive, the individual learns early to make distinctions between in-groups and out-groups, and habitually learns to value the former. These factors all interact to produce high social cost associated with international images, and therefore they contribute to the contrast effect which produces hostile images.

Conditions of contact between groups. It is a rather common-sense idea that the less knowledge a person has about another nation, the more likely that his images will be distorted. This does not imply that familiarity *per se* will produce accurate and realistic images, for the *nature* of the contact affects the accuracy of perception.

However, one possible benefit from any kind of contact, is that at least the most ridiculous and extreme image distortions may be removed. If an individual believed that members of another group grew horns on their heads (by way of analogy), at least such an extreme image could be destroyed with a single contact. However, any contact which serves to sharpen perceptual differences between the individual and the contact group contributes to negative images. This is especially true where the contact emphasizes ethnocentric symbols of minimal or no meaning to the individual. Thus, depending on the type of contact, interaction with members of other groups may produce either a contrast or an assimilation effect.

Information complexity. There is a body of evidence which shows that variety, volume, and complexity of information and experience (being exposed to, being confronted by, and evaluating many aspects of the same problem) lead to differential evaluation of other people (nations) and therefore less proneness to develop negative stereotypes. Under conditions of emotionality, a person is more apt to make rash, polarized judgments. Scott (1963) showed that the greater number of attributes (dimensional complexity) a person had available, the less likely the person was to think emotionally (the greater the ability for non-affective cognition).

Scott and Withey (1958) showed in another study that people who are well informed about world affairs are more sympathetic toward internationalist positions in foreign policy and tend also to support the United Nations to a greater extent than people ignorant of world affairs. They suggest that having only a minimal amount of information about the world leads to simplistic thinking (unidimensional structure), which is conducive to ethnocentric attitudes and the maintenance of the maximum psychological distance from things perceived as being foreign.

Perhaps complexity of experience reduces the perceived social cost of interacting with foreign people or nations, and thereby reduces the psychological distance. Information complexity disconfirms the ethnocentric point of view. For a person in possession of a complex international viewpoint, the nature of the aversive stimuli (foreignness) is disconfirmed, the threat of foreignness reduced, and the significant-other support sought is shifted from ethnocentric groups to a broad identification with humanity and world institutions.

That increased knowledge of a foreign group leads to more positive images is suggested by the work of de Sola Pool (1965). He showed that a lengthy stay in a foreign nation tends to produce a U-shaped curve of changing attitudes. Initially the individual had very positive attitudes toward the host country; then, within the first year, the visitor experienced problems of adjustment. However, if he remained in the country beyond a certain time, the visitor gained a deeper and more positive image of the host country. These findings are also supported by Lysgaard (1955), Coelho (1958), Morris (1960), and Selltiz and Cook (1962), whose studies all suggest that increased contact produces more favorable images.

One may speculate that initially all inexperienced visitors possess black-white stereotypes about a potential host country. Since they presumably choose to visit the country, the assumption may be made that, although undifferentiated, the image is probably favorable. Problems of adjustment shatter illusions, but increased experience produces empathetic identification and favorable images. Since these latter images are closer to reality, they are less likely to be disconfirmed and more likely to endure.

As Coelho (1958) points out, the effect of first-hand experience is the reduction of stereotyping; and, as time passes, the visitor develops a more differentiated image. Sophisticated and differentiated insight is associated with favorable images, probably because such insight increases the likelihood of empathetic identification. Ignorance facilitates negative stereotyping.

Intelligence may be defined as the ability to adapt to changing environments. Both genetic and environmental factors influence the level of intelligence. By the same token, the level of intelligence probably also influences the number, type, and complexity of experiences a person is exposed to. Rosenberg (1965) suggests that, with the application of intelligence, even distant matters and events are perceived as being personally relevant. It could be argued that the ability to adapt and the ability to reduce psychological distance is mediated by the empathetic process of identification.

Intelligence is related to favorable international images because it is related to the ability to empathize. Intelligence is functionally related to complexity of information. A complex differentiated environment stimulates comparatively higher levels of intelligence; conversely, high levels of intelligence may encourage the searching out of complex environments. Such curiosity motivation, that is, getting beyond the dulling constrictions of familiar routines, is related to positive images (Rosenberg, 1956). Chesler and Schmuck (1964) showed students who favored intellectualism rejected the need for heavy national armaments, whereas anti-intellectual students favored such a policy. Low levels of information complexity predict the contrast effect in image formation.

Paranoid values and ethnocentrism. Being intelligent and cognitively complex implies the ability to overcome the perceptual distortions resulting from emotion-laden values and conformity pressures. That values may distort perception was clearly demonstrated in an experiment by Bruner and Goodman (1947). These investigators asked ten-year-old children to estimate the size of various coins by adjusting a circular spot of light until it was the same size as a given coin. They compared children from well-to-do homes and from poor homes and found that poor children tended on the average to overestimate the size of coins to a greater extent than "well-to-do" children. Similar results have been found by other investigators (e.g., Ashley, Harper, and Rynyon, 1951; Secord, Bevan, and Katz, 1956).

Values in particular determine the aspects of the environment which we attend to and therefore act as a selective filter of information. Values which are relevant in the formation of international images include those parts of the personality syndrome known as chauvinistic nationalism and, more broadly, ethnocentrism.

Basic to the ethnocentric attitude is a favorable evaluation of the in-group and a condemnation of out-groups. These attitudes grow in strength with the psychological and cultural distance *between* the in-group and out-group. The intensity of this attitude may partially be attributed to the moral nature of the evaluation (we are good; they are bad) and to the fundamentally paranoid outlook the attitude expresses. As is well known among clinical psychologists, the paranoid outlook is extremely difficult to modify and is closed to incongruent information.

The paranoid outlook is circular, and it selectively filters information according to the "we good — they bad" dichotomy. The two chief elements of paranoia closely follow this dichotomy. The delusions of grandeur are attempts to bolster the "we good" aspect (and since there is a considerable amount of identification and conformity in this outlook, one may assume that the "we good" also means "I good"). Associated with delusions of grandeur (in fact, imperative to their existence) are the delusions of persecution. A paranoid reasons that greatness is not realized because the out-group is constantly looking for opportunities to block or destroy the aspirations of the in-group. Basic to ethnocentrism is the extreme and morally evaluated in-group—out-group dichotomy, expressed in delusions of grandeur and persecution. It is superfluous to say it, perhaps, but a paranoid value system contributes to the contrast effect.

Conformity and ethnocentrism. When a nation as a whole is ethnocentric (and this author is led to suspect that nearly all nations and groups are), the major obstacle to favorable international images is identified. Conformity pressures based on the fear of significant-other rejection (social cost), may begin to exert themselves even at a very early time in a child's life. (To get an intuitive feeling of these pressures, try to remain seated next time you attend a public affair where the national anthem is played! Since conformity in behavior toward symbols of flags and anthem are constantly a required part of life, they lead to a corresponding ethnocentric image formation.) The laws of cognitive dissonance (Festinger, 1957) have clearly shown a correspondence between public behavior and internal attitudes. If behavior and attitudes are dissonant, this condition is felt as psychologically uncomfortable, and the individual is motivated to change one or the other. Since behavior is under pressure to remain ethnocentric, beliefs and images for most people are congruent with their ethnocentric behavior.

People are especially subject to conformity pressures where they have little first-hand information. The average person gets nearly all his information from secondary sources: books, people, and other forms of news media. Since the media itself represents, to a greater or lesser extent, the ethnocentric outlook, it is not surprising that this world perspective is seldom questioned by adult citizens. Children are thoroughly indoctrinated by emotional conditioning to chauvinistic symbols; and, as they grow to adulthood, this world view is constantly reinforced by the media. Horowitz and Horowitz (1938) indicated that even in early primary grades children learned to evaluate their own national flags as "most attractive" and "nicest looking."

This extensive ethnocentric experience may affect the foreign policy of the nation in several ways. Leaders, too, are products of their actions and share the ethnocentric perspective. In fact, it is quite unlikely that a leader would become a leader (whether in the United States, U.S.S.R., or any other country) if he did not express his country's ethnocentrism. These attitudes are in turn directly related to war and armament production, as well as other offensive and defensive policies. In addition, leaders are also restricted by ethnocentric conformity pressures. The relative intensity of this pressure limits how cooperative a leader may be with an out-group before his policies are perceived as treacherous. Ethnocentric conformity pressures make it less likely that another people's beliefs and habits will be considered within the assimilation range.

Insecurity, conformity, and aggressiveness. Most people are reluctant to suffer the social cost derived from ignoring group norms. Probably nothing causes more psychological discomfort than being rejected by a valued reference group. Conforming to group norms serves several important social-psychological functions, including social acceptance, achieving a social identity, and being able to function ("get along") in a society. While conformity is a phenomenon affecting all people's lives (and in some ways this is a positive thing; without some conformity, modern societies could not function), there are individual differences in submitting to conformity pressures. Some sections of society are more vulnerable to social cost and hence tend to conform more.

Bell (1963) notes the anxieties associated with moving up into middle-class life, especially in those who come from minority groups and who perceive themselves as having suffered from social rejection. Such segments often tend to become super-Americans in their attempts at becoming acceptable. Few religious groups have been rejected as often as the Mormons (driven out of a number of states before finding a refuge in Utah), yet probably few areas of the country surpass Utah in ethnocentrism and anti-communism. The students at Brigham Young University, the Mormon Church's major institution, are required to stand at attention every school day as the national anthem is played over the loudspeakers.

Larsen (1969) noted the relationship between personal insecurity and dogmatic closed-mindedness. Paul and Laulicht (1963) showed that religious dogmatism is associated with an acceptance of bigger military forces, favoring the spread of nuclear weapons and a hostility to coexistence. Personal insecurity may exaggerate the threat of potential out-groups leading to the acceptance of military solutions and preparedness. In addition, the cost of war is lower in groups which predict the inevitable "second coming." If the world is going to end in cataclysmic splendor, there is not much to do but resign oneself to it. The danger is that such pessimism may lead to its confirmation as expressed in the self-fulfilling hypothesis (if you believe in something and act accordingly, you thereby verify it).

Allied with this pessimistic view are the common-sense theories based on man's innate predisposition to go to war: "There have always been wars, there always will be wars;" "My country right or wrong, but my country;" "Let us get it over with." These conceptions tend to reflect an almost fatalistic belief that men of good will can do little to affect the probability of war.

Personal security is probably related to status factors, such as job satisfaction and a stable economic life. Campbell (1947) found that those who were dissatisfied with their jobs were more likely to be anti-semitic. A decade later, Kosa (1957) investigated the attitudes of Hungarian immigrants to Canada and found that favorable attitudes toward the British were associated with job satisfaction. Supporting evidence was also found in a study by Spilka and Struening (1956), who noted that ethnocentrism was related to a low sense of social worth and poor social adjustment. This discussion suggests that certain socio-economic experiences lead to a sense of low self-esteem and personal insecurity, which in turn predisposes the individual toward an authoritarian and ethnocentric world view.

The ethnocentric outlook may help the insecure person overcome some of his fears of failure and lack of self-esteem by identification with the "glorious" and powerful nation. Adorno, Frenkel-Brunswik, Levinson, and Sanford (1950) noted that the authoritarian personality is especially characterized by strong acceptance of conventional norms combined with an intense interest in the immoral behavior of others. Other symptoms include compulsive submissiveness to parents and exaggerated expectations of punishment resulting from personal aggressiveness toward persons perceived as positive. In other words, while all people are motivated by fears of social rejection, authoritarians are particularly vulnerable to such rejection. Out-groups which are not capable of rejecting the individual therefore become easy targets of hostile images and behavior.

The reason out-groups become targets may be explained in terms of displacement. The insecure and ethnocentric person, having experienced a great deal of personal frustration but being fearful of the in-group, displaces the aggression toward an out-group. Support for the displacement hypothesis may be found in the work of Hovland and Sears (1940), who showed that lynchings of the blacks in the

South fluctuated with the frustrations associated with the rise or fall in the price of cotton. When the price of cotton was low, economic hardships and frustrations were expressed by attacking scapegoats, and blacks often suffered. The massacre of the Jews by the Nazi machine served a similar function of avoiding internal stress by blaming a minority group for all the ills in the nation.

Such displacement behavior is a dominant phenomenon, because most of the populations of nations tend toward ethnocentrism and authoritarianism. Displacement also would be less likely were it not for the early emotional conditioning to ethnocentric symbols which are called into play in time of internal stress. However, insecurity may also serve to produce the contrast effect which justifies the displacement. Insecurity leads to approval-seeking, motivating the insecure person to become a super-patriot. These factors all contribute to the contrast effect which supports the cognitive-perceptual distortion known as ethnocentrism.

Personal belligerence and chauvinism. Eysenck (1953) noted the F-Scale designed to measure authoritarianism is also a measure of personal aggressiveness. Gladstone (1955) found a hostile orientation toward other nations is associated with interpersonal belligerence, while, conversely, non-violent attitudes toward nations is associated with pacifism. Levinson (1957) reports moderately strong correlations between the F-Scale and his Scale of Nationalism, and Sampson and Smith (1957) found a negative correlation between nationalism and world-mindedness. Simmons, Larsen, and Fajardo (1972) found militarist students were less world-minded and more in favor of "hard" institutional solutions to world conflict in comparison to pacifist students.

For a summary on studies relating authoritarianism and internationalist attitudes, see Titus and Hollander (1957) and Katz (1965). The results as a whole lend strong support to a relationship between personal belligerence and chauvinistic attitudes. The ethnocentric world outlook is as much an expression of interpersonal hostility as of international hostility. Personal belligerence widens the contrast range to include the beliefs and habits of nearly all persons except the belligerent individual.

Threat and hostility. Threat may be productive of international hostility. Mulder and Stemerding (1963) noted that, under threat, a group tends to become particularly cohesive and tolerant of strong leadership. Individuals are related to national policy by identification with the nation. Through national policy, the individual advances his economic well-being and obtains vicarious gratification from the status of the nation (grandeur and prestige) in the international community. Perceived threat to the national group is therefore perceived as a threat to the self, as a result of the identification process. As the nation mobilizes for resistance against the threat, morale and cohesiveness increase, making it extremely difficult for the individual to resist national policy.

Threat is also the stimulus for eliciting the paranoid outlook (delusions of grandeur and persecution) along with the associated defense mechanisms. The ego defense mechanisms serve to protect the individual from unpleasant reality and, therefore, to some extent, distort the truth. A number of these have been identified as functioning in all people to greater or lesser extents. Repression protects the individual from a complete awareness; rationalization involves the search for "good" reasons for behavior rather than the real reasons; projection is the attribution of our own undesirable qualities in exaggerated amounts to other people; reaction-formation is expressed in giving strong support to the opposite of what one really feels; and substitution involves having socially unacceptable motives find expression in acceptable forms.

A fictitious case history may provide an example of how these mechanisms may operate to facilitate hostile images. Nation A declares its intention to include nuclear weapons in its arsenal for defensive purposes only. Nation B perceives this action as directed against its interest and represses the official reason given by Nation A. Having long desired the territory of Nation A (real reason), Nation B uses the pretext of the threat (good reason) to attack. Nation B's decision-makers attribute their own aggressiveness to Nation A (projection), while professing their deep devotion to the cause of ultimate peace. Since nations are above the moral restrictions of individuals, the resulting war becomes an acceptable substitute for otherwise unacceptable aggressive motives. Students of history will likely find many examples of conflict resulting from perceived threat;

such threat is often magnified out of proportion to its real nature by paranoid thinking and ego defense mechanisms.

Threat also produces perceptual distortions. There is general recognition among psychologists that rationality is lost under tension and threat, making the probability of extreme, polarized responses more likely. Hostility grows out of fear and, if unresolved, may add to the tension under which the only option is perceived to be conflict. This is even more effective when the pressure of the ethnocentric group is felt with the appeals to national honor and threat to the nonconformist. As noted in earlier arguments, such threats may overcome even the fear of personal destruction.

Ethnocentrism, then, is an over-reliance on the contrast effect brought about by a number of factors just discussed. Conditions of contact which serve to make more salient group differences, low information complexity, a paranoid value system, conformity pressures, individual insecurity, and threat also serve to heighten the social cost of interaction. High social cost in turn produces a perceptual contrast effect, so other people's habits are seen as more foreign than they objectively are. This contrast effect is the justification for the rejection of out-groups.

It is time now to structure these factors within more formal models. The first model we will discuss emphasizes the social-psychological factors predicting hostile images. This model is a facet of a larger socio-cultural model, which indicates levels of preponderant influence, starting with the essential competitive nature of our economic system. Social cost is an intervening and integrative variable in both models.

The essence of the social-psychological model is that certain child-rearing procedures (emotional conditioning to ethnocentric symbols, punitive child-rearing, and simplistic experiences) lead to cognitive-perceptual habits characterized by paranoid and ego defensive cognitions which find their chief outlets in displacement of anger toward out-groups. These experiences also produce personality traits of insecurity, low self-esteem, and authoritarianism, which, combined with ethnocentric group pressures, produce high social cost for contact with other groups and therefore produce hostile images of other categories of people.

The social cost involved here is both the psychological

discomfort experienced by fear and rejection of things foreign and the very real rejection which may occur from significant others if such contacts are made. For these reasons, most societies today are ethnocentric and produce populations vulnerable to social cost and hence individuals *who value approval above all else.*

MODELS FOR HOSTILE INTERGROUP IMAGES

The previous discussion points to several etiological factors predisposing an individual toward hostile international images.

A social-psychological model for hostile images. Figure 8.1 suggests a sequence (or levels) of social-psychological influences leading to hostile images. The critical child rearing elements include early emotional conditioning to ethnocentric symbols (e.g., flag, anthem). Since these symbols are conditioned at an early age without cognitive evaluation, the assumption is made that these symbols remain powerful reinforcers of chauvinistic behavior. Ethnocentric symbols take on the nature of the sacred, and attitudes toward them are absolute and not subject to questioning. The emotional conditioning is continually reinforced during the life of a person by means of the mass media, sporting events, and other activities. Therefore, they have considerable motivational properties which can be used to mobilize a population at the shortest possible notice. They are powerful motivators, since the children were inoculated with chauvinistic attitudes at a time when they possessed little cognitive evaluation and were under the pressure of maximum moral identification with the purveyors of nationalist doctrine — parents and teachers. The moral evaluation of symbols (and hence the nation) must of necessity lead to the lower evaluation of other nations.

Allied with this condition is the effect of punitive child-rearing procedures which have been shown to relate to aggression (e.g., Bandura and Walters, 1959; Lyle and Levitt, 1955; Radke, 1946; Whiting and Child, 1953) and to chauvinistic nationalism and closed-mindedness (Larsen and Schwendiman, 1969). Such severe aggression training is undoubtedly experienced as frustrating by children, but coupled with the frustration is a fear of parents and other forms of authority.

Aiding these processes are the effects of simplistic experiences.

Figure 8.1
A Social-Psychological Model for Hostile Intergroup Images

Child rearing practices A	Cognitive perceptual habits B	Personality traits C
1. Emotional conditioning to ethnocentric symbols	1. Paranoid and ego defensive thinking expressed in displacement	1. Insecurity
2. Punitive child rearing	2. Cognitive simplicity	2. Low self-esteem
3. Simplistic experiences		3. Ethnocentrism and authoritarianism

Social cost E		Images F
Group pressures D		Hostile
Ethnocentric group identification	Increased social cost of foreign contacts as a function of increased psychological and cultural distances and intimacy of contact	

Direction of Influence

"Simplistic experiences" is both a qualitative and quantitative concept. It is defined by the absence of the uncommon, the lack of cognitive stimulation in general, being limited to one cultural experience with little or no experience with foreign cultures, especially those very exotic and discrepant. Such a deprived cultural background leads to cognitive simplicity and to low thresholds for experiencing "cultural shock." The latter is characterized by fear and disorientation on exposure to the foreign, and as I have already noted, fears and threats lie at the base of hostility.

The cognitive-perceptual habits which emerge from these fears become relatively permanent parts of the individual's repertory. The habits are expressed in the form of paranoid, ego defensive thinking and displaced through hostility toward minority out-groups or other nations. This process is aided by the contrast effect previously discussed.

These cognitive-perceptual elements, in turn, are basic traits in the personality syndrome reflected by insecurity, low self-esteem, ethnocentrism, and authoritarianism. Personality traits may be thought of as those cognitive-perceptual elements in an individual which endure despite changing situations. In the case of the aforementioned syndrome, however, it is broadly representative of national character and furthermore reinforced by group pressure. These cognitive-perceptual habits are therefore representative of the modal person in most modern societies.

A word of caution is necessary: The intent is not to imply that *all* the elements in a given sequence of influence must be present to produce the indicated results. The rule is one or more, although it appears that the influences at each level are highly correlated.

With respect to the group pressures experienced as a result of ethnocentric group identification, note that the child-rearing practices and cognitive-perceptual habits listed also contribute indirectly to group pressure by making the individual more vulnerable to these pressures. These influences are indicated by the dotted arrows. This influence is also indicated by the arrow between the personality traits (which are inclusive of the cognitive-perceptual habits and partially attributed to these and the child-rearing practices) and group pressures.

The combined result of the personality traits and group pressures is to increase the social cost of foreign contacts. The cost involved here is both psychological discomfort experienced by fear and rejection of things foreign and also the very real rejection which may occur from the social environment if such contacts are made. In general, social interaction lies at some point between the very intimate and non-intimate behavior. The Bogardus (1925) Social Distance Scale represents this range, where the very intimate contact is represented by the willingness to marry the foreign national, and non-intimate contact is represented by the willingness to have the foreign national visit one's country. Clearly the social cost will depend on the relative intimacy of the contact, with the more intimate forms of interaction producing the highest social cost.

Another variable affecting the social cost is the perceived psychological and, in general, cultural distance between the native and foreign culture. The contrast-assimilation phenomenon would suggest closely allied cultures would be assimilated and present little, if any, social cost, whereas the more distant cultures would be contrasted and represent high levels of social cost. Therefore, to briefly summarize the theory: If the indicated personality traits and group pressures are present, and if the social cost is high (interaction intimate — psychological and cultural distance wide), the individual is likely to have hostile images of the foreign nation.

A final brief word on the relative importance of personality traits versus group pressure in contributing to social cost: It is the consistent bias of this volume that group pressure (potentials of rejection from significant others) will, as a rule, modify any tendency in the individual to act contrary to the norms of the group. The personality traits listed only reinforce this tendency and make the individual more vulnerable to rejection.

A socio-cultural model for hostile inter-group images. A complete analysis of hostile inter-group images must take into account the economic structure of a society, as well as its socio-cultural superstructure. Economic structures have varied through history from feudal to modern forms of capitalism and communism. Capitalism is characterized by competition. The point of this review is only to point to some consequences of competition as a mode of human interaction.

If the world is looked upon as a zero-sum game with scarce resources, the outcome of human interaction is such that the gains of one person or group are at the expense of another. It is the outcome of this economic interaction, where competition is the mode, which is the basis of socio-cultural hostility toward members of out-groups. Personal aggressiveness (competitiveness) is related to hostile international attitudes, especially where right-wing authoritarianism plays an important role (Katz, 1960; Titus and Hollander, 1957). Right-wing authoritarianism may be expected to engender status concerns. Putney and Middleton (1962) showed that status concerns were related to hard-line approaches toward communist nations.

Competition creates a simplistic structuring of all human relationships in terms of in-groups and out-groups. Katz (1965) has pointed out that ethnocentric identification is readily developed by a people with a homogeneous culture in competitive contact with other nations. That competition leads to hostile attitudes and behavior is implicit in the writings of many authors. It needs, however, to be stated explicitly: Competition for perceived scarce resources is the root cause of aggression. It has produced a situation where mere membership in another category, even where the category is nonsensical, is the minimum and sufficient cause for rejection by members of an equally nonsensical category (Doise, et al, 1972).

Competition affects the social structure at at least three points. First, as already pointed out, it creates ethnocentric group identification through chauvinistic traditions. Secondly, it creates a philosophical world view which is characterized by threat. Finally, it affects the child-rearing patterns of parents and teachers to exact obedience and conformity to the dominant ideology which emphasizes competition as a mode of interaction. Grades and other incentive systems are means by which the individual derives self-esteem in a competitive society. Self-esteem is derived by ranking higher than a minimum number of other individuals on some socially important dimension. In a competitive and hierarchal society, the individual must compete to be attributed esteem.

The combined effects of competition on the social structure is to make the individual vulnerable to social cost by extending approval or disapproval for all actions. The individual in a competitive society values approval as the end reward of competitive interaction. This in turn creates dogmatic and chauvinistic attitudes which affect perception and create hostile international images. Depending on the situation, the images may either result in latent action such as prejudice, or overt action such as joining, voting, or otherwise exerting behavior on behalf of aggressive chauvinistic groups. This structural model would look as follows in Figure 8.2.

In terms of human values, an aggressive society is a society which values approval above all else. Approval-seeking motivation underlies intergroup hostility, although such conflict may be couched in other terms. At the level of rationalization, men may go to war "to make the world safe for democracy" or "to end all wars;" at the level of reality, however, men go to war because they value approval and wish to avoid social rejection.

The two models are interrelated. For example, the social structure is partially defined by the child-rearing practices in society. However, we must also recognize the chauvinistic traditions and threatening world view which is an inheritance from the past. The cognitive-perceptual habits and personality traits of the modal person in society are the outcome of social reinforcement and group pressures, which make individuals vulnerable to social cost and therefore lead to approval-seeking. The factors which contribute to hostile images are preponderant levels of influence, leading to approval-seeking values. The degree to which approval-seeking (or social cost) elicits hostile images is a function of psychological and cultural distances and the intimacy of the contact, both of which contribute to the contrast effect. The contrast effect is the justification for hostile images defined by ethnocentrism.

CHANGING IMAGES AND SOCIAL COST

Festinger (1957) observed a person's belief structure serves as a source of stability, and de Rivera (1968) noted the belief structure is the foundation for a person's social judgment. The decisions a person makes are, to a large extent, determined by what a person believes is true, that is, his images. Since beliefs and images serve to ensure personal stability and continuity in a constantly changing world, it

Figure 8.2
A Socio-Cultural Model for Hostile Intergroup Images

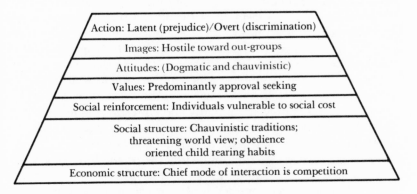

Action: Latent (prejudice)/Overt (discrimination)

Images: Hostile toward out-groups

Attitudes: (Dogmatic and chauvinistic)

Values: Predominantly approval seeking

Social reinforcement: Individuals vulnerable to social cost

Social structure: Chauvinistic traditions;
threatening world view; obedience
oriented child rearing habits

Economic structure: Chief mode of interaction is competition

could be assumed that any threat to these will be strongly resisted. Beliefs get close to the definition of what a person is, and abandonment of beliefs without conversion to a different system implies chaos and disorientation. Cultural shock experienced as fear and disorientation may be partially explained as a challenge to a person's habitual images which conflict severely with the new experience. Rokeach (1960) has indicated that belief incongruence is the primary variable producing rejection, provided that the effects of social cost are held constant.

All this suggests that images once firmly established will become extremely resistant to change. Berelson and Steiner (1964), in their study on the effects of environmental pressures, noted almost nothing in the world seems to be able to shift the images of 40 percent of the population of most countries. People will call upon support of their social groups to defend images and beliefs and will resort to perceptual distortion or deny reality in defense of these.

Recognizing the difficulty of changing images, there are nevertheless some conditions which will facilitate such change. Festinger (1957) observed a force which tends to make a person's beliefs consistent with each other. Awareness of inconsistent beliefs produced "cognitive dissonance," which is experienced as psychologically uncomfortable, and which consequently motivates the individual toward reducing this dissonance. This would suggest that one way to change images would be to confront these with incongruent images under conditions where it is difficult to refute the latter.

In addition, the perception of the other group must be free of ambiguities and cross-pressures. For example, it makes a difference whether you are a guest in South Viet Nam of the Saigon government, or the Front for National Liberation, or whether you visit as a "neutral" observer. A condition of "no pressure" would lead to maximum change of distorted images, as the images have a greater chance of being evaluated rationally and with less emotional bias.

Pressure from significant others mobilizes resistance to image change. Images serve to help the individual function in society. They assist in preventing rejection, by telling the person how to behave appropriately toward out-groups and the valued in-group culture and traditions. Images are developed out of the constraints and pressures of significant others. Images may define the world of reality, but social cost is the core around which the structure of subjective reality is built.

To modify or change these images would of necessity imply the need for changing the impact of potential rejection. Allport's (1958) group contact conditions discussed in Chapter 6 are relevant here. Implied in these conditions is an attack on ethnocentrism itself and a securing of the positive sanctions of authority for a change in the relationships between groups. Many prejudicial images in the U.S. have been modified in recent years, particularly in the South, since the behavior based on these perceptions is simply not functional anymore. Blacks are viewed from different perspectives, because the conditions of interaction have been changed, reducing the social cost of the contacts.

Ethnocentrism itself is largely a result of conditions of contact which emphasize group differences, low information complexity, paranoid values, and conformity pressure. These causes suggest several other remedies: More contacts with foreign nationals may reduce the most extreme stereotypes and, if the conditions of contact are right, may lead to more positive images. Also, it is obviously more difficult to maintain an ethnocentric viewpoint when people assume cross-national loyalties. Joining international organizations, whether cultural, special interest, or political, may reduce ethnocentrism. Education, especially a liberal education, increases a person's ability to make differential social judgment, and enables him to appreciate the complexity and value of national and ethnic differences. These characteristics make it more likely that the educated person will resist ethnocentric conformity pressures.

Today there are many forces wishing to reduce the number of people experiencing higher education. There is little argument that an elitist system may be more efficient, but are the educator-technocrats who advocate this approach aware of the possible social consequences? One serious consequence is a society more resistant to change and more likely to accept conflict and war — in short, more ethnocentric.

Some sections of society play leading roles in image change primarily because they possess power and are therefore less subject to pressures than less powerful sections. Lazarfeld, Berelson, and Gaudet (1948) observed that mass communication was carried out by means of a two-step process: The initial step (a) proceeds from the mass media to a human network of opinion leaders, and (b) these leaders interpret the communication for society. These opinion leaders (doctors, lawyers, labor and religious leaders, etc.) decide on the credibility of the information — what can or cannot be believed. It is clear, therefore, that any change effort must be directed toward these opinion leaders, since the public will remain unconvinced if these leaders' images are not changed.

Galtung (1964) advanced a structural theory of society in some respects analogous to the Lazarfeld et al. proposition. Society is divided into a center and a periphery, in which the center is the relatively privileged section, and the periphery consists of the rejected section. As a result, perceptions of social reality and attitude formation in the periphery "lag" behind and to a large extent follow the center. This may partially be attributed to the fact that the periphery is removed from both the communication and decison-making nucleus of society. The concept of social position could be applied to research in most countries in the world today regardless of formal economic structure, as it is based on ecological, geographical, educational, and occupational, as well as age and sex, variables.

It now becomes clear why it is so difficult to change images held by large proportions of the population. Public images are changed as a result of image change among opinion leaders; (a) opinion leaders represent the privileged sections with an interest in the status quo and (b) there is a time lag (when change does occur) between image change of opinion leaders and image change adopted by the larger periphery.

In some manner, therefore, the center must come to accept the value of favorable international images and to pass these along to the periphery. Travel and other forms of informal contacts may aid in this. However, it would seem the perception of common interest, whether in altruistic cultural-political pursuits (music, associations, or the UN) or the more selfish economic interests (international trade cooperations), would be especially helpful in promoting more positive international images. Since some of these contacts may, for obvious reasons, fall along ideological channels, it is especially important to overcome this factor by strengthening the exchange and trade between east and west.

THE SOCIAL PSYCHOLOGY OF AGGRESSION AND NATIONAL DECISION-MAKERS

The importance of the perceptual-cognitive views expressed is based on the assumption that nations do not make decisions, but that national decision-makers do. National decision-makers are human beings subject to the same psychological laws as other human beings. It is true that they are restricted to some extent by roles, by the behavior expected of them. Unfortunately for peaceful relations between nations, the role expectancies often facilitate hostile behavior. This may be attributed to the ethnocentric outlook of most groups, which national decision-makers must express if they are to survive as leaders. Leader roles therefore restrict cooperative behavior while facilitating hostile behavior.

It could be argued that national leaders closely identify with the nation as a source of ego gratification through the achievement of power and grandeur. If this assumption is correct, national decision-makers may be more susceptible to influence by the ethnocentric outlook expressed in paranoid and defensive thinking, as compared to the population they lead. To the extent that ethnocentrism becomes an influence in national policy, international images are distorted in the less favorable direction. This situation calls strongly for the presence of an institutional adversary group within each national government to correct for this distortion and bring about a more realistic appraisal of the world. The emphasis is on institutional, since such an adversary process must be imbued with considerable prestige and postive sanction (and lack of reprisals) in order to be successful.

SUMMARY

The all-pervading influence of fear of rejection from a person's social group in producing the syndrome of personality traits known as ethnocentrism has been examined. Gross distortions of images may be corrected by mere contact, but enduring positive changes in images are brought about by conditions which reduce perceived differences between groups, the paranoid values of the in-group, and the perceived threat of the other group. At the same time, the possession of more complex information about the other group, coupled with resistance to conformity pressures, predicts more positive inter-group images. The models proposed attempted to take these factors into account in outlining the levels of influence which lead to high levels of social cost for "foreignness" and consequently to hostile images. The social cost of foreignness is particularly high if the perceived psychological and cultural distance between the native and other nation is wide and if the proposed contact is intimate. Under these conditions the contrast effect plays a highly salient role in developing and maintaining hostile images.

Since our images help to define reality and our stability, it is little wonder that they are highly resistant to change. Any change process must induce dissonance of images under conditions in which it is hard to deny reality. The positive sanction of authority is also essential. Since innovations proceed from the center to the periphery, concerted attempts at change must first be directed to opinion leaders. International contacts leading to perception of common interests are of particular importance.

For those apt to dismiss a social psychological interpretation of international relations, let it be remembered that nations do not make decisions, but national decision-makers do. Subject to role limitations, decision-makers are subject to the same laws as any other individual. Profound and enduring changes toward more positive international images must come about by means of moderate and graduated steps taken by leaders, along with structural changes making the international community more interdependent. In the following chapters, we shall discuss in more detail the factors which contribute to international conflict and its resolution.

9.

Conflict Management: Moving Toward a Convergent World

We live in a world of nearly continuous, open conflict. True, some conflicts appear to be far away and for that reason do not concern us directly. The world, however, is increasingly interdependent. New advances in communication and weapons development make it impossible to ignore even the slightest conflict. Such a conflict is potentially the spark inside the gun chamber. The coining of the term "Spaceship Earth" connotes this interdependence of all the people on our planet. History teaches us that nations cannot maintain stability for long with unresolved internal conflicts.

In the past, conflicts were resolved on the battlefield with a tremendous loss of human life. Today, however, war could very realistically mean the end of civilization. Perhaps life of some forms would remain — perhaps even human life. Realizing what happened at Hiroshima and Nagasaki makes us believe that the living would envy the dead. War has caused nearly all deaths which have occurred from lethal violence. Prosterman (1972) noted that nearly four-fifths of all deaths from violence since 1820 have occurred from large scale conflicts of over 30,000 participants apiece. Yet these conflicts are minor, compared to the potential horror which looms in the future.

In this chapter we shall be concerned with the processes which lead to war and to conflict management. The terrible cost of war demands that we find ways of dealing with conflict in nonviolent ways. The management of conflict is a complex process and, depending on other variables, leads the conflict actors from negotiation to arbitration. The average person in society can participate if he knows the techniques of conflict management. In the final section of this chapter we shall discuss the Clark-Sohn proposal for reorganizing the United Nations and bringing about total disarmament.

WAR

In this section we discuss the problems which are inherent in the concept of mutual deterrence. Is the balance of power really fail-safe? What are the implications of crisis psychology on this problem? Efforts at arms limitation are positive steps in the right direction, yet the nuclear stockpiles which remain may destroy civilization many times over. Certainly the arms race cannot be considered productive work for the benefit of any of the nations involved. The waste of human resources staggers the imagination. Why then do men go to war? There are real reasons for war, but these are usually clothed in rationalizations. A great deal of conflict theory has been based upon the idea that wars are fought between actors who are equal in resources. However, some conflicts are symmetric and some are asymmetric.

The cost of the balance of terror. Can we assume, as did many of the developers of the A-bomb and the H-bomb, that the very terror involved in these weapons would prevent their use? Terrible weapons have been used throughout history, and there is no guarantee that nuclear weapons will not be used in a future war. Is mutual deterrence effective? Mutual deterrence is a condition where several powers possess nuclear weapons of sufficient quantity and quality to withstand an initial attack and then retaliate. The balance of terror in the world is based on the concept of mutual deterrence. However, mutual deterrence is not fail-safe. The potential for war remains.

The mutual deterrence system is supposed to prevent the triggering of accidental wars; yet we know of near misses. As Raser (1969) has stated, a fail-safe system depends on two factors: (1) carefully chosen individuals will retain cool and calm judgments in intense crisis conditions, and (2) if one individual fails (loses sound judgment), others will step in and act as a fail-safe device. Research in behavioral science indicates both assumptions are faulty. As we know, crisis situations can create feelings of panic, terror, and hysteria. These feelings all lead to impairment of judgment and to potential over-reaction, which could lead to nuclear war. Raser also reports research by Torrance on B-26 crews, which showed the crews nearly always conformed to the captain's decision, whether the decision was correct or not. Most individuals, and especially those trained in military discipline, exhibit an overwhelming drive to obey those perceived as possessing legitimate authority.

Admittedly, some steps have recently been made to reduce world tensions. The positive steps to limit armaments must be lauded, for they bring the world temporarily back from the brink. Yet it should not be forgotten that if the nations retain only their *present* armaments, and make no superior weapons for the future, the potential remains to destroy the world many times over. Thee (1972) noted that, during the last decade, world arms spending has risen by two-thirds. The current sum runs about 200 billion U.S. dollars per year, out of which the United States expends 84.3 billion. These budgets have assured a colossal nuclear overkill by the superpowers, soaring to tens of tons of TNT *per each person in the world.* Thee observed that, not only has the quantity of weapons increased, but the quality has developed to a level of fearful sophistication. The range, speed, precision, intensity, technology, and extent of automation tends to make these weapons truly fearsome.

The waste of human resources staggers the imagination — not only in the manufacturing of weapons, but in the fact that nearly 25 percent of the world's scientists are engaged in the arms race. Fifty million people now directly or indirectly serve the military establishment. Half of these are soldiers, and 37 percent of these are in the developing countries which can ill afford them.

The longer the arms race lasts, the stronger the probability of nuclear warfare. Stone (1972) wrote that, if the past trend continues, by mid-1975 we will have over 20,000 nuclear warheads for 180 cities in the Soviet Union with populations in excess of 100,000. "The gap in missile warheads is widening rapidly in our favor to the point where the Soviets must fear that we are trying for some kind of counterforce, preemptive or first-strike capacity." Should the current disarmament talks succeed, there still would remain a stockpile of weapons large enough to destroy the world many times over. Such is the era in which we live. If we are to leave a more peaceful world to our children (or leave a world at all), we must tackle this problem with all possible commitment and speed.

The causes of war. International conflicts occur for several reasons. A nation may covet the territory or something else of value of another nation and attempt to expropriate it. The war initiated by Germany for "life space" during World War II was partially of this type.

After World War I, Germany was in a state of political and economic collapse. National socialism changed this situation by focusing (displacing) the anger caused by the situation on its internal and external enemies. The Nazi leaders pointed with effectiveness to the unfairness of the treaties concluding World War I. They blamed equally the allied countries and the internal traitors (all viewed as Marxist-Jews) for Germany's defeat. The displacement served the function of reintegrating a society which had been on the point of collapse. Internal conflicts may therefore be projected outwards upon other nations and thereby suppress the internal contradictions.

During World War II, Germany sought to "save" the Western world from bolshevism. World War II was also a conflict over values and ideology. In many people's eyes, the war concerned political principles thought crucial to the welfare of man. War, therefore, is caused by a combination of the coveting of territory, by attempts to solve internal conflicts, and as a result of ideological differences. To what extent any of the aforementioned sources may be considered a primary cause for war is difficult to conclude. They all interact, and each reason in turn may be used as a rationalization for the other.

The justification for war. In fact, it is fair to say the real reasons for war are often completely obscured by various justifications for entering the conflict. For example, the real reason the Americans intervened in Korea was to prevent the collapse of a strategic area thought important to the defense of Japan and Asia. The justifications used included such slogans as "containing communism" and "preserving democracy" in South Korea. The effect of using justifications is to lock the conflict into morally absolutistic terms, scuttling hopes for a negotiated end to the war.

The reasons many soldiers go to war may be to avoid heavy penalties for desertion or refusal to participate. However, fears of penalties alone are not sufficient to induce men vigorously to engage in war. To maintain high levels of motivation and morale, men must have rationalizations or justification to fight. Rationalizations are "good" reasons rather than the "real" reasons for behavior. To have meaning, rationalizations must be related to people's needs and values within the framework of their particular culture or society.

Doob (1964) has reviewed extensive historical records pertaining to war and listed four causes for war arising from nationalism: (1) self determination and irredentism — wars are fought to create a nation state free from foreign domination and to recover all the people of the nationality in that state; (2) solidarity and prestige — for pride in national prestige and expansionism and as instruments of national solidarity; (3) self-sufficiency and isolation — to seek security from attack and stabilize the economic life of the nation, and to develop its own unique national character as expressed in economic isolation and self-sufficiency; (4) mission and expansion — nationalism creates an attitude of superiority and, therefore, seeks to expand its culture and ignore the demands of other nations and the world community.

Derived from the historical record, Doob lists twenty-three justifications for war, as follow: divine sanction, destiny, nature, humanistic responsibility, peace, freedom, security, sovereignty, justice, contract, majority superiority, birthright, consanguinity, culture, duration, status quo, posterity, need, achievement, public opinion, revenge. Nationalism is a primary cause of war, creating its own rationalization.

It is extremely difficult to change attitudes toward these justifications, since nationalism serves many important psychological functions in the individual. For many impotent people, the nation provides a sense of belonging and vicarious achievement. Yet nationalism remains one of the serious causes of war. A change toward internationalism and world government is necessary, if difficult. Most of us are trained to perceive differences in peoples and objects, forgetting the all-pervading fact: people have more communalities than differences. All people face the same existential problems of life, such as, security, death, love, and the anxieties derived therefrom. Cultures and societies have found different ways of dealing with these similar problems. Training people to perceive the common core of humanity and the relativity of human values must be the first step toward internationalism. Later we shall discuss improving an already existing institution, the United Nations, to make it a prototype of world government.

Types of conflict. Galtung (1969) discussed basic types of conflicts and how these might best be managed. Conflict is defined as a property of a system of action, in which there are incompatible goal-states between the actors. The realization of the goal of one actor would exclude wholly or in part the realization of the goal of the other actor. If the goals are held by the same actor, we are dealing with intra-actor or psychological conflicts. If held by different actors, we are dealing with interpersonal, inter-group, or international conflict.

Not all actors are of the same rank. A symmetric conflict is a conflict between actors of equal rank. According to Galtung, this involves two things: (1) the actors are more or less of the same kind (e.g., both are nations), and (2) they have roughly equal resources at their disposal. Both of these variables would imply a relative equality of power and no clear advantage of one actor over the other. Asymmetric conflicts, on the other hand, are between actors of different (unequal) rank who have different resources and/or are different in kind.

These two conditions result in three types of conflicts. If actors of high rank are referred to as topdogs, and actors of low rank as underdogs, the following conflicts are possible: (a) between topdogs (symmetric), (b) between underdogs (symmetric), and (c) between topdogs and underdogs (asymmetric). It makes a difference whether the conflict is symmetric or asymmetric. If strongly asymmetric, a conflict would usually not last long, as one of the actors would probably quickly overcome the other.

It should be kept in mind, however, that resources of one type on the part of one actor, may be compensated for by resources of another type by another actor. The material superiority of the American side in Viet Nam was well compensated for by the stronger motivation and consequently higher morale of the other side. It is difficult to find a common standard to apply by which resources can be measured. The standard would have to be some sort of energy yardstick, measuring the ability to maintain or improve on the status quo.

Two indices of energy are possible — the long-term destructive capability of the armed forces and, related to this, the long-term productive capability of the nation. The latter would include the ability to compensate for losses and keep up with the productive capability of the enemy. A criterion for a symmetric conflict must be a stalemate of some sort. The wars in Korea and Viet Nam appear to be conflicts of this type.

A great deal of conflict theory is based on the assumption of symmetry. Yet a great number, if not the majority, of the conflicts in the world are asymmetric. A theory of violence focusing primarily on symmetric conflicts between topdogs will overlook the asymmetric nature of structural violence between unequals. Poverty, hunger, and inadequate treatment of disease are just as lethal and absolute as being killed by a bomb. The suffering and feelings of impotence derived from this situation have similar results.

Furthermore, since the violence is structural and part and parcel of people's daily life, the suffering is often accompanied with ignorance. This makes struggles against asymmetric structural violence particularly difficult. It is difficult for people to be objective, to stand apart and analyze the many small and interrelated facts which cause oppression. This is especially true when the system is clothed in rationalizations of equality at another level. Poverty is real in America for a large number of people, and inflation prevents security for a great portion of the remainder. Yet our parliamentary democracy claims that all people are equal before the law. This formal equality has relatively little meaning as long as structural violence remains.

CONFLICT MANAGEMENT

In managing conflicts, there is a choice whether to focus on the real source (or interaction of sources) or on the manifest rationalizations. Both levels must be dealt with if the conflict is to be resolved. If the real sources are ignored, the conflict will remain despite efforts at resolving the rationalizations. Let us not forget, however, that rationalizations are the conscious reasons for which most people fight. Political leaders cannot, for reasons of popularity, end a

SOCIAL COST AND CONFLICT MANAGEMENT

Social cost is a variable which affects both the causes of war and the processes of the management of conflict. One reason we cannot be secure with the so-called "fail-safe" system is that the assumption that decision-makers will remain cool in a crisis situation when others fail is not valid. The conformity pressures from significant others in the decision hierarchy could cause the outbreak of war. Nationalism and ethnocentrism as causes of war are largely determined by social cost pressures. The attempt at reintegration of society in Nazi Germany was largely brought about by the displacement process determined by social cost. Furthermore, the rationalizations of war are resistant to change, because they are deeply related to approval-seeking motivation. Likewise, the group standards which support war are also rooted in approval-seeking ethnocentrism. Wars occur because they are accepted institutions. The fight against structural violence is a difficult struggle, because social cost motivation leads to ignorance on the part of the oppressed, and because of an unwillingness to struggle directly with those in status and power. In fact, a large part of the resistance to institutional change is caused by the conformity pressures seemingly essential for the survival of the less powerful.

conflict without satisfying the justifications which led to and maintained the conflict.

Resolving the real sources of conflict involves the question of justice. Negative peace is defined as conflict management, that is, preventing conflict from breaking into open violence. Positive peace, on the other hand, involves the resolution of injustice in society. The management of conflict does not necessarily help the cause of justice. The "real" reasons for the conflict may still remain. Consequently, conflict management is inherently unstable. Those concerned with positive and enduring peace (peace with justice) must therefore struggle against structural violence and for symmetric relations between groups and nations.

According to Galtung (1969), conflict management may be supervised by the parties involved in the conflict (endogenous) or by actors outside the conflict system (exogenous). Solutions which are arbitrarily imposed are not lasting. Arbitration frequently means an unsatisfactory solution for one or more of the actors in the conflict system. It is therefore desirable that solutions are negotiated by the conflict parties themselves. At times, the hostility may be so severe as to make direct contact impossible. In such a situation, mediation by a third party may be helpful in clarifying the issues and thereby helping the conflict parties to formulate a decision. Arbitration ought to be the last solution sought when all other alternatives have been exhausted.

The essential concern of conflict management is to prevent conflicts from becoming overt. The management of conflicts does not imply the resolution of conflict. Yet, since our survival in the nuclear age depends initially on the skills of conflict management, this field is an important area to study in its own right. Informal strategies for conflict may solve issues between friends, but group conflict requires a knowledge of the processes of negotiation. Solution paradigms cover the range from coercion of one party by another through attempts to reduce the sources of conflict to lasting solutions. We shall discuss the importance of empathy in mapping out areas of agreement and disagreement. Some responses to conflict are autistic and some are constructive. It is important to recognize there are two sides to a coin, and a solution is mutual responsibility. A model which predicts preferences for the type of constructive solutions sought in a conflict will be briefly discussed.

Models for conflict management. Prosterman (1972) outlines several peace paradigms. The control paradigm is the situation where one country or group of countries order, or in some fashion coerce, an end to conflict. An example is the U.N. Security Council resolution pertaining to the 1967 Mideast War. (Unfortunately there is little power presently in the U.N. to back up such resolutions.) Another problem is, if one party has the power to coerce for peace, they may (unless properly safeguarded as in the Clark-Sohn proposal for revision of the U.N. Charter) also have the power to coerce for selfish or anti-social goals. Power may lead to exploitation and moral corrosion. A power solution may still be necessary, but one with effective checks and balances.

The agreement paradigm describes the situation where the

parties to a conflict agree to end it or its cause. Examples include the various arms control agreements and the ceasefires in Korea and Viet Nam. To induce cooperation, it is essential that the agreement contain better conditions for each when compared to the continuation of the conflict. The initiative model is like Osgood's gradual tension reduction approach (to be discussed later in this chapter). One of the parties takes a unilateral step devised to remove threat and increase the chance that the other party will cooperate.

The amelioration paradigm involves an attempt to get to the root of the conflict. Examples would be social security, medicare, and land reform. The utopian models describe the ideal structure of society and how this structure affects conflict. The marxist and anarchist understanding of history blames structural relationships themselves for much of the violence. The ultimate utopia for marxists and anarchists is represented by the absence of structure, as exemplified in "the withering away of the state." To many people, utopias imply impossible dreams. However, utopias play an important role in motivating people to change the present society toward the ideal. Without utopian ideals, societies would stagnate.

To reach agreement by unilateral initiative or amelioration is not a straightforward matter. Bixenstine, Potash, and Wilson (1963) found the level of cooperation on the part of one player in non-zero-sum games did not affect the level of cooperation of the other player.

Larsen (1972c) asked his participants to play three games. Unknown to the participants, they were playing with an ally of the experimenter. In one game the ally was 100 percent cooperative; in the second, 100 percent competitive; and in the third, 50 percent random cooperative-competitive. None of these strategies had any effect on the cooperation of the other player. These results question the role of the carrot and stick approach. It is important to specify the conditions under which unilateral cooperation leads to reciprocal cooperation. The factor which is important is a clear communication of intent on the part of the party who takes the unilateral initiative. *The process of negotiation.* At times, the parties to a conflict may agree it is better to get part of the cake than endure the possibility of having no cake at all. Sawyer and Guetzkow (1965) have extensively discussed the process of negotiation. Negotiation is a voluntary agreement to try to resolve differences between two or more parties. The underlying assumption is that the essential part of each party's objective can be met thereby.

Sawyer and Guetzkow have identified five parts to negotiation. The first part is the identification of the goals over which the parties are in conflict and which cannot be achieved fully unless some agreement is reached. Peace in Viet Nam was presumably a goal for all the conflict parties and was clearly dependent upon an agreement by all.

The second part is the process of negotiation, itself. Here, research in the area of communication is especially appropriate. Conflict often creates distortions in perceptions and judgment, making it extremely difficult to communicate. The question is, how to ensure that the position and message of each party is understood.

In the process of negotiation there is no substitute for empathy. Negotiators should be specially trained people, trained in taking the sides of potential opponents and thereby being able to map the areas of agreement as well as those of disagreement. In training for negotiation, it is a good idea to have people repeatedly debate, taking the opponent's view. Each debater should restate the opponent's position until the opponent is satisfied that the other person understands, and vice versa.

To help an opponent to understand the position of the other party, Rapaport (1970) suggests three steps. First, convey to the opponent that his message was heard and understood. Second, make an attempt to define the areas where the opponent may have a valid point. Third, help to induce feelings of similarity about this region of agreement, and invite the opponent also to go through steps one and two. Misunderstandings and misperceptions often occur as a result of threat. It may reduce threat if similarities are discussed before differences are evaluated. This may create the positive attitudes necessary to resolve conflict.

The process of negotiation should lead to certain actions. Hostilities stop, men return to work, the estate is properly divided, etc. The actions have certain outcomes for each of the conflict parties. This third part concerns "how the pie is cut up," who gets what territory, the size of the salary increase, or the division of responsibility.

The fourth part is the effect of the preexisting background on these outcomes. What is the influence of cultural traditions and/or the relations between the parties? It has been a long tradition to fight in Viet Nam against foreign invaders. To what extent will this affect not only the war, but also the peace?

Finally, there may be specific situational conditions influencing the whole negotiation process. Teacher salary negotiations may have to be completed by a certain deadline. Renewed bombing might be threatened if "reasonable" progress is not made toward peace. Negotiation consists of these five variables, which must all be taken into account if we wish to predict the eventual outcome.

Constructive and nonconstructive responses to conflict. There would seem to be five possible responses to any given interpersonal or intergroup conflict, three of which are constructive, solution-oriented responses, and two of which seem to be autistic or nonconstructive responses (Larsen, Simmons, Coleman, 1971). The constructive solutions all assume the essential mutuality of the conflict crisis and can be arranged on a voluntary-involuntary continuum. The position on the continuum is characterized by the degree to which the conflict partners control the conflict resolution themselves or permit (or are forced) to have third parties participate or make binding conflict resolution decisions.

Negotiation, as indicated, implies direct contact between two parties. This situation is characterized by bargaining. Negotiation assumes the conflict parties can obtain at least minimal goals and suggests some equality of power. If one or several of the parties fail to come to terms and/or fail to agree on a minimum solution, they may permit a third party to enter the decision-making process.

In mediation, a third, supposedly neutral, party enters to help resolve the conflict. Such a party may search for alternatives and negotiate separately with the parties, but it is limited to suggestion and persuasion. If all good efforts of the mediator fail in attempting to build common ground, the next alternative is arbitration.

In arbitration the parties give up the right to make a decision and turn this decision over to a mutually respected third party. The arbitrator may hear out both parties, gather facts, and will finally render a decision which, regardless of feelings of justice or injustice, is binding on the parties in conflict.

The two nonconstructive responses are withdrawal from solution to the conflict and aggressive attack. Both of these responses deny the essential mutuality of conflict and are responses designed to "solve the problem" of one of the participants. If the conflict is perceived as relatively unimportant, both participants in the conflict may withdraw after negotiation has failed to solve the conflict. If the issue is important, the parties may continue through mediation to arbitration. High power and the perception of the conflict as important may lead to an aggressive attack, after the attempt of an imposed solution has failed. The attempt on the part of one of the parties to *impose* a solution by withdrawal or aggressive attack can be judged autistic in its denial of the mutuality of the decision-making process in conflict resolution. A diagram of the various points presented here would look much like Figure 9.1.

Apart from the autistic responses, what are the factors which may determine the preference for a given mode of conflict resolution (negotiation, mediation, arbitration)? The point of view to be advanced here is a perceptual one and thus is not concerned with the "objective" truth. The perceptual view argues truth is in the eye of the beholder and responses to conflict depend on the conflict parties' perception of the situational components of the conflict.

Three components are deemed of crucial importance in the perception of conflict situation and, thus, in determining the response to the situation. Whether the conflict parties are perceived as open or closed to solution alternatives is one determinant. If the parties perceive a possibility of influencing the opponent, they would probably prefer negotiation where they can best exert such influence. As the positions close, the preference will be for gradually introducing third parties through mediation and arbitration procedures.

A high power position may also be indicative of a preference for voluntary decision-making (negotiation). High power would seem to be best exercised in direct influence attempts, while the introduction of third parties is admission of lack of power to influence. Lack of power to influence may be an absolute lack or it may be a power balance deficiency. As power to influence decreases, the respondents move toward mediation and arbitration.

Urgency is the third factor which affects preference for conflict

Figure 9.1
Responses to Conflict

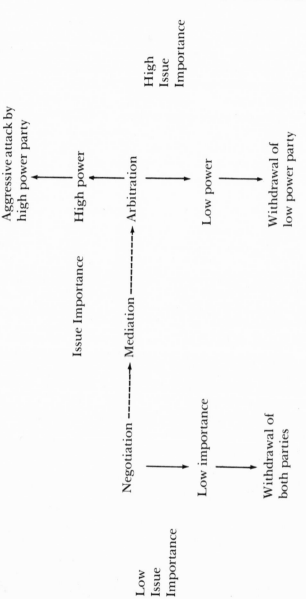

resolution strategies. Some conflicts are perceived in a vacuum with no great urgency for a decision. Others are infused with tension and time pressure expressed in the demands of the "now" movements. A high degree of urgency may lead to direct negotiation attempts, since this may, under proper conditions, lead to the quickest decision (witness the hot line between Washington and Moscow).

A combination of the perception of high power, open position, and high urgency would be the most predictive of a preference for negotiation; whereas low power, closed position, and low urgency would lead to a preference for arbitration. Middle values of these variables would be predictive of mediation. Larsen et al. found support for the predictive efficacy of this model when tested in a survey employing six distinct samples.

TECHNIQUES FOR CONFLICT MANAGEMENT

The complex world we live in calls for specific techniques in reducing the possibility of war. Since conflicts will remain in this imperfect world for the foreseeable future, we need to find non-violent solutions to these problems. We need to know more about the politics of conflict.

Perhaps we can check up on the leadership traits which lead to peace and reward peace leadership. The role of the media in war prevention is discussed in this section. Some conflict situations tend to accentuate the type of conflict which could be reduced and localized. We need a system for gradually reducing the tensions of the world and preparing the nations for a world order of conflict management.

The politics of conflict management. Prosterman (1972) noted that an effective commitment to eliminate war must demand both intellectual and emotional involvement. He suggests we need disarmament to have a lawful world, but we also need law to have disarmament. There is a need to strengthen a sense of a world community. Provisions must be made for developing non-violent channels for resolving conflict and improving the quality of life. We need to develop an understanding of how to motivate other nations to move toward disarmament. Peace research is essential to develop techniques for dealing non-violently with the conflict, which will remain even in the disarmed world.

He also suggests we need to take a sobering look at our national leaders, who make international decisions. Those personality elements which make power desirable to a person frequently are different from the traits which help a leader to exercise power wisely. It may therefore help to have mandatory psychological testing before any national decision-maker is permitted to take office. Prosterman suggests leaders and their families should be located at the most exposed and dangerous positions in the country, as this may induce some restraint. Encounter groups may be helpful for leaders to re-establish the human contact so frequently lost in the abstract and rarefied atmosphere of a decision-maker.

Military leaders are awarded high honors and distinctions for their service to the country. Perhaps it is time we recognize on a national level the distinguished efforts for peace on the part of national leaders. Such social recognition may promote peaceful efforts on the part of our national leaders.

Moderating the media. Television popularizes the use of the gun, by both criminals and law enforcement, to the point where the loss of human life by gunfire is quite accepted. That violence is accepted here to a larger extent than in Europe may be exemplified by the recent outcry in Great Britain over the police shooting of a hold-up suspect. It was the third case in twelve months! Compare this to the hundreds killed under similar circumstances in this country.

Without advocating censorship, what can be done to moderate the media? In particular, what can be done when the media is used to whip up a public hysteria against potential foreign enemies? Singer (1970) suggested using a feed-back model to create awareness in the media as to the number of friendly, neutral, or hostile information units addressed to each nation from within another nation. For example, if the number of hostile comments rises drastically, the media may wish to tone down these comments to permit decision-makers to work in a less hysterical atmosphere. It may also provide an opportunity for the state to deny a relationship between the press hostility and official relations with the other nation. In countries where there is less press freedom, there would naturally be a stronger relationship between press hostility and official policy. The afore-mentioned proposal would therefore be more valuable in a country with media freedom.

Beyond moderating violence in the media, it may also be possible to use media to promote solutions to conflict in crisis situations. Galtung (1968) suggested the setting up of a telesatellite communication system, over which an international panel of experts could discuss crisis situations. Such a panel may contribute to a more complex and less stereotyped understanding of the problems. Having a world-wide audience, the panel's discussion may present a background against which any policy-maker would have to evaluate his own decisions.

Why not also make efforts at popularizing peace? This may be done by dramatically appealing to people as is now done in the case of violence. Is not Gandhi's non-violent struggle for independence in India an epoch-making story, rich in material for movies or television serials? Other themes of struggle from history, in which individuals and groups have achieved noble and daring objectives by peaceful and cooperative means, could surely be found.

Isolate and reduce the impacts of conflicts. A West German truck is moving on the highway between West Germany and Berlin. Moving up to a road block, the driver is ordered to halt and get out while the truck is inspected. In the course of the inspection, the guards find literature considered undesirable in East Germany. As a result the truck is confiscated for bringing enemy propaganda into East Germany. Whether this fictional account has any merit or not, it illustrates an international incident which might be typical of scores of others.

The question now is, at what level, and therefore with what intensity, will the reaction be made by the West German authorities? The incident could be dealt with at the state level in the form of a stern protest or by sending armed convoys through the corridor. We can also guess what would be the response of the East Germans to such aggressive action. Threats induce counter-threats, and a relatively minor incident could be blown way out of proportion to its importance and perhaps lead to serious conflict.

Fischer (1968) indicates an alternate procedure. He suggests fractionalizing conflicts; that is, split subsidary conflicts which arise from the central core of contention, and treat these as separate matters. Rather than treating the aforementioned incident as a state matter involving the rights of access to West Berlin, it could be treated as a matter between the guards and the driver, or between the driver and some lower level bureaucratic office in both states charged with resolving these incidents.

Conflicts can be enlarged or made small; what happens depends upon the level at which the problem is resolved. One obvious yardstick for choice of level is the potential threat to the security of a nation. In addition, some appropriate weight must be given, depending upon whether the incident is a repetition or an isolated act. An isolated incident may be the work of isolated individuals who have misperceived state policy, or in the absence of policy, have made a judgment of their own. If the act is isolated, it is clearly in the interest of both parties that the level for resolution of the incident be the lowest possible commensurate with a nonarbitrary and just solution.

The United Nations could create a roving corps of ombudsmen whose function it would be to investigate incidents and determine if they are isolated or state policy. If the incident is isolated, an attempt would be made to resolve the problem by appeal to national and international law. To facilitate the work of the United Nations ombudsmen, each concerned nation should appoint a corresponding ombudsman, perhaps with the rank of a police inspector. The national ombudsman would be authorized by law to make a settlement of the case, unless it involved a serious breach of national or international law. If the former, the matter would be settled in the national court of the host country, with the United Nation's ombudsman filing a brief as a friend of the court. If the office of UN ombudsman carried sufficient prestige, it may be assumed that this brief would carry considerable weight.

If the matter concerns international law, the United Nations should create regional courts where these matters could be settled quickly. The ombudsmen of the nations involved could represent respective interests, and the United Nations ombudsmen could once again file a brief as a friend of the court. This procedure could take a host of potentially hostile acts out of the relations between states and place them at the levels where they belong: between the parties directly concerned or within some lawful lower level framework.

Gradual tension reduction. To a large extent, World War I was the result of misperceiving the intentions of the opponent. The conflict actors were locked into an interacting system of threats and counter-threats prior to the conflict. This system eventually required hostile actions. The German military system was of such a nature that, once mobilization had begun, there was no way of preventing war. This was attributed to the problem of logistics and supply. Once the trains started rolling toward the front, they could only be stopped at the cost of great dislocation and a vulnerable defensive position if the enemy should attack. The threats and counter-threats did not work, and we know now that threats are not conducive to changing the attitudes or behavior of people. Threats create fears leading to defensive reactions. The military is taught the best defense is offense. This, in a nutshell, is what happened during the tragic and inconclusive war in Europe.

From experimental studies discussed elsewhere in this book, we know also that, if aggression is "successful" in obtaining some desirable value, the activity itself may be reinforced and lead to further hostility. In the long run, successful or semi-successful aggression may lead to a habit of militarism, perhaps best expressed in the Prussian militarist traditions. The millions of Jews who died during World War II are a testimonial to the futility of patient suffering when dealing with a brutal and cynical dictatorship. In fact, the rise and fall of the Nazis is a clear historical example that appeasement leads to increased aggression, leading to further appeasement, until the breaking point is reached.

To achieve peace in the world it is necessary to avoid the misperceptions which are derived from threats and appeasements. Osgood (1962) has made a proposal which would permit the gradual reduction of tension without taking inordinate risks or weakening a country's military potential. The essence of the plan is that a nation takes a unilateral step toward disarmament in the hope that the enemy would be induced to follow suit. The step might be, for example, the disarmament of a division or some other military reduction clearly disadvantageous to the side making it. To obtain the desirable effect, the step must be clearly perceived by the enemy as somewhat reducing the military threat against him. Consequently, all other things remaining equal, it would be more significant if a nuclear force were disarmed in Turkey (lying on the borders of the Soviet Union) than if a similar reduction were made farther away from the Soviet heartland.

While the step should be significant, it should not be of such a size to seriously increase the enemy's threat to the initiator's heartland. The step should clearly indicate to the opponent what steps he might take to disarm and reduce tensions. Every attempt should be made to announce the plan in advance to allied, neutral, and enemy countries; but the announcement should not demand prior willingness to reciprocate as a condition for taking the step. Such, in brief, is the plan. It has the advantage of dealing with the world of reality we are living in. It decreases the possibility that nations would be caught up in interlocking threats and provides a real incentive for the opponent also to move toward disarmament. Any future disarmament steps would be conditioned on some measure of reciprocation on the part of the enemy. Osgood outlines the procedure thusly: "1) If he tries to change the status quo by force, we will firmly resist and reestablish the status quo; 2) If he tries to reduce the status quo by means that reduce tensions, we will reward him by steps having similar intent; 3) If he tries to take advantage of initiatives we take in his favor, we will shift immediately to firm and punishing resistance; 4) If he reciprocates to our initiative with steps of his own, having similar intent, we will reward him with somewhat larger steps designed to reduce tensions" (pp. 25-26). This carrot and stick approach is the essence of operant conditioning procedures. Disarmament is gradually shaped by means of mutual rewards and punishments. The plan has also the advantage that it does not require a high level of mutual trust to be initiated. Rather, mutual trust is built as a result of reciprocation, assuming that disarmament serves one's own as well as the other's interests.

MOVING TOWARD A WORLD ORDER

Many people value peace as a possible goal. However, positive attitudes toward peace must be linked to some action, either educational or political. Political institutions, once established, are difficult to change, for several reasons; but they must be changed if we are to move toward a structure of peace. We must define the goals which require cooperation and are compelling to actual and potential conflict actors, because working toward these goals will reduce conflict. World government is possible despite ethnocentric resistance. A plan for limited world government, the function of which is to manage conflict, is discussed.

Positive attitudes toward peace are not enough. Attitudes toward peace are often mere abstractions for many people in the periphery. In fact, peace has frequently been used as a justification for war! Doob (1964) reviewed public declarations of war, and found that peace ranked high on the list of justifications. The declarations all agree on one point: wars are only justified if the other party threatens or actually begins the conflict. The UN Charter, the Cominform, NATO, and The Council of Europe all express a responsibility and need for maintaining the peace. Ironically, this sentiment is also expressed in most declarations of war.

Attitudes toward peace must be linked to peace action to contribute to a world order of peace. For convenience, peace action can be divided into persuasion efforts and political activity. Persuasion efforts should be directed at the center of society by means of the arts, crafts, and other educational efforts. This can be accomplished partially by developing "peace" courses from kindergarten through the university. Washburn (1971) estimates that nearly 150 institutions now have courses which are related to peace. This is progress but really a drop in the ocean, considering the thousands of institutions in the United States.

Political activities must focus on electing and retaining legislators who are favorable to a world detente. Officials must be elected who are ideologically disarmed and who understand that no peace is stable without social justice. Effort must be made, in lobbying and working on behalf of international organizations, to strengthen bonds of friendship among nations.

Overcoming resistance to institutional changes. Patterns of human relationships which fulfill important functions tend to become semi-permanent, or in other words, institutionalized. Institutionalization is characterized by formal reciprocal role relationships. In the nation, a citizen is expected to support the state, by paying taxes or going to war; and the national decision-makers, representing the state, in turn promise him prosperity and a share in the glory of the nation. The problem with institutionalization is that human needs may change; yet, despite these changes, it is extremely difficult to change relationships, once they are institutionalized. People often suffer from simple inertia. The path of least resistance in life is often to do nothing; and in the absence of catastrophes, most people are happy with the status quo.

There is also genuine fear of the unknown on the part of many people, which acts strongly as a brake to change. The story is told of the rebel condemned to death by the Sultan's court. Prior to the execution, the Sultan presented the prisoner with two choices. He could either face the firing squad or walk through a black door. The rebel chose the firing squad, after which the Sultan was asked what was behind the black door; "Freedom," the Sultan replied.

Part of the fear of the unknown is undoubtedly based on the fact that so few of the common people of the world have been trained in or given an opportunity for decision-making. Feeling impotent about what is known magnifies the fear of the unknown. Not participating in decision-making creates a lack of interest in understanding the short and long term effects of institutional actions. Since the interest and opinion of one man does not affect the whole, there is little incentive to be involved.

Related to these problems is the inability to observe the entire institutional process. Many people, whose concerns revolve around bread-and-butter issues, fail to see that a temporarily expedient policy may be disastrous in the long term. The armaments race may bring temporary prosperity but may also lead to its logical conclusion — war. In addition, in-group pressures are constantly in operation to reward those deemed loyal and to punish potential rebels. Significantly, many of these reward and punishment contingencies are held by the status quo powers. The president may call out the troops; the chairman of the corporation may fire the individual. Conformity is necessary for the sake of survival. The end result is that nearly all pressures are lined up behind the status quo. Apathy is mistaken for consent, leaving the status quo powers nearly impregnable.

Faced with this situation, there are two basic conditions under which institutional change might occur. The policies of the established forces may be so detrimental to the population as a whole that a drastic realignment of forces takes place in the nation. Revolutions occur when the present institution is hopelessly inadequate in solving the needs of people and channels are available for the people's anger. The other alternative is to take over the status quo institutions. This may be done by such means as coup d'etat or boring from within. A reform wing may take over a single party by playing the game better; of course, it is to no avail if they do not also learn, for example, how to play the election game better as well, as the McGovern forces failed to do in 1972.

Common goals and international cooperation. Angell (1962) suggested that common beliefs are not essential to obtain international unity. If the people of the nations cooperate on tasks of mutual concern, they will, in the long run, learn to trust each other. At a very elementary level, we ought to have a concern in survival. By cooperating in reaching total disarmament, presently hostile nations may change by getting closer and developing a greater number of cross-national bonds. The developing areas of the world need assistance in many ways to cope with rising populations, to say nothing of improving on the status quo. There are many worthy goals which can be achieved only by the cooperation of the major powers in the world. These goals are superordinate, as discussed by Sherif (1966). A superordinate goal is a goal compelling to both parties — but which is impossible for either to achieve without the cooperation of the other.

A primary task for peace research and education is to define and rank order for the most pressing superordinate goals. Goals such as disarmament, control of pollution (which recognizes no national boundaries), and preservation and extension of democratic institutions must be placed high on the list. Existing international organizations, in particular the United Nations, must be strengthened and take on the shape and function of an embryo world government. A great deal has been said about the impotence of the United Nations. This impotence is in direct inverse relationship to the strength and predominance of the concept of national sovereignty. Efforts must be made to shift people's loyalties from narrow nationalistic frameworks to a broader concern about humanity.

This cannot be achieved overnight, but must derive from gradual development. Perhaps initial steps must lead to stronger regional identification. An African, European, or Asian consciousness may have to precede a world consciousness. What can be done in the next decade to strengthen the regional apparatus of the United Nations and take such apparatus out of ideological conflicts? Conscious planning must evaluate how each region can best serve themselves and other regions at the same time. Past history is replete with exploitation. The search for complementary goals must take on a new form of equality of relations.

Homans (1961) stated, "The open secret of human exchange is to give the other man behavior that is more valuable to him than it is costly to you, and to get from him behavior that is more valuable to you than it is costly to him" (p. 62). Regional developmental offices could, in cooperation with national governments, define complementary and superordinate goals, both within and between regions.

There is no internal political stability, or stability in international relations, as long as large discrepancies in wealth exist between nations. National sovereignty will maintain these discrepancies. In Yugoslavia, the more developed sections of the state look with jealousy upon aid given to brother nations within the federation. The problems of nationalism must be dealt with by defining superordinate and complementary goals and by a gradual movement from national to regional to world consciousness.

Boulding (1966) stated, "the major task of the political scientists, the philosophers, the journalist, and the prophet: to give the people an image of changes in the international system which seems small enough to be feasible yet large enough to be successful" (p. 89). He suggests stages moving the community of nations toward world government. Stage one is the stage of tacit contracts, for example, a mutual suspension of nuclear tests. The second stage would involve formalized agreements, as exemplified by arms control organizations. If a freeze of armament levels is not to occur, it is vital that arms control move fairly rapidly into disarmament. Arms control by itself will remain unstable. Having disarmed does not imply that conflict will disappear. Conflicts will remain, so some system of conflict control and processing must be developed. The last stage is the development of true world government. In particular, this government should be "capable not only of controlling conflict, but of expressing and developing the common concerns and aims of mankind" (p. 89).

Do superordinate goals aid in the reduction of inter-group hostility? Sherif, Harvey, White, Hood, and Sherif (1961) did an experiment testing this hypothesis, creating conditions which led a group of boys to form "in-groups." Other competitive situations developed hostility between the groups. The experimenters then tried several approaches in removing this hostility. Initially, they introduced a common enemy or increased contacts. These procedures had limited success. The experimenters decided to utilize goals which appealed to both groups and would require the cooperation of both (superordinate goals). The camp's water supply was made dysfunctional, and the two groups of boys had to cooperate in fixing a plugged valve. Other "problems" were introduced requiring cooperation, for example, the purchase of a movie, collectively pulling a truck that was made unoperational, and separating intermixed camping equipment.

These cooperative tasks resulted in the gradual reduction of inter-group tensions, as evidenced by less derogatory name calling and the integration of the groups during meal times. After six days of superordinate goals, the boys were asked to express their choice for friends and rate each other on a series of adjectives. The percentage of friends chosen from the other group rose from six to thirty-six and from seven to twenty-three in the two groups.

There are no apparent reasons why these procedures could not also help improve relations between nations. True, the task is infinitely more complex. It would involve overcoming the effects of leader role requirements, hostility developed from ideological warfare, and different perceptions of reality based on varying cultures. Yet the hope for a converging world must, to a large extent, depend upon the elucidation of such goals.

To move away from war and toward a convergent world must depend upon several requirements. Superordinate and complementary goals must first be defined within nations, to insure internal integration, and then between regions, to promote international cooperation. The nature of these goals must be such that they are clearly perceived as superordinate or complementary and also concrete, in the sense that they can be completed within a specified time limit. It would be best to start with simple problems, to insure a feeling of accomplishment and success, before tackling the more difficult. This must be moderated by the possibility that the more difficult problems are frequently also the more urgent. A compromise would be to subdivide the more difficult and urgent problems and then tackle the task systematically and sequentially.

Is a world government possible? Frank (1966) notes that individual psychopathology cannot cast much light on why men fight wars. It is sufficient to observe that mentally healthy leaders frequently lead a nation to war. In addition, individuals may fight, but they do not wage war.

To eliminate war, it is necessary to modify the group standards which support it. According to Frank, these standards include: the concept of national sovereignty, the concept that war is a proper way of pursuing group interest, the equation of armed strength with determination and courage, and the labeling of adversaries as non-human. The institutional change needed to oppose these ethnocentric standards is to build a sense of world community.

Gaitskell (1966) echoes this sentiment when he writes: "we have got to set up and operate institutions which will mean nothing less than a major advance towards world government. Global solutions of this kind which not long ago were dismissed as the cloudy fantasies of well-meaning cranks have today become the necessary condition of our survival" (p. 143).

Levi (1960) stated that war occurs because it is an accepted institution. The reason it is accepted so easily is that there is no common loyalty to one community (world) and, therefore, no agreed-upon procedure for settling conflicts.

The Clark-Sohn proposal for reorganizing the United Nations. World institutions must be established which will create optimal conditions of contact between the nations of the earth. A plan which has the advantage of utilizing an existing institution, and which makes very specific recommendations with respect to changing them, has been advanced by Clark and Sohn (1966). The plan is outlined in a 535-page book, so the following summary will be less than complete.

According to Clark and Sohn, peace is not possible without law. The law of a world authority must be developed. The law should be uniformly applied to all nations and should forbid violence as a means of solving international conflicts. There are six underlying principles to the plan: (1) An effective system of enforceable world law in the limited field of war prevention must be developed. (2) This law must be explicitly stated in constitutional law with appropriate penalties. (3) World judicial tribunals must be established to interpret and apply world law. (4) A permanent world police force must be created. (5) There must be complete universal and enforceable disarmament. (6) A world machinery designed to reduce or eliminate the economic disparities between various regions of the world must be developed.

The plan involves a comprehensive reorganization of the United Nations. Before the revised charter comes into effect, it must be ratified by five-sixths of the nations of the world with five-sixths of the total world population and including the twelve largest nations. The general assembly is responsible for disarmament and the maintenance of peace and is given sufficient powers to accomplish this. The system of representation is revised, abolishing the one vote for one nation; the new representative system takes into account the relative population of the nations — the larger nations have a relatively larger number of representatives. No nation would have more than thirty nor less than one representative. The representatives would be selected by means of a three stage plan: Phase 1, chosen by the national legislatures; Phase 2, half chosen by legislatures and half by popular vote; and Phase 3, all are chosen by popular vote.

The present Security Council would be abolished in favor of an executive council composed of seventeen representatives elected by the General Assembly. The council would have no veto power, and votes carry with a 12/17 margin. Written into the selection procedures are provisions to have various regions of the world represented. The proposal outlines a detailed plan for a general and complete disarmament. Disarmament is to be carried out over a six year period, under the supervision of an inspection service. In each six month period after the acceptance of the revised charter, each nation would destroy 10 percent of its military organization and 10 percent of its armaments. To maintain peace (e.g., since personal guns are exempted), a world police force would be created, recruited mainly from the smaller nations. These would be stationed in such a way that there would be no undue concentration in any one area of the world. A peace force reserve and a UN military supply and research agency would supplement the force capabilities of the General Assembly. Directing the police force would be a five member military staff committee under the supervision of the General Assembly.

Conflicts may be settled by the judicial and conciliation system. Disputes based on legal principles may be settled by an international court of justice, and disputes of other than legal character may be referred to a world equity tribunal with power to recommend settlements. It is expected that the latter would have a world prestige similar to the national prestige in the United States of the Supreme Court, and therefore its recommendations would have the force of law. For trials of individuals accused of violating the disarmament provisions or laws enacted by the General Assembly, UN regional courts would be organized. The inspection service would be aided by a force of civil police in the detection and prosecution of disarmament violators. The options of the General Assembly would range from ordering economic sanctions to ordering the UN peace force into action.

The plan recognizes a perpetual source of conflict in the economic inequities between nations. Therefore, the proposal provides for the establishment of a world development authority to assist in the social and economic progress of the developing areas. The UN revenue system would provide 9 billion U.S. dollars for the peace force, $2 billion for the General Assembly and Executive Council, and $25 billion for the world development act, for a total budget of $36 billion. This provides for development and represents a considerable saving over the current military budgets. To avoid a UN tax bureaucracy, each nation would assign to the UN a proportional tax assessed under national law. After the General Assembly adopted a budget, it would decide the amount to be assessed to each member nation.

The revised charter also has a section dealing with rights and privileges of UN personnel and a bill of rights. The latter specifically states that rights not claimed by the revised UN Charter are explicitly reserved by the member nations and has provisions preventing the UN from violating the basic rights of the individual. The plan also includes formulas for amending the revised charter and the strengthening of existing organs of the UN.

The plan is realistic, since it is based on an existing institution and does not interfere in the basic rights of nations, except in the area of disarmament. The chief obstacle (besides the psychological factors discussed previously) is vested interest. Such a basic change would be a direct challenge to traditional diplomacy and our military traditions. The armament workers would suffer some temporary dislocation until plants could be retooled for peaceful use. Considering the alternatives of war and destruction, these are small challenges to meet.

SUMMARY

In this chapter, we have analyzed the cost and causes of war and the management of conflict. By conflict management we refer to the strategies and techniques which are useful in preventing a conflict from becoming overt. Conflict management does not imply the resolution of conflict — the causes of war may remain. In the nuclear age, however, the limited efforts at war prevention take on great significance. The resolution of the problems of social injustice would make little sense in a world devastated by nuclear warfare. Any step which brings the world closer to disarmament must be applauded.

The probability that war will break out in a world armed to the teeth is very high. But disarmament also has very important economic consequences. The resources which are squandered on arming the nations of the world could, if applied, solve the problems of social injustice in a short time. In fact, the world cannot begin to deal with the problems of injustice unless this struggle is linked to the movement for total disarmament.

The causes of war as well as conflict management are strongly affected by social cost motivation. There are objective reasons for war, but these are closely tied to justifications based on ethnocentric values. Ethnocentrism is an expression of social cost motivation. Likewise, the resistance to instititutional changes is strongly affected by ethnocentrism and conformity pressures. Conflict management must take into account the importance of having highly respected national leaders, with impeccable records in expressing ethnocentric values, negotiate detente. Such leaders can model effectively the changes in attitudes necessary to bring the world to disarmament.

In the near future, the limited objective of peace educators, researchers, and activists must be to bring the monster of nuclear warfare under control. Negotiation, mediation, and arbitration are all constructive responses to a world beset with conflict. In the complex and interrelated world in which we live, there are reforms that both decision-makers and citizens can work for.

It is important to understand the contributions of the behavioral sciences in the shaping of human behavior. Just as some conflicts become accentuated by interlocking systems of threats and counter threats, they may also be reduced by localization and gradual tension reduction. These are important preliminary and parallel efforts to limited world government in the area of disarmament. The distant future, however, looks for conflict resolution, that is, a resolution to the problems of social injustice. In a world of conflict management, social injustice will cause continual instability. To achieve conflict resolution requires a peace ideology. In the next chapter we discuss a peace ideology leading to integration.

10.
Conflict Resolution: Synergetic Integration, an Ideology for Peace

---

Peace like any other desired end state may be defined as a value. Rokeach (1973) wrote, "a value is an enduring belief that a specific mode of conduct or end state of existence is personally or socially preferable to an opposite mode of conduct or end state of existence" (p. 5).

That the vast majority of people in the world hunger and yearn for peace is undoubtedly true. Yet peace is as elusive today as yesteryear. Part of the elusiveness may be attributed to the conceptual confusion in understanding peace — as a human value, peace means different things to different people. Little wonder that this end state is difficult to achieve when disagreements exist concerning the essential nature of the peace. An enduring social peace, however, must be defined as peace with justice.

To achieve the goal of peace requires an understanding of the processes of attitude and structural change. Both structural and attitude changes for peace must be correlated to achieve maximum results. Different individuals and sectors of society respond differently to appeals, depending upon the motivational basis of the appeal. However, for people who belong to the periphery of society, structural change (e.g., conditions of contacts between groups) precedes any attitude change. One goal of attitude change toward peace is the development of empathetic sensitivity. Empathy enables the individual to include widely varying groups or cultures within the assimilation range of his own beliefs and habits. Altruism, or the unselfish desire to do good for others, is a necessary state of mind for peace. This value is largely brought about by the empathetic processes. We shall also discuss the conditions and norms which facilitate altruism.

Any peace which is broken tomorrow because of unresolved conflict fails the lofty promise which is the meaning of this value to most people. The hope of peace is that it will be lasting. The goal for which we strive is the permanent resolution of conflict between the peoples in the world. Conflict resolution requires a synergetic integration of the beliefs and cultures throughout the international system. Synergetic integration refers to the cooperative and correlated integration of beliefs and habits in the creation of a new and superior world culture. The creation of this culture will ensure an enduring peace. The processes leading to synergetic integration are discussed in this chapter. These processes define a peace ideology sorely needed to direct the efforts of peace researchers, educators, and activists in pursuit of a peace with justice.

THE NATURE OF PEACE

In this section, we shall discuss several definitions of peace. Peace is more than just the absence of war or the management of conflict. Positive peace is defined as peace with justice. Peace is the operationalization of the values of equality and freedom. The radical critique of contemporary peace research is well founded. Conflict management often protects the status quo and therefore promotes structural violence, that is, the violence which happens to a person as a result of his socio-economic membership. There are just wars because structural violence may extort a greater number of victims in both the short and long run. Yet, in changing unjust relations between people, we must not forget that we live in a nuclear age.

Differences regarding the end state of peace affect the means-ends, the methods used to achieve the goal. These differences can be generally summarized into two broad classes: (1) *Internal peace.* Seaver (1967) notes that peace, to some, means unity of mind within the individual person. Peace then, refers to the absence of internal conflicts and the presence of internal harmony. Internal peace may be independent of social structure and is the ultimate goal of nearly all religions and philosophies of man. (2) *Objective peace*. This refers to peace among individuals and between groups. In this category of peace there are two subdivisions. To Galtung (1969) we owe the definition of negative and positive peace. Negative peace is the absence of overt conflict; positive peace is peace with justice. The values which define positive peace will be outlined in this chapter. The management of conflict was the topic of the preceding chapter.

Peace is not only the absence of war but also the absence of conflict. Why are conflicts eliminated? Because, in the utopian society, certain values are paramount in directing human interaction. These values include equality (meaning the perception and acceptance of equal status among people) and freedom (meaning maximum conscious decision making participation in society). This utopian definition integrates both the subjective and objective definitions of peace, for how can an individual experience internal peace in a world overflowing with injustice and conflict? Since only positive peace is lasting, we shall refer to it simply as peace for the remainder of the chapter.

A value definition of peace: equality and freedom. Peace is dependent on the absence of the hierarchal structure which is the root cause of nearly all human conflicts. This permits the individual to pursue self-relevant goals without obstructions. Peace means making the political and socio-structural changes necessary to achieve these values.

To change the world toward equality and freedom requires first and foremost that the future is no longer treated as a forgotten dimension. Our political and educational focus must be aimed at the immediate, intermediate, and long-range future. We must also recognize there is no science apart from values. If we refuse to take values into account in future planning, this means support of status quo values frequently favoring social inequity. Recognizing the importance of values does not imply the absence of scientific ardour. The medical profession is highly dedicated to scientific procedures in the pursuit of a human value: health. Likewise, those of us who are concerned about peace must dedicate our efforts toward creating the social structure which permits the fulfillment of two basic values which are the foundation of a positive peace: equality and freedom.

Unfortunately, most of man's efforts have been devoted mainly to the management of conflict, leaving future planning perpetually to the future. Negative peace characterizes portions of the world we live in today and the function of UN peace keeping forces, for example, in Cyprus or the Middle East. In our day, when the world can literally be destroyed by nuclear warfare, such limited but important efforts at war prevention need not be belittled.

There are those (Hamon, 1965) who think that peace research should focus on clarifying the factors which continue the absence of overt conflict, on the assumption that such a state of warlessness, if continued, would eventually become a habit. Yet the presence of warlessness does not imply the absence of conflict. A system of negative peace is inherently unstable, and overt conflict is dependent upon the presence or absence of certain factors in the conflict actors (e.g., changes in the power balance and the introduction of new weapons). Boulding (1967) has argued that the outbreak of World War III is virtually certain on the basis of probability alone. Therefore, peace without justice is not peace at all; it is merely a delay of the inevitable conflict.

The radical critique of peace research and just wars. The traditional patterns of thought about peace have focused on conflict management. This is primarily because of the vacuum caused by the absence of a peace ideology. Indifference to the value questions implied in the concept of structural violence is the basis of the radical critique of peace research.

Hayden (1967) points to the conservative nature of peace research in the United States. Since research grants are distributed by government institutions, he argues that much of this research clings to the conservative rather than radical modes of thought.

Schmid (1968) began a wave of New Left criticisms of peace research. The essence of these criticisms is that peace researchers have also been confounded by the dominant ideology of the country in which they work. In the west, this means peace research has largely ignored the structural basis of conflict. In attempting to be scientifically unbiased, peace researchers in the west frequently view opponents in conflicts as equal in power and resources, when in fact many conflicts are of the type between master and slave.

As long as inequality exists between different sectors of a population, supporting the status quo does, in fact, not imply a lack of bias, it is, in fact, a bias in favor of the privileged sections of society. If conflict is inherently in the structure of the society, then the traditional emphasis on control and management is at best a short-term solution. Death from structural violence (hunger, disease) is just as real and devastating as death from a bomb. The radicals claim, not without justification, that peace research which focuses on control and management is largely pacification research and suggest that these efforts should be redirected into revolution research aimed at eliminating injustice.

This critique should indicate that the enforced absence of war (negative peace) is inherently unstable because the conditions of justice are not fulfilled. On the other hand, revolutionary wars may lead to nuclear confrontation if they represent a serious threat to the status quo powers. The dilemma of our generation is gradually to shift the balance of power in favor of equality and freedom without risking thermonuclear destruction. This ought to be the essence of peace research and peace education. Whenever a peace research or education project is contemplated, the initiators should ask themselves the question: What effect will the project have on facilitating a change in the balance of power toward equality and freedom? That in a nutshell sums up the problem confronting peace research and education.

THE CHANGING OF ATTITUDES TOWARD SYNERGETIC INTEGRATION

To change the world toward peace requires an understanding of appropriate structural conditions and attitude change processes. Peace thinking reflects different approaches to peace. Segregation is not a viable construct in an increasingly interdependent world. Assimilation, however, should not be confused with integration. Synergetic integration respects the contribution of all people and depends on cooperation rather than force. To achieve integration requires large shifts in attitudes on the part of both opinion leaders and followers.

Traditionally, theories of change have focused on the consistency principle and the creation of cognitive dissonance. The underlying hypothesis of this approach is that dissonance is experienced as uncomfortable and that people therefore will change in the direction of cognitive congruence. There are three reasons why dissonance is an effective change agent in laboratory studies, which do not apply to real life. First, dissonance is more salient in the laboratory than in real life. Secondly, the subjects used in laboratory experiments are college students of relatively high cognitive sensitivity. Finally, there is a conceptual confusion between stereotypes and attitudes. Stereotypes are changed relatively easily because the strong emotionally conditioned component of attitudes is absent.

Social position theory suggests that attitude formation and change are dependent on socio-economic factors. Functional and social influence theories leave unanswered the important question of what parts do attitudes play in various socio-economic groups and the functional relationship between influence processes and group membership.

The goal of change processes should be to develop the empathetic processes in individuals and society as a condition for altruism. It is important to remember, however, that, in the periphery of society, social changes usually precede attitude change.

The peace thinking continuum. Galtung (1969) discusses a basic continuum of peace thinking, anchored at the one extreme by total isolation and at the other extreme by total integration. Between these two end points are located the disassociative school and the associative school of thought. The modern nation state is based on the disassociative school. This school of thought advocates that the best thing to do under all circumstances is to keep the potential conflict actors as far apart as possible. This may be done either spatially (e.g., goegraphical distance) or by means of social distance (the internalized bigotry expressed in "birds of a feather flock together").

One of the basic training functions of groups or nations is this predominant emphasis on differences between the in-group and out-groups; yet this emphasis overlooks the much larger share of characteristics we have in common. A predominant result of the large scale international study (Larsen, 1972b) was the strong similarities between people of different nations and cultures (rather than differences). We must reverse the trend of thinking which is based on differences. In preserving our cultural integrity, let us not forget what we all have in common.

The system of nation states in Europe is an example of the disassociative school. These states are kept apart spatially, often by natural geographical borders, and socially, by different languages and customs, engendering bigotry and prejudice. The associative school, on the other hand, argues that conflict actors should get as close together as possible. The more closely interacting, the more interest in common, the less likelihood of conflict.

Integration is the only reasonable course for our modern age. Even if people desire segregation, it is impractical and impossible for several reasons. Our modern and instant means of communication make what happens in one group or nation pictorially available to

---

SOCIAL COST AND CONFLICT RESOLUTION

If the world is to change toward the unselfish concern for others, the norms which facilitate altruism must become stronger than those which facilitate aggression. Attitudes are formed in the interaction with, or through the pressure of, significant others. Likewise, important social attitudes are changed in the population at large through opinion leaders.

The structural changes required in society can only be achieved if an ideology of a positive peace is accepted by the powerful or the aspiring powerful. Social cost motivation dictates an elitist approach to change and a realistic appraisal of power relationships. In the world characterized by synergetic integration, social cost motivation will play a decreasingly smaller role, as the assimilation range is increased to include the whole human family. In this utopian world, approval for individual differences will be the rule, and conformity pressures will decrease. Equality and freedom will be achieved when social cost is no longer an over-riding motivator of human behavior.

other groups or nations. At the same time, our modern weapon systems make every part of the globe vulnerable. We cannot live apart, so we must sink or swim together.

Integration is the only correct, *long-term* policy, but not necessarily the best short-term approach. Forced integration between powerful and less powerful actors frequently means assimilation and the destruction of the cultural integrity of the less powerful. Assuming there is something valuable in every culture, which is expressed in unique cultural products, forced integration between unequal actors destroys the culture of the less powerful and produces assimilation. Synergetic integration depends on the creation of symmetric relations between peoples.

The best policy for the present is cultural pluralism between asymmetric partners and synergetic integration between partners equal in rank. Synergetic integration would insure the inclusion of the cultural values of all groups, thereby producing a superior culture in a dialectic fashion. This culture would take advantage of all the progress of mankind and would also have learned from all the mistakes of history. This is the type of integrated world toward which we must move.

Consistency theory. It is an imperative task to change the syndrome of attitudes and war justifications which are detrimental to stability and peace with justice. To change these attitudes, it is necessary to understand attitude organization and functions. An attitude is an intervening variable between some attitudinal object (stimulus) and some measurable dependent variable. The attitudinal object may be an individual, a racial or ethnic group, or an issue of contemporary concern.

There are three components of an attitude: affect (i.e., positive or negative feelings toward the object), cognition (i.e, beliefs concerning the object), and overt behavior toward the object. The relationship between these components is characterized by consistency. For example, a person may feel negative (affect) toward communism (attitudinal object), believe that the system represents a threat to the "free enterprise" system (cognitive component), and therefore vote for the candidate who appears most anti-communist (behavior).

Consistency is the most common theory of attitude organization in psychology. The typical person is viewed as having a set of central values around which are organized a closely interrelated set of attitudes. The authoritarian person has his attitudes organized around power, security, and perceived in-group morality.

Most people feel that their values and attitudes are consistent with each other. This is rarely completely true. The bigot may have positive feelings toward democracy, but only for whites, for example. All kinds of defense mechanisms are brought into play to enable the individual to remain unaware of these inconsistencies. We invest considerable time in rationalizing these away, or we maintain rigid separation between attitudinal categories, or we may simply repress the inconsistency. These defenses are brought into play by the need to feel consistent.

Most theories of attitude organization or change proceed from the principle of consistency. Heider (1946, 1958) first proposed a theory of balance. A person may be positive or negative toward another person, and this attitude tends to be in balance with feelings toward the attitude object. A state of balance exists if all three relations are positive, or if two are negative. For example, John likes Peter and they both like Jews (attitude object):

$$\text{Jews}$$
$$+ \qquad +$$
$$\text{Peter} + \text{John}$$

or John doesn't like Peter or Jews, but Peter likes Jews:

$$\text{Jews}$$
$$+ \qquad -$$
$$\text{Peter} - \text{John}$$

Osgood and Tannenbaum (1955), Newcomb (1953), Cartwright and Harary (1956), Festinger (1957), and Rosenberg and Abelson (1960) have all proposed theories making use of the consistency principle.

The basic idea of consistency may be summarized as follows: (1) There is a tendency for the elements of an attitude to have the same sign. For example, negative feelings toward an object will be associated with negative cognitive elements to support the feelings and, all things being equal, will result in negative behavior. (2) Attitudes tend to be related to each other in some logical and consistent manner. If a person doesn't like Jews, chances are that he will not like black people either. (3) Attitudes toward attitude objects tend to be consistent (in the same direction) with attitudes toward people. If person A feels favorable toward American intervention in Viet Nam while B feels negative, B is also likely to feel negative toward A.

Research on attitude change has proceeded from the consistency principle also. To induce attitude change, a person must perceive a "dissonance" in terms of the above three principles. The dissonance will be experienced as psychologically uncomfortable and will induce change in the direction of consistency. The primary assumption underlying attittude change toward consistency is that the individual must be aware of the inconsistency. Most attitude change studies go through considerable effort in creating this awareness. Also, most of these studies are carried out on populations possessing relatively high cognitive sensitivity.

These two factors favor attitude change in the laboratory, but are they representative of the real world? In the real world, there are real pressures supporting attitudes. Conformity to norms, based on the fear of rejection, is the rule and not the exception. The majority of populations are vulnerable to conformity pressures. Social cost motivation is supported by belief in external control of life, authoritarianism, cognitive rigidity, and low self-esteem. These social-psychological conditions call forth a host of defense mechanisms to repress or rationalize the feelings of dissonance. The result is a low level of awareness. Because of this condition of unawareness, attitude change based on cognitive dissonance is difficult to achieve in real life.

Stereotypes or attitudes. Another reason why some laboratory or field studies show that dissonance is an effective change inducer is the conceptual confusion between stereotypes and attitudes among researchers. The La Piere (1934) study showed little correspondence between responses to symbolic social situations and responses to actual social situations. He asked a number of establishments whether they would accept Chinese as guests. Despite an overwhelming number of negative replies, only a few actually rejected Chinese when confronted with a well-dressed couple. Minard (1952) studied white and black miners who worked together. The results showed that the integrated white miners achieved more favorable "attitudes" toward blacks on job-related items but that this did not carry over to non-job items.

Several conclusions about the lack of congruence between verbal and behavioral reactions and the lack of transfer of "attitudes" may be drawn. A verbal reaction cannot, by itself, define an attitude. People may be reacting to stereotypes, that is, systems of beliefs concerning attitude objects with little emotion attached to the object. Since there is little emotional involvement in stereotypes when confronted with incongruent stereotypic objects, people may readily change in the direction of congruency.

Attitudes, however, are rooted in affect and especially in the fear of social rejection or on the desire for acceptance. A great deal of so-called attitude change demonstrated in attitude change studies is probably only a change in stereotypes. Larsen and Schwendiman (1969) wrote:

> These results may be interpreted as a change in stereotypes due to exposure to incongruent stereotype behavior. These changes then are not changes in norm-relevant social attitudes, but rather changes in stereotype. . . . A primary fact of social attitudes apparently is that they are well grounded in reference group norms. We suggest this is the most salient difference between stereotypes and social attitudes. (P. 157)

The results of the study suggested that, if people have a stereotype of blacks as "slovenly," for example, exposure to a well-dressed, educated black will change this stereotype. Changes in stereotypes do not necessarily lead to changes in attitudes, which are supported by affect, rationalizations, and reference group support. Cognitive dissonance as an instrument for change should therefore be primarily directed to those who have sufficient cognitive sensitivity to respond to the dissonance.

Social position and attitude change. Galtung (1964) divided society into two broad classes. The center is the more privileged group close to communication and decision-making structures, whereas the periphery is removed from these. The people in the periphery are located in rural areas, have less education, and are disadvantaged in such areas as occupation and economic status. Consequently, perceptions of social reality and attitude formation are influenced by limitations of knowledge and information. The vast majority of people in most nations are in the periphery. They must rely to a large extent on information from the center for support of their attitudes. Consequently, attitude change of broad social importance proceeds from the center to the periphery. This dependency is made especially acute by the personality characteristics generally present in the periphery which tend to support authoritarian attitudes (Larsen, 1972b).

Broad social change, for example, in moving away from ethnocentrism toward a world order, must be supported by a two-pronged attack. People of the center have the cognitive ability to be sensitive to logical inconsistencies and, because of higher self-esteem are presumably less dependent on social approval for their attitudes. While attitudes may be firmly held, they are held within a framework of flexibility and open-mindedness. For the center, therefore, attitudes serve the function of organizing social reality, whereas for the periphery, attitudes are organized primarily to defend the ego. In serving defensive purposes, there are natural and interrelated relationships between attitudes in the periphery and various defense mechanisms, such as rationalization and repression.

The center, therefore, is more open to attitude change efforts based on logical persuasion, cognitive dissonance, and apparent inconsistencies in its moral code. The peripheral people are more likely to respond to apparent legitimate models of authority. Social cost primarily determines attitude formation and change in the periphery. Educational efforts to change the world toward peace should be directed toward the center, which may gradually change the periphery via opinion leaders. There is a time lag between the initial change of social attitudes in the center and the follow-up change in the periphery. The length of the time lag will depend on the extensiveness and importance of the attitude change. The changing of attitudes toward the war in Viet Nam on the part of large segments of the center in the U.S. brought about a gradual change in the periphery in the late sixties. The hard hat marches of the early seventies serve to remind us, however, of the resistance of the periphery when ethnocentric attitudes serving many important needs are aroused.

Functional and social influence theories of attitude change. Katz (1960) and Katz and Stotland (1959) advanced a functional approach to the study of attitudes. They suggested that only by understanding the motivational basis of an attitude is it possible to understand change and resistance to change. The key question is what function the attitude is serving in the psychological economy of the individual. According to Katz, attitudes serve four major functions. The first is the instrumental, adjustive, or utilitarian function. This function is closely allied to the social cost idea: a person seeks to adjust or "get along" with his significant others. Attitudes may also have ego defensive functions; that is, they may serve to maintain an unawareness of unpleasant facts. As has already been noted, ego defensiveness lies at the base of prejudice. The value expressive function is served by attitudes which spring from the personal values of the individual, those attitudes which are appropriate to the person's self-concept. The peace activist may gain satisfaction from expressing his views. Finally, attitudes serve to organize our experience. We need to structure reality and, thereby, reduce inconsistency and ambiguity. Attitudes, therefore, have also a knowledge function.

Implications of functional theory for attitude change suggest persuasion may be appropriate to certain attitudes; for example, attitudes serving instrumental and knowledge functions. Attitudes which serve ego defensive purposes, however, are probably best changed by methods which reduce anxiety or make use of powerful significant others. Katz's theory does not deal with the crucial question of what *proportion* of attitudes serves a given function in the average person. Nor does it deal with the structural distribution of these functions in society, that is, the proportion of attitudes serving a particular function as a result of membership in socio-economic groups. For people in the periphery, most attitudes probably serve ego defensive functions; and the approach to attitude change must therefore be different in the periphery compared to the center.

Kelman (1961) suggested three processes of social influence. A person complies when he accepts influence from some other person or group in the hope of obtaining some favorable reaction. This is another way of saying that social cost motivation, or the need for "significant other" approval, is necessary in order to obtain attitude change. The expression of attitudes or opinions is helpful in obtaining rewards and avoiding punishment. Identification is the acceptance of influence, because behaving this way is important in establishing or maintaining a satisfying relationship with some person or group. Once again, the importance of social cost is emphasized. Internalization is the process whereby the individual accepts influence, because the changed behavior is consistent with his value system. This is somewhat similar to the value expressive function suggested by Katz.

Power is the important variable in Kelman's theory. Control over rewards and punishment is the necessary condition for compliance and identification. Kelman does not evaluate what proportion of attitudes are maintained or changed by compliance or identification versus internalization. Neither does he consider the appeal of these influences as a function of social structure. Social cost theory would suggest compliance and identification are primarily influence processes in the periphery, whereas internalization implies a more sophisticated influence process characteristic of people in the center. To map strategy for social change, it is necessary to relate the functions attitudes play and the corresponding influence processes effective in different sectors of the population.

It is well to keep in mind strong resistance will be displayed against persuasive messages which are highly discrepant from the person's own view. This point is summarized by the contrast-assimilation effect discussed in Chapter 6. Strong resistance will be induced in particular if the communicator is not a friend (Zimbardo, 1960). The argument produced by a communicator may produce dissonance, which is resolved by rejecting the message of the perceived unfriendly communicator. To obtain attitude change, it is critical to develop the perception that both the sender and receiver have much in common apart from the communication. It is difficult to attack someone who appears similar to oneself, since such an attack may be perceived as an attack on oneself. In order to communicate effectively, the message must not be highly discrepant and must be presented by someone having a sociometric attraction to the receiver. *The importance of empathy.* History is replete with examples of conflicts which have arisen from communication difficulties. An important obstacle to successful communication is the difficulty inherent in projecting oneself into the frame of reference within which the opponent operates. Klineberg (1971) notes,

> The quality most urgently needed in connection with international understanding is that of empathy. . . . Can we teach attitudes that question the validity of national or ethnocentric perception and judgment, and that involve an empathetic response to the positions held by others, even hostile nation-states? (P. 128)

Being empathetic (literally trying to understand reality as the other person sees it) is not easy. It is the task of social psychology to delineate the conditions which are productive of empathy. In particular, the danger of extreme polarity of categorical thinking should be stressed. Without open-mindedness reflected by the willingness to change one's mind as the evidence changes, there is little hope for empathy. Minorities or other nationals are often hated blindly. There is a need for more communication and travel to develop a minimum of empathy and to remove at least the worst stereotypes.

Since we know that ethnocentrism serves many important psychological needs, we must try to satisfy these needs. In the long run the insecurities which underlie ethnocentrism must be dealt with. This can best be accomplished by creating conditions where people feel the joy and responsibility of making important decisions affecting their own lives. The vicarious satisfactions of achievement and power which ethnocentrism provides play a role only as long as people feel impotent.

The glorification and desensitization of violence must be eliminated from the media. Pain is real, and yet our history books persist in glorifying tales of gore. The news media, television, and movies are guilty of creating an acceptance of violence. The acceptance of violence is partially accomplished by making few attempts at portraying violence and pain with empathy.

In order to create an attitude of empathy, then, it is imperative to remove illusory perceptions of social psychological differences between people and create appreciation for communality. Empathy implies that deviations and differences can be tolerated and understood as well. Empathy produces a respect for individual differences. On the international scene, efforts must be made to strengthen relationships and interests which all nations have in common, and at the same time to develop a greater acceptance of pluralism so as to move the world toward ethnocentric and ideological disarmament. Today closed-minded ideological attitudes may lead us to catastrophe. It is necessary to have realistic conceptions of how the opposition sees the world, in order to move toward tension reduction.

Structural change and attitude change. Eckhardt (1967) has drawn a model for future peace planning. The long range view calls for the effort of peace researchers, whose results would gradually become a part of the literature and therefore influence opinion leaders in the intermediate future. In the short range, what is needed is peace legislation, that is, strengthening the United Nations and laying the foundation for a world government. The immediate future calls for peace action, that is, non-violent demonstrations. In this scheme, peace research is at the top of the pyramid and gradually changes the attitudes of the population through the pressure of opinion leaders.

The interaction between attitudinal and structural change is apparent. However, of the two, structural change is the more important. Attitude change in the general population (apart from the intelligentsia) follows structural change, and not vice versa. An excellent example of this is the attitude change which has occurred in Southern United States toward blacks.

Relatively speaking, attitudes toward blacks have improved more there than in any other section of the country (Larsen, 1971b). Why is that so, considering the previous negative attitude of whites? Did the southern whites become more Christian or converted toward a more compassionate outlook toward their fellow man? There is no evidence to indicate this is so. However, there is evidence of the fundamental structural changes which must precede attitude change.

Starting with Eisenhower sending federal troops to Little Rock, Arkansas, the power of government has been used to enforce the civil-rights laws of the United States. No longer do blacks eat at separate restaurants, drink from different fountains, or sit in the back of public transportation. These structural changes directly challenged many of the myths and stereotypes of white southerners and have in large measure improved racial attitudes.

The four structural changes which precede any large scale attitude change are: equal status between groups; common goals, which are valued by both groups; interdependence between groups, in the sense that efforts by members of both groups are needed to reach common goals; and the positive sanction of some legitimate authority on behalf of these changes (Allport, 1958). Pettigrew (Larsen, 1971) called the southern whites latent liberals, because he thought correctly that their attitudes would change in a relatively short period of time if legitimate sanctions were brought to bear. This is the rationale behind bussing to achieve racial balance in schools. The essence of the whole argument is that we do not change the world (structure) by changing the hearts of men. We do change the hearts of men by changing the world.

ALTRUISM: A NECESSARY PRECONDITION FOR SYNERGETIC INTEGRATION

The empathetic processes are crucial in order to bring one people's beliefs and habits within the assimilation range of another people. We like those we believe are similar to us, with the result that we want to act altruistically toward them. Altruism is a function of feeling empathetic toward a wide range of people and is a necessary condition for synergetic integration. We shall discuss the conditions and norms which facilitate altruism.

Injustice and personal responsibility. In many parts of the world, as well as within the American society, there are appalling inequities which remain a constant source of conflict. Galtung (1972) discusses the presence of structural violence in modern society. Social structure may kill people by means of poor nutrition and inadequate health facilities. The cost of health care in this country has risen to astronomical heights, leaving vast numbers of poor people unable to provide good medical care for their families. Peace must be understood as the presence of equalitarian, non-exploitive cooperation between groups and the absence of suppression. Galtung suggests peace research has gone beyond the point of impartial objectivity, because the absence of taking sides actually favors the structural violence of the status quo. Peace researchers and all concerned individuals must take sides against unjust structure and should not only develop policy research, but also take concrete actions for peace.

Lasting peace and stability is impossible as long as immense disparities in economic development exist between countries. To reduce these discrepancies, it is necessary to stop the arms race. By reducing the huge armament expenditures and reallocating part of these funds for the economic development of developing countries, the gap could be narrowed. International structural violence (economic inequities) parallel the inequities within society and require similar remedies.

We have a personal responsibility for removing injustice. This is especially true of scientists who, in the name of "pure science," have helped to bring the world to the brink of destruction. A scientist's responsibility does not end with research and invention. To refuse to be concerned with the policy implications of scientific research is an abandonment of personal responsibility to the human race. Such an "ostrich in the sand" attitude has caused untold suffering in the world.

Frisch (1970) invites scientists to take individual pledges not to do war work or anti-social work of any kind. He suggests that a special government agency be created to process and referee technical-political decisions. A court should be set up with prominent scientists to evaluate the political implications of technical decisions. Each scientist has a responsibility to make his views known, directly, in writing. In removing injustice and the dangerous conditions which threaten the world, scientists and all conscious people have a personal responsibility and a personal stake in becoming altruistic.

The development of altruism. What conditions are productive of altruistic behavior? Why are some people concerned with and desirous of helping others? It would seem an attitude of altruism is learned much in the same manner as are other forms of social learning.

It has been a consistent argument of this book that social cost (seeking approval of or avoiding rejection by significant others) is an important human incentive. Altruism, as well as aggression, may therefore be affected or reinforced by social cost. Other reinforcers, such as physical rewards (money, candy, etc.), may also be effective in shaping behavior.

Fischer (1963) gave marbles to nursery-age children in an experiment. Subsequently they were shown a picture of another child who had no marbles and asked if they would like to share some of their marbles. Some of the children were given bubble gum after sharing and some were given verbal praise by Fischer. The results showed that those children given bubble gum were more likely to repeat their behavior than those receiving verbal praise. As Kaufman (1970) observes, Fischer had no previous relationship with these children, so consequently praises had little effect. For social cost to be an effective motivator, the approval or rejection must be experienced from *significant* individuals or groups. The Fischer experiment is therefore not a critical test of the relative importance of social cost versus physical rewards.

Midlarksy and Bryan (1967) investigated the effectiveness of verbal praise after the child had already developed a positive attitude toward the experimenter as a result of a hug. The child had a choice of two levers where one led to candy and the other to verbal praise. In this situation the child preferred the lever leading to verbal praise. How did the Fischer and Midlarsky-Bryan experiments differ? In the latter, positive feelings were developed toward the experimenter prior to reinforcement. In other words, the experimenter had become a *significant* person, and praise therefore became an important reinforcer.

Aronfreed and Paskal (1965) supported these findings. Children who received hugs and joyous responses from the experimenter when they gave candies away tended on subsequent occasions to be more generous also. These findings would suggest that altruistic behavior in children may be developed by using various forms of reinforcement. For altruism, as for aggression, social cost is an especially effective reinforcer.

Norms facilitating the development of altruistic behavior. Kaufman (1970) discussed several norms important to altruistic attitudes. The first is social responsibility. There is a widespread understanding in most societies that people are supposed to help those who depend upon them. In a narrow sense, this may mean the immediate family. It would seem a particularly important task to transfer this concern for the immediate family to concern for less fortunate people everywhere in the world. A bond of dependency appears to be the key to feelings of social responsibility.

Berkowitz and Daniels (1963) found that their participants worked harder in groups if the supervisor of the group had an opportunity to win prizes (was dependent upon them). In addition, Adams (1967) showed that the closer people's kinship, the greater the likelihood of help. The more variety of bonds and the greater the strength of bonds which are established between people, the greater the chance that reciprocal dependent relationships (interdependent) will be developed. This points once again to the need for moving toward integration, through business, travel, and international organizations.

The second norm is reciprocity. Most people feel an obligation to return help they have received from others. Here, a different form of assimilation function operates. Goranson and Berkowitz (1966) suggested people feel debts to others in direct proportion to their resemblance to some previous benefactor. If a member of another race or religion has saved a person's life, the goodwill engendered may generalize to the whole group.

The third norm affecting altruism, according to Kaufman, is distributive justice. This norm reflects an economic model of human behavior. People in groups have the tendency to compare the rewards and costs they incur with the rewards and costs of other individuals in the group. If the costs of some individuals in the group are higher than others, it is expected that rewards will also be higher (Homans,

1961). Altruism is therefore moderated by social justice. May we thus expect greater altruism on the part of those who have a larger proportion of rewards compared to costs? It is possible social attitudes are, in general, based on such utilitarian functions. In time, however, the attitudes may become independent of the functions and self-sustaining. Initially, however, it is important that people feel a stake in helping others.

In primitive times, when social units were small, the feeling of responsibility was more immediate. To a large extent, the family depended upon each other for survival; and, if one member shirked his duty, everyone else suffered. Today, the larger society has taken over many of these protective functions. Social security protects the survival of the individual, not the family. This has caused a diffusion of responsibility. As Darley and Latane (1966) stated, the more people who are within a crisis, the less responsible each individual feels. However, this feeling of lack of responsibility may be attributed to more than diffusion of responsibility. The structural relationships in most larger groups create feelings of alienation and powerlessness. How can the individual feel altruism toward other members of a society when his judgment and decisions count for little? A necessary precondition for altruism in our modern society is the removal of this alienation and powerlessness.

INTEGRATION

Synergetic integration is indeed the answer to inter-group conflict. The failure of past integration attempts can be placed squarely on the failure to evaluate the importance of values in integration schemes. In the vacuum caused by the absence of a peace ideology, competition between groups is a factor even in integration efforts. Integration is not assimilation. We must respect the cultural integrity of all groups.

The first step toward respect for the cultural integrity of each group is equality of relations between groups. In the struggle for ideological integration, we must overcome the exclusivist positions of ideological systems. Today, the structure of a positive peace requires ideological integration rather than the victory of ideology.

Integration: the answer to inter-group conflict. As Galtung (1969) has pointed out, peace thinking has generally fallen at some point between the opposing policies of integration or segregation. There are those who feel that sufficient distance between conflict actors leads to peace. National boundaries and racial or ethnic ghettos are based on this school of segregation. In a naive and primitive sense, the rationale of this school is logical and straightforward. If distance is created between conflict actors, it is impossible for a fight to occur. Unfortunately, there is a problem in the concept of distance.

In the past, natural boundaries, such as rivers or mountains, did provide real defenses and, therefore, distance between groups. Our age, however, is characterized by spectacular changes in transportation and communication. No longer is it possible to hide behind natural barriers, because mountains represent no obstacle to rockets or Telstar communications. *Segregation, therefore, no longer serves a functional purpose in preventing conflict.* Yet, despite its lack of functional utility, segregation characterizes the world we live in today.

Integration, on the other hand, assumes that conflict can best be eliminated by bringing potential conflict actors into contact with each other. The essence of integration is that people from different groups begin to perceive a common fate (assimilation effect) with members of other groups. It is also based on the truism that we human beings, regardless of our background, have more in common than what separates us. Finally, and most importantly, integration is based on the assumption that human values are relative and not absolute in nature; and, therefore, people with different value systems can get along and have respect for each other. Unfortunately, in our world, ideology or religion as expressions of human values are frequently seen as absolute and, therefore, not subject to compromise or reevaluation.

A value approach to integration. Lawler and Laulicht (1970) have observed the few successes and the many failures of social, economic, and political integration in various parts of the developing world. The multiple reasons for failure in various integration schemes are:

(1) These attempts have been made within the scope of competition. The result has been that each party has tried to maximize the social, economic, and political return within a zero-sum model.

(2) Two universal values have not been satisfied in these integration attempts. *Where failure in integration is apparent, the values of equality and freedom have been violated in some fashion.* The two values are interdependent and equally important. It is impossible to have freedom (defined as the exercise of maximum decision-making ability) without equality (defined as equal status). It is also impossible to achieve equal status without removing the decision-making obstacles inherent in a hierarchal system. The practical or functional attempts at integration have ignored the fundamental nature of these two values across national, religious, cultural, and even ideological boundaries.

(3) The meaning of freedom and equality has been perverted by self-protective ideological considerations, resulting in lost operational meaning for both decision-makers and the population alike. To the capitalist apologist, freedom means the right to express opinions and vote for representatives, even if the reality of political situations shows that the media and vehicles for election are totally under the dominance of one ideological viewpoint (and therefore not conducive to change). Likewise, the value of equality may have lost its meaning in East European countries through the development of new status hierarchies. Integration attempts must show explicit, operational definitions of equality and freedom.

(4) The conditions of contact between members of different groups which best facilitate equality and freedom (as outlined by Allport, 1958) have not been met. These conditions emphasize the importance of equality, interdependence, common goals, and the positive sanction of perceived legitimate authority.

Value obstacles to regional integration. To the extent that obstacles to equality and freedom are removed in plans for integration, will integration, itself, be successful. The question is not regional integration versus immediate world government. Rather, the question is, to what extent does any plan for integration between groups, whether functional, amalgamative, transactional, regional, or universal — social, economic, or political — overcome obstacles to equality and freedom?

Etzioni (1963) has noted that no economic union in the developing countries had achieved the records of the European Common Market. This disparity in economic integration has led others (Haas, 1961) to suggest international integration is best facilitated as an expression of the rational interests of the urban-industrial society. One reason is that the role of nationalism is different in the developed and developing countries.

Haas notes that nationalism in the developing countries was formed in opposition to colonialism, without clearly defined positive values of its own. In some cases, this modern form of nationalism has developed a xenophobic zeal which approximates that of a religion (Hayes, 1931). Nationalism, therefore, means competition in behalf of narrow national interests in a world of competition. Competition has an end goal, high ranking in some form of hierarchy. Any regional system, therefore, which is entered in the hope of only improving short-term national interests will neither produce equality nor freedom. Competition leads to conflict, and integration under conditions of competition is paradoxical and may intensify inequalities between groups and nations.

Integration theories. Integration theories up to this point have chiefly been characterized by their functional approach to integration, independent of values. Functionalism contains the idea that national sovereignty will gradually be replaced by a commitment to internationalism. This commitment is brought about by internationalizing specific tasks and objectives which are no threat to national sovereignty. Functionalism is basically an economic pressure group or technocratic approach with a gradually expanding network of ties which at some magic moment, becomes political. However, if these technocratic networks serve competitive functions, we can expect national political leaders to be sensitive to their own national interests and not the interest of the regional or world system.

Functionalism is a method of bringing about integration through the back door, in an atmosphere of low awareness. The approach might be useful, if its modus operandi were changed to deal with the issues of equality and freedom in a conscious way. Failure to do so leaves functionalism with little hope of success, beyond narrow special interest integration.

Whereas functionalism focuses mainly on economic interaction, transactionalism seeks integration by means of non-economic contacts (e.g., traveling and cultural exchanges). This approach is helpful in eliminating extreme negative group stereotypes. Transactionalism, likewise, deals only with values in an implicit way; and its success is limited. In either case, functionalism and transactionalism seek to change public opinion toward integration, by means of increased contact.

We have already noted that for the major portion of the population, attitudes are best changed by structural changes. The amalgamationist position is that centralized political institutions are most conducive to the development of an integrated social and economic community. However, the problems of Nigeria, for example, have clearly shown the obstacles in imposing a common government without supportive public opinion. Clearly, both structure and attitudes have to be congruent for maximum results in integration.

International (world wide) approaches to integration have featured UN Charter revisions and a host of partial or utopian measures such as constitutional conventions, a disarmament organization apart from the UN, and various forms of international cooperation (Newcomb, 1967). These measures all suffer from the same failings: ignoring the value problem in human interaction and not realizing that power relationships are changed by power, not by appeal to goodwill.

Integration and cultural integrity. The aforementioned strategies all have as a goal some form of integration. Integration may be either positive or negative. It is negative if it occurs under conditions of unequal status and power of the system actors. The result of integration under conditions of inequality is the loss of the cultural integrity of the less powerful group. Integration under conditions of disparity of power may lead to the loss of cultural traditions or a people's particular view of reality. The loss of unique cultural values diminishes all mankind.

Assimilation as a form of integration is a fact of modern life, but too often this process has negative consequences. Assimilation which is based on power serves to destroy the cultural values of subnational or national groups. Assimilation attempts are paradoxical in a sense, for the assimilation is never complete. While the majority culture may in many aspects be imposed (language, dress, etc.) on the minority group, there is ample evidence that core elements of the minority culture may survive for centuries. The journey of the Jewish people through history is but one obvious example among many. It would appear that the choice is between either synergetic integration based on equal status or the maintenance of ideological alliances and the strong probability of war.

Synergetic integration of the values of all cultures is positive and will produce a new and more advanced world culture. In the process leading to eventual synergetic integration, there is a need for increased confrontation of the cultural values of group and nations. This confrontation implies an evaluation of these cultural values. The criterion for retention of values in an integrated world is what contribution these values have made to peaceful relations between people. Do they represent realistically the world of the twentieth century, or are they artifacts of a mystery-ridden, ignorant past?

There is an additional need to teach the relative rather than the absolute nature of values. An awareness of the relative nature of values makes it easier to resolve value conflicts or reduce value discrepancies between groups. Different values may have been functional at previous points in history, as they arose in response to different socio-economic conditions and development. However, in today's world, with the introduction of technology and the spread of mass communication, the socio-economic conditions are becoming more uniform. What is needed is the development of a common value hierarchy which would serve the function of leading all cultural groups toward synergetic integration based on equality and freedom. Such a value hierarchy would reduce the perceived differences between nations, which contribute to the contrast effect of hostility and negative international images.

First step toward synergetic integration — equality of relations. To eliminate conflict in the long run, it is critical that the underdogs in society change the condition of the interaction toward equality. In a system of inequality, the cause for conflict will always remain ready to break into open violence when oppression becomes unbearable. This has happened in Watts and other ghettos in the United States in recent years.

Carmichael and Hamilton (1967) stated the conditions which would have to change for black people in America before they could compete in an open society. The black people would first have to close their own ranks and develop group solidarity before they could operate effectively from a bargaining position of strength in a pluralistic society. The internal forces would all have to be marshalled and coordinated for this struggle.

The concept of black power expresses an attempt to develop bargaining power. Black power means proper representation and sharing of control. It is an attempt to create a power base to change varying patterns of oppression. Group solidarity, therefore, begins with the preservation of the racial and cultural personality of the black community. True freedom is not assimilation, but rather the preservation of cultural integrity as a basis for attaining equality. As Killian and Grigg (1964) stated, negotiations are effective only if the black community musters enough power to require white leaders to negotiate.

Exclusivism or integration of ideology. As a step toward an integrated world, we must recognize the futility and fallacy of insisting one system of political thought is "absolutely" superior to another. An initial step, perhaps, is expressed in the slogan Willy Brandt made popular in his drive toward rapprochement between the Democratic Peoples Republic and the Federal Republic of Germany: "Change through getting closer."

No one has a monopoly on truth. Ideological systems have grown out of the experiences of people and, therefore, are subject to all sorts of human error, misperceptions, and misjudgments. Unfortunately for peace, both capitalism and communism have been invested with absolute moral righteousness. This has created a great deal of closed-mindedness and rigid thinking precisely at a time in history when tolerance and flexibility are required.

Dogmatism, as Larsen has shown (1971c), creates considerable distortion of social reality. Dogmatic thinking is a fear response derived from personal insecurity. People assured of the soundness of their belief systems would welcome a dialogue providing both an opportunity to learn from others and to teach others. Dogmatic rhetoric, however, accomplishes neither. It is best represented by the analogy of two record players playing simultaneously. The record players may make lots of noise, but they receive no message.

Open-mindedness does not imply one social system may not have many advantages over another. It is, however, impossible to discern what these advantages are in an atmosphere of dogmatism, hostility, and mutual suspicion. The desirable thing would be to have an open dialogue between systems.

Rapoport (1969) suggests the importance of looking for what has proved humane and useful in each system. While values are rarely realized to the fullest extent, western democracy has shown a greater restraint on the power of the ruling group and greater tolerance of ideological diversity. Yet, Rapoport observes, the complex features so important to a modern society — a greater sense of social responsibility and a historical vision, which are largely lacking in western democracies, are basic values in communist countries. These values are not in conflict with one another but are, in fact, complementary. Recognizing the complementary nature of these values would be an initial step toward eventual ideological integration.

What is needed is a new look at the values of each ideological system. Each ideology should incorporate those values which are complementary and recognize the relativity of other differences. The chief obstacle to achieving ideological integration is the historical legacy of mutual hostility. This hostility is based on special interests in capitalist countries (the strata to whose advantage it is to prevent an integration of social systems and maintain the hostility and instability of international relationships) and the dogmatic interpretation of Marxist philosophy and ideology in the communist countries.

A giant step toward peace was taken with the adoption of the peaceful coexistence policy in the Soviet Union and Eastern European countries. However, the ideological conflict remains, ever ready to be used as a rationalization and cover-up for real conflicts of interest. Why not move the ideological conflict toward a genuine dialogue? The historically more advantageous ideology would make the correspondingly larger contribution to the advancement of society. Many issues must await the development of society to be resolved. Meanwhile, the channel of debate should remain open for the verification or disconfirmation of the opponent's or one's own position.

Ideological systems are not endowed by God but represent the best effort of thinkers in each generation. Bourgeois philosophy developed at a time when feudal relations were developing into capitalist society. Marxist philosophy grew out of the age of the industrial revolution. Both express values which are enduring and are not mutually exclusive. Where is the ideology of the twentieth century? Marxism recognized the dialectical process and hence the need for ideology to develop in accordance with objective contemporary conditions.

The most frightening spectre of our era is the possibility of very real destruction by means of nuclear warfare. While peaceful coexistence in relations between states is a step in the right direction, it does not go far enough. Since ideology remains a convenient motivation and rationalization for violence, ideological conflict must be replaced by ideological dialogue. This, in turn, may help create a better blueprint of a peaceful and happy future. As U Thant (1970) stated:

> Is it so difficult to admit that ideologies and political systems are perfect only in theory, that each system has good and bad aspects, that nations should enrich each other with what has proved good in the art of governing human societies and that such art must be highly flexible and nondogmatic in a rapidly changing world?

U Thant (1971) noted that the world must change from its present course of international hostility toward common concern and a new unity of purpose. The crisis of the world, expressed in the armaments race, war, and underdevelopment, requires that the United Nations become universal and that we revise our priorities which result from the world's divisions. All nations can improve in the art of government.

Toynbee (1971) has observed that our hearts are still blindly devoted to national sovereignty, yet we know that, in this age, national sovereignty spells mass suicide. The practical alternative to nationalism is ecumenism. According to Toynbee:

> The task of the present generation is to put the out-of-date sovereign national state in its place before one of the chronic conflicts between these antediluvian monsters releases the precarious catch that holds the bomb back from dropping. (P. 331)

Two alternatives for achieving integration: the victory of ideology or ideological integration. Two roads to a positive peace are discernible at this point in history. It is either in the victory of Marxism on a worldwide basis or in the realization of the relative nature of ideological systems. Ideological integration is the necessary precondition for synergetic integration.

Two things we owe to Marx. One is the materialist conception of the development of society. According to Marx, at each level of history, society is structured in such a fashion that the exploiting class and exploited class have antagonistic interests; and in dialectical terms, the classes present the thesis and antithesis at that point in history. These contradictions are resolved by means of revolution (meaning a restructuring of society), thereby eliminating the power of the exploiting class. This process of thesis, antithesis, and synthesis will continue until society has developed into communism. In this ultimate utopian society, there are no classes and therefore no contradictions. It is the end point of history characterized by equality and freedom.

The second point we owe to Marx is an understanding of capitalist economy. In capitalist economy is found the contradictions of capitalist society. Laborers in capitalist society are paid only a fraction of what they produce, for all things are created by labor. Consequently, they can buy back at the market place only a fraction of the products of their labors. This is the primary reason for the periodic recessions and depressions in capitalist society. As long as capitalism is expanding, moving into new markets in the developing countries where trade exchanges favor the developed capitalist nations (lower real wages), the working classes of the developed countries may survive these temporary disruptions. However, as struggles for national liberation succeed, the markets of capitalism will shrink, causing serious economic disruptions. This is the necessary objective precondition for revolution in developed countries.

World government may be achieved by the victory of Marxism over bourgeois ideology. History is replete with examples of integration and unity being achieved by force, from the spread of Christianity and the Muslim religions to the Nazi adventures during World War II. These schemes have all been based on the misconception that value differences between ideological groups are absolute rather than relative to time and place. The dogmatic approach to value integration also overlooks the obvious; namely, that, while historical experiences of peoples have produced different emphasis of certain values (different hierarchies), these values, rather than being mutually exclusive, may, in fact, be complementary. For example, liberal parliamentarism in the West has emphasized individual freedom, whereas the communist nations have emphasized social responsibility and future planning.

Ideological integration can take place by recognizing the relative and complementary nature of values, rather than the dogmatic and antagonistic nature of ideological positions. Since it is very difficult for the average person to achieve this recognition (value change follows structural change), it is important that leaders of governments and institutions recognize this point of view as a necessary condition leading to a positive peace. The success of such a scheme would depend on the development of a truely supra-ideological organization.

The UN of today is frequently only a forum for ideological conflict and debate. Perhaps the emerging so-called third world force could develop an integrated ideology taking into account the complementary values which have been found useful in the development of capitalist and communist societies (by useful is meant moving these societies closer to equality and freedom). A stronger UN, with enforcement power based on such an integrated ideology, is the structure needed to achieve a positive peace.

The structure of a positive peace. This structure expresses the values of equality and freedom, which cannot be achieved on a personal or national basis. Communication media and weaponry have made international interaction a fact of our age. Segregation as a means of conflict prevention belongs in the museums of thought as a relic of a bygone era. The values of equality and freedom must be expressed world-wide, or the potential for conflict remains. This calls for the following three-point structure.

First, through technology, create a world of relative abundance, and thereby eliminate the motive for selfishness and competition. Under conditions of competition, the individual achieves esteem by ranking higher than someone else, usually on some material or power basis. This creates exorbitant and conspicuous life styles, alienating the individual from society and himself. Needs for social goods may be expected to change drastically in a society which is characterized by cooperation and, through technology, by material abundance. When the need for exorbitant and conspicuous life styles has been removed, there will be an abundance of technological know-how and energy to meet human needs of life sustenance and culture.

Secondly, we must develop a world-wide institution which is characterized by moving away from political functions and toward purely administrative functions (the distribution of goods and services). The political functions of government imply the suppression of certain groups, classes, or nations in the world, by means of power. Power can only be dealt with by power. The transition regime moving from the political to the administrative world system must therefore be political; that is, exercise suppressive power. The actual structure of the administrative world system is an Industrial Union Congress, whose functions would be the planning and distribution of goods and services on the basis of equality and need. The world's resources would be considered to belong to the people of the world, and the consumer goods derived from these resources would be evenly distributed across the population of the world.

Finally, parallel to these efforts, we must work toward ideological integration. The essential process called for is the synergetic integration of complementary value systems. A preliminary condition is the destruction of mythological components used to maintain religious or chauvinistic traditions. This applies especially to ethnocentric symbols (flags, anthems, and other emotionally conditioned symbols). Secondly, an open-minded tolerance for what differences exist after these artificial and nonsensical barriers between people have been removed. Finally we must ensure the establishment of the basic norms of equality and freedom as ideological axioms.

Awareness of values in future planning. As a precondition for any successful program of synergetic integration, there must be an acknowledgment of the predominant importance of equality-freedom in human interaction. The question which must be asked of any plan is: What is the contribution of the plan to equality-freedom? If that question is asked, any plan may contribute toward eventual world-wide integration. In other words, the value problem must be brought out of the mothballs and made explicit as a standard for success of integration. A mutual recognition of equality-freedom as a standard for success would orient the various efforts in a common direction and eliminate conflict between integration orientations. Apart from the most reactionary regimes, equality-freedom is already an accepted standard throughout large sections of the world. What is needed is the operationalization of these values in meaningful ways between leaders and members of different groups. If not, the various schemes for integration are just so much meaningless malarky, for they lack an ideological basis and, therefore, motivation for success.

The problem of power for the enforcement of integration schemes is a different and difficult dilemma. Historically, man has devoted loyalty to increasingly larger political units from the family to the UN. The problem with our current UN structure, as everyone recognizes, is that it lacks enforcement power. Integration is therefore primarily a political problem, whether it is attacked at the supranational regional level or at the world level. The short range goal must be a revision of the UN Charter of the type advocated by Clark and Sohn (1966), which has the power to enforce equality-freedom on a world-wide basis. By means of dynamic interaction, all integration schemes can contribute to synergetic integration if based on a deeprooted and basic value orientation. The ideology of a positive peace found in synergetic integration outlines the values which must be realized in human relationships to resolve the conflicts between peoples and nations. Peace is more than the absence of conflict!

SUMMARY

In this chapter we focused on outlining the processes leading to synergetic integration. Peace is more than conflict management. Conflict resolution requires the creation of a world culture composed through the creative and cooperative integration of all cultural values. This chapter was therefore concerned with the development of a peace ideology, that is, the values which define peace and the processes which lead to synergetic integration.

Although there are several definitions of peace, any lasting social peace must solve the problem of social injustice — that structural violence from which a person suffers because of an underprivileged position either in the national or international social structure. The values of equality of status and maximum decision-making freedom must partially be operationalized by an equitable redistribution of income and resources in the world. To achieve these goals requires large scale attitudinal and structural changes.

Attitude change efforts must be directed toward the development of keen empathetic processes and the development of the value of altruism. Attitude change is characterized as a two-phase process, with the initial change occurring in opinion leaders. It is important to remember that, for large segments of the population, structural change precedes attitude change. However, for maximum results, both attitude and structural change efforts should be parallel efforts.

The structural change required for a lasting peace is synergetic integration. In the ultimate sense, this requires the operationalization of the values of equality and freedom. It is, perhaps, historically too early to evaluate the effectiveness of various integration schemes. However, we can hypothesize that the lack of success of many regional integration efforts is caused by the absence of an integration or peace ideology. The consequence is that the national actors in the system still try to maximize their own utility returns within a competitive zero-sum model.

Synergetic integration may not be equated with assimilation. The cultural integrity of each people must be respected. Integration succeeds on the basis of equality of relations and the open-minded realization of the relative and not absolute nature of ideological systems. Achieving the values of equality and freedom may come about as a result of the victory of ideology; but, in the nuclear age, there is a greater hope that ideological integration may serve as a model for the future. Of course, any ideology will be victorious to the extent that it fills a vacuum of ideas.

The structure of a peace with justice requires the elimination of the private ownership of the tools for social production. This is necessary for the just redistribution of goods and services on a world-wide basis. The structure of peace requires a world-wide institution characterized by moving away from suppressive political functions and moving toward administrative functions. To aid these structural changes, belief systems must move toward ideological integration.

The integration of ideology is achieved by the elimination of ideological myths, the open-minded tolerance for differences which remain, and the establishment of the basic norms of equality and freedom as ideological axioms. The realization of these goals is, perhaps, in the distant future; however, the direction we must travel is not an arrow in the blue.

We have now outlined models for both conflict management and conflict resolution. The future will tell the extent to which these models are realistic. What do people in various parts of the world think of war and peace? The preceding chapters have suggested the importance of power, both in the control of violence and in the solution to conflict. Power as a theoretical variable will be used as an interpretive tool of a large scale international survey on images of the future, reported in the next chapter. We will have an opportunity to examine what people throughout the world believe concerning the future.

11.

How People of the World View the Prospects of Peace and War

This study was carried out while the author was a research associate at the International Peace Research Institute, Oslo. Parts of the study have been presented at the annual meeting of the Peace Research Society (International), Vancouver, B.C., March 1970 and at the World Congress of Psychology, Tokyo, Japan, August, 1972. Articles based on the project are published in *The Journal of Cross Cultural Psychology* and *Social Behavior and Personality*. Thanks are expressed to Åke Hartmann for extensive help in the data analysis, and to Johan Galtung and Helmut Ornauer for helpful criticisms and suggestions on the manuscript.

This chapter presents the results of an international survey project entitled, "Images of the Year 2000," jointly sponsored by the European Coordination Centre in Social Sciences and the International Peace Research Institute, Oslo. We begin by discussing a theory of future images, in which the concept of power plays a key role. Various aspects of objective and subjective power and the hypotheses which link the power concept to peace proposal agreement, pessimism-optimism, and expectation of conflict are reviewed. A description of how these variables are measured is briefly outlined in the measurement section. The results of the data are discussed in connection with three hypotheses. International comparisons of peace proposal agreements follow. The chapter concludes with an examination of the data relevant to an extension of social position theory to the international system and the perception of conflict between potential conflict groups.

INTRODUCTION: A THEORY OF FUTURE IMAGES

Among all the areas in which future-oriented research is justified, the field of conflict resolution is one of the most important. In preparation for war, there has been no lack of future-orientation; and the very real threat of war is partly a result of this extensive preparation. Future-oriented research focusing on conflict resolution may, therefore, be partially corrective, in the sense of contributing to the understanding of conflict management. Furthermore, such research could establish the conditions which are productive of a real peace, which must include solutions for problems of social justice.

The situation in the world is such that positive attitudes toward peace among all peoples are very important. Not all levels of society, however, have an equal impact on policy decisions; some individuals and groups are more powerful than others. It may therefore be said that it is more important to find positive peace attitudes in certain groups of individuals than others. Ideally (at least for those who favor peaceful solutions), those who wield power should also be most strongly in favor of peace. This would probably ensure that peaceful alternatives would be pursued, since those possessing power are more likely to consistently realize their attitudes.

Unfortunately, one is induced to suggest that it is the people low in power who tend to have more overall positive attitudes toward peace. There are at least two good reasons for this. One is the moralist perspective found among extremely powerless persons in society. Low power individuals frequently have utopian notions about the paths to peace and view peace, itself, abstractly, as a socially desirable issue. A utopian perspective, coupled with peace as a highly emotional personal goal, should logically lead to greater agreement with a variety of peace proposals (whether these are related in content or not).

The other reasons for positive peace "attitudes" among low power persons may be found in their inability to differentiate effectively among different paths to peace and therefore their willingness to accept almost any proposal. Such acquiescent responses are a function of punitive or non-rewarding social experiences causing low self-esteem and personal insecurity. Conversely, it is expected that high power persons would critically evaluate proposals for peace and develop more individualized patterns of peace agreement. The aggregate result would be that high-power persons, as a group, would show lower agreement on a series of peace proposals, whereas peripheral individuals would show a higher level of agreement.

In the study reported here, we had the opportunity to look at the relationship between a set of indexes measuring subjective and, to some extent, objective power dimensions, and the agreement to a set of peace proposals, pessimism-optimism, and the expectation of war. If future expectations of high power persons are optimistic, their goals might be achieved. Conversely, it is of less importance to find optimism among low power persons, since they have less influence and, therefore, make smaller contributions toward reaching socially valued goals such as peace.

There are several reasons to expect greater optimism among high power persons. Such individuals have experienced a great deal of personal success; and since the past is likely to repeat itself, there is good reason for high power individuals to be optimistic. Personal success may also affect the high power person's perception of his ability to conduct his own life and promote his interests in society. Combined, these factors should produce a greater optimism in the high power person. This optimism on the part of people high in power may also affect the expectation of war in the future. In general, higher power individuals should be less likely to expect war.

OBJECTIVE AND SUBJECTIVE POWER

The following predictor variables were considered to reflect both objective power (the ability to exercise power) and subjective power (feeling powerful) and thus be related to the predicted variables as suggested in the introduction.

Predictor variable 1: Social position. Social position is a structural variable which reflects the individual's location in society with respect to such things as communication and decision-making

structures. As has been previously discussed, Galtung (1964) developed a structural theory of society, in which society is divided into a
center and a periphery. The center is the relatively privileged group,
whereas the periphery consists of the rejected sections. In this model,
the periphery is a victim of insufficient communication and isolation. As a result, perceptions of social reality, attitudes, and attitude
formation proceed along a different path in the periphery than in the
center. The periphery is isolated from both the communication
networks and also from the decision-making nucleus in society.
Consequently, individuals belonging to the periphery are lower on
social participation and, as a result, have less knowledge concerning
significant social events. Social position (center-periphery) must
therefore of necessity have certain consequences for attitudes toward
peace proposals, pessimism-optimism, and expectation of conflict.

Due to lack of knowledge, lack of social participation, and
inadequate communications, it is expected that the extreme periphery will have difficulty making evaluations of public issues. This
lack of differential evaluation can be represented as a gradient rather
than as a strict dichotomy.

In Galtung's terms, there are three stages. In the extreme
periphery, there is no cognition of alternatives and consequently no
evaluation. In stage two, there is some cognition of alternatives,
which has, however, not yet become the basis for differential evaluation, but rather predisposes the individual toward thinking in
absolute terms and thus to rigidly favor one policy. Finally, in the
center, there is not only a cognition of alternatives, but also a
differential evaluation.

The lack of differential evaluation in the periphery should
predispose individuals in this group toward rigid response patterns,
or, more specifically, toward agreement response sets. Being alienated
from the communication network as well as the decision-making
nucleus of society may induce peripheral people to accept peace
proposals to a significantly greater extent than persons in the center.

While Galtung does not believe that the content of opinion is
predictable from social position, he is suggesting a basic difference
between the center and periphery. This difference concerns the mode
of cognition or the cognitive style in the center which, when com-

pared to the periphery, finds the latter characterized by moral absolutist thinking. This must of necessity have consequences for the peripheral person's perception of the past, present, and future. The point is that moral absolutism may act as an intervening variable predisposing the peripheral person toward a more pessimistic outlook. This is due in part to the obvious discrepancy between the ideal and life as it really is. An additional element is his rejected position in society, which is likely to be loaded with feelings of personal insecurity, powerlessness, and latent aggressiveness. These factors will probably influence the peripheral person's view on the past, present, and future of his own life, his country, and the world. In all cases, it is to be expected that the periphery will be more pessimistic when compared to the center.

Predictor variable 2: Social activity. How active an individual is in society is likely to influence his perceptions and attitudes. For one thing, an active individual has shown his motivation and concern for social problems by his activity, by being involved. This indicates a preliminary set of attitudes and opinions characterized by optimism. In addition, a person's activity demonstrates that he believes he can do something about his attitudes and opinions, that he has a sense of personal power and self-esteem. Since active individuals are involved in organizations, they are also often at the center of communication networks and therefore may have more knowledge and a better sense of social reality upon which to base their judgment.

In a sense, a person's involvement in society tells us a great deal about the extent to which he is influenced, but more important, the extent to which he is concerned and therefore wishes to be informed. By definition, he belongs to the center of society, in the sense of Galtung's Center-Periphery Theory; and, by necessity, he has more knowledge. These traits (personal power, self-esteem, center position, knowledge, and concern) are helpful in predicting the response of active persons to peace proposals and expectations of the future. An active person has the information and cognitive ability to evaluate peace proposals more critically, while displaying optimism about the future and the probability of conflict.

Predictor variable 3: Alienation-satisfaction. Being alienated in the sense of being dissatisfied with one's present life situation may also have certain personality and motivational properties. For one, the alienated individual has experienced personal adversity tending to make him devaluate his personal and social worth. Low self-esteem, in turn, is reflected in an acquiescence response such that individuals high in alienation will agree indiscriminately to peace proposals. Beyond that, alienation is not an independent construct but may also be related on an *a priori* logical basis to low knowledge and a peripheral position in communication networks and social structure. The result of these influences may, as indicated, produce an agreement response set across many types of peace proposals.

Alienation from one's present status within society may also be a potent variable in affecting questions of national importance and international images. Feeling dissatisfied with one's job or country reflects a feeling of powerlessness to affect the future. The alienated person sees his own life as less than fulfilling. In addition, he perceives himself as unable to improve his lot. This personal pessimism may be projected to the status of his country, the world, and expected conflict.

Predictor variable 4: Knowledge. The more knowledge an individual possesses, the more expertness he feels in a given field. A sense of expertness is a source of resistance to persuasion and is thus an anchor for the stabilization of social attitudes. Degree of knowledge not only affects perceptions of present and future, but affects these perceptions in a particular positive or negative manner. As for activity, knowledge reflects concern about social problems and, consequently, involvement, at least at the cognitive level. In addition, this variable also suggests a position that is central to the communication structure, and a central rather than peripheral position in society.

Thus, knowledge not only is an index of the assimilation of facts, but also has motivational properties. The self-esteem derived from expertness, a central position in the communication and social structures and his social concern, may lead a person high in knowledge to evaluate critically various proposals for peace. Conversely, persons low in knowledge are less capable of differential evaluation; and, because of this and other factors (lack of expertness, peripheral position in the communication and social structures), they are more likely to show an agreement response set.

At the same time, knowledgeable persons have, because of feelings of expertness, a sense of personal and social power. The attainment of knowledge not only is an indication of a motivation to know but also reflects an ability to do, to actively and successfully intervene in one's own life as well as larger social systems. This sense of expertness should logically produce a greater optimism about one's own life, as well as the past, present, and future of one's country and the world. Such optimism may also lead to lower war expectations.

Predictor variable 5: Dogmatism. The development of the construct of dogmatism can perhaps be viewed as the end product of a series of dialectical processes, beginning with Frenkel-Brunswik, Levinson, and Sanford's personality-centered approaches to perception (1947). The central concept is emotional ambivalence, a notion derived from psychoanalysis, which is viewed as the main intervening variable between the cognitive spheres and social or emotional spheres of behavior. Relative emotional ambivalence is a function of specific child-rearing procedures in which extreme punitiveness may create ambivalence toward parents, which in turn affects cognitive and social dimensions as well. The point is that the person who through punishment and fear is unable to express normal ambivalent feelings toward parents develops a generalized need to structure his world rigidly, as well as an inability to tolerate perceptual and cognitive ambiguity.

The next major step was the work of Adorno, Frenkel-Brunswik, Levinson, and Sanford (1950), which culminated in the publication of their book, *The Authoritarian Personality.* Although the original work began with a study of anti-semitism, it soon became clear that prejudice toward minority groups could be defined as a syndrome of traits appropriately entitled ethnocentrism. An attempt was made to develop an indirect assessment of prejudice and a tendency toward a fascistic outlook on life, which culminated in the development of the F or fascism scale.

The popularity of this contribution is evidenced in the

numerous studies carried out in which the F scale has been used to measure general authoritarianism. According to Rokeach (1960), this caused a conceptual confusion, since the F scale was developed to assess fascistic authoritarianism and not general authoritarianism. He advanced to the point that authoritarianism may be found at any point in the political spectrum and indeed across all socially important dimensions (religious, academic, philosophic, etc.). The significant point for Rokeach was not the content of belief systems, but rather the structure, that is, whether a person (regardless of his beliefs) had an open or closed mind about his own and others' belief structures.

The genesis and structure of the dogmatic personality makes it possible to make some predictions about each individual's attitudes toward a given range of peace proposals, as well as their perception about the past, present, and future. The genesis of the dogmatic person may be found partially in a punitive child-rearing pattern, which then is reflected in personal abasement, subservience to authority figures, and a preoccupation with status. The overall effect is a deep sense of personal insecurity, in which low self-esteem plays an important part (Larsen, 1969). The personal insecurity is likely to play the role of an intervening variable and produce an acquiescence response, that is, an agreement response set. The result would be that dogmatic persons may show greater agreement on socially desirable topics.

This agreement pattern predicted is not necessarily an indication of a greater optimism about the past, present, or future. In fact, quite to the contrary, it is expected that highly dogmatic persons will show greater pessimism. Important to this prediction is precisely the personal insecurity pattern mentioned above and, with that, feelings of impotence in affecting one's personal life or the affairs of one's country or the world for better or for worse. The lack of personal power, and collateral perception of the world as a threatening place in which to live (therefore dependence on authority figures) is productive of an overall pessimism, expressed in perceptions of one's life and the past, present, and future of one's country and the world, and in higher war expectations.

In discussing social position, activity, alienation, knowledge, and dogmatism, these constructs have repeatedly been described using such overlapping terms as center-periphery, relative motivation, and self-esteem. These descriptive terms all suggest that the same variables reflect relative objective and subjective power dimensions in the individual described in those terms.

Power as an integrating variable. An integrating construct which relates social position, activity, alienation, knowledge, and dogmatism in a consistent manner to perspectives of the future is the amount of power attributed to or residing in an individual. Minton's (1967) conceptual differentiation between manifest and latent power makes the distinction between objective and subjective power clear. Power actually exercised, based on various sources, is termed manifest (objective) power, whereas latent (subjective) power refers to the individual's feelings or attitudes about his power. While the two are positively related, there is not necessarily a one-to-one relationship between them.

A peripheral position in society is a position of powerlessness both at the latent and manifest levels. Such an "underdog" will be absent from the central decision-making processes and its supporting communication structure which, in turn, may relate to his own sense of powerlessness.

Homans (1950) suggested a relationship between social activity and power. Increased activity leads to increased interaction and collateral positive feelings from others. Since liking is one critical dimension (Fiedler, 1965) which enables a leader to exercise influence in a group, activity may be indirectly related to power. Alienation has been directly related to power, and Seeman (1959) suggests that one dimension of alienation is a personal sense of powerlessness. Knowledge and information are related to bases of power, according to Raven (1965). Informational power is held when the influencing agent is in possession of information and the content of the information (not the influencing agent) is considered important. Expert power, however, is based on the attribution of superior knowledge to the influencing agent. Dogmatism has been related to low self-esteem and feelings of powerlessness (Larsen 1969).

The foregoing suggests that a peripheral position, low social activity, alienation, low knowledge, and high dogmatism are consistently related to low power, at both the manifest and latent levels. Having power should in turn affect perceptions of the future, and high power persons would have the feeling that they could actively intervene to shape the future according to their desires and expectations. The common factor of power suggests the following general hypotheses:

H1. Low social power is related to peace agreement.

H2. Low social power is related to pessimism.

H3. Low social power is related to expectation of war.

METHOD

As spelled out above, the model looks like this:

Figure 11.1

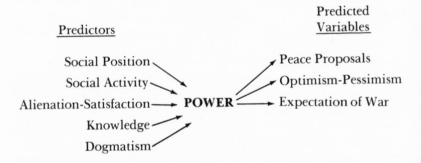

THE MEASUREMENT OF THE VARIABLES

In this section, we discuss the measurement of the variables used in the study. Correlational studies do not answer the question of cause and effect. Nevertheless, we do consider the variables which are related by the power construct to be antecedents or predictors of the variables which measure peace proposal agreement, optimism-pessimism, and expectation of war. The statistical relationship between the predictor variables will be discussed.

Predictor variables. The various assessments of power were measured as follows:

Social position: The interviewed person's relative central or peripheral position was measured by an eight-item index dealing with ecological, geographical, occupational, educational, economic, age, and sex variables.

Social activity. A six-item index was developed to measure social activity by asking respondents to indicate membership in political and other organizations and extent of involvement in those and other forms of social involvement.

Alienation-satisfaction. This variable was assessed by a four-item index asking the interviewed person to respond to questions dealing with perceived influence in public affairs, preference to live in home or foreign country, and satisfaction with one's occupation and income.

Knowledge. The specific knowledge assessed concerned international systems. The persons interviewed were asked if sixteen different countries belonged to NATO, the Warsaw Treaty, or neither.

Dogmatism. This construct was assessed by seventeen items derived from Rokeach's dogmatism scale (short form) (Rokeach, 1960), and three items especially designed for the study.

Predicted variables. One concern of the survey was to ascertain the relationship between the aforementioned variables and agreement with peace proposals, pessimism-optimism in the future, and expectation of war.

Peace proposals. The following twenty-five peace proposals, representing a variety of ad hoc suggestions to bring about peace or reduce conflict, were presented to the respondents for their agreement or disagreement:

To obtain peace:

1) People must become more religious all over the world.
2) One has to start with the single individual everywhere and make him less aggressive.
3) One must create more peaceful relations in the family, at school, and at work.
4) The colonial system must be abolished all over the world.

5) Hunger and poverty must be abolished all over the world.
6) It must be possible for people freely to choose their governments all over the world.
7) All countries must stop completely from intervening into the internal affairs of other countries.
8) Countries must be (politically, economically, socially) more similar to each other than today.
9) An economy based mainly on private ownership must be introduced all over the world.
10) Developed countries must give much more technical assistance and aid to developing countries than they do today.
11) An economy based mainly on public ownership must be introduced all over the world.
12) The gap between rich and poor countries must disappear.
13) An economy based on a mixture of private and public ownership must be introduced all over the world.
14) Countries must be members of military alliances so that no country or group of countries dare attack others.
15) We must have general and complete disarmament as soon as possible.
16) Countries must withdraw from military alliances.
17) Countries will have to keep national armies.
18) Countries should have less to do with each other and become self-sufficient.
19) We must have increased trade, exchange, and cooperation between countries that are not on friendly terms.
20) Poor countries all over the world should unite to obtain a bigger share of the wealth of the world.
21) Small countries all over the world should unite to have more influence on the affairs of the world.
22) We must improve the United Nations so as to make it more efficient than it is today.
23) A world language that can be understood in all countries should be adopted all over the world.
24) We must have a strong international peace-keeping force that can stop aggression from any country or group of countries.
25) We must have a world state with disappearance of national borders and an efficient world government.

People's views of the past, present, and future. The Cantril (1965) self-anchoring scale, a nine-step ladder, is shown to the person interviewed so that he can indicate on the ladder where he personally, his country, and the world stand now, stood five years ago, and will stand five years from now and (in this study) by the year 2000. In a sense, this scale reflects a person's optimism-pessimism across time using his own assumptions and perceptions regarding social reality.

Expectation of war. The question asked was, "Thinking of war and disarmament, what do you think the world situation will be like in five years, twenty years, and in the year 2000" with five response categories — world war, more armament, about as now, partial disarmament, and total disarmament.

Power as an intervening variable. As has already been mentioned, it is not likely that the various predictor variables used in this study are independent from each other. The common components reflecting low power which may account for mutual variance are the acquiescence response and pessimism which we expect to find in the person high on dogmatism, low on activity, low on satisfaction, low on knowledge and located in the periphery. Having this variance in common, it is predictable that the independent variables will intercorrelate. Specifically, it is predicted that activity, knowledge, satisfaction, and social position will correlate positively, and dogmatism will correlate negatively with all of them.

Table 11.1 shows the number of significant correlations in the predicted direction. Many of the correlations appear to form a consistent pattern from country to country as shown. In general, there is a positive relationship between social position, activity, knowledge, and inverse correlations with dogmatism. Dogmatism in turn correlated negatively with both activity and knowledge. The alienation-satisfaction index is on the whole unrelated to any of the other variables. One reason for this may be found in the poor operationalization of this construct. For example, dissatisfaction with job or country does not necessarily indicate powerlessness. Authoritarianism has, in the past, been shown to be related to intellectual inferiority (e.g., Restle, Andrews, and Rokeach, 1964). It is therefore no surprise that dogmatism correlates negatively with social position or activity. Neither can the inverse correlations between dogmatism and the knowledge index be surprising, since dogmatic subjects have in general been thought to be in possession of a simplistic construct system, differentiated in extremely polarized categorical terms. In other words, high dogmatism, low social activity, knowledge, and peripheral position go together, partially confirming our expectations. It may also be noted that these results lend some validity to Galtung's Center-Periphery Theory, since it is predictable from this theory that the peripheral person should be low in activity and knowledge and, because of his inability to make differential evaluations (cognitive rigidity), high in dogmatism. These findings also add further construct validity to the theoretical rationale of dogmatism and suggest that individuals characterized by dogmatic traits tend to be low in social position, activity, and knowledge.

Table 11.1

Number of significant correlations ($<.05^*$) in
predicted direction between independent variables
for Britain, Czechoslovakia, India, Finland, Japan,
Norway, Spain, and Yugoslavia

Social Position			
Activity	6		
Alienation-satisfaction	3	1	
Knowledge	7	6	1
Dogmatism	7	6	0	6

*The significant correlations ranged from .09 to .47; maximum number of correlations is 9.

RESULTS AND DISCUSSION

We will now examine the results and evaluate the three hypotheses previously discussed. To what extent is power related to peace proposal agreement, pessimism-optimism, and the expectation of war?

Power and peace proposals. Using this finding, the first of the three hypotheses can now be explored. In Table 11.2 we have the total number of significant correlations and the total number of positive and negative correlations. As may be observed. dogmatism is by far the best predictor of agreement with peace proposals, with social position, activity, and knowledge taking intermediate positions, and the alienation-satisfaction index accounting for little more than chance level correlatiòns. Hence, the model of the "peace advocate" (not to be confused with pacifist or other concepts) seems to be as follows: he is high in dogmatism, tends to show little activity, is low in knowledge, and belongs to the periphery of society. This result confirms hypothesis number one (H1), although there are large differences in the efficacy of the various predictors.

Two things must be kept in mind, however. First, on the one hand, the number of significant correlations is spread over a wide, varied range of peace proposals containing, undoubtedly, several independent dimensions. Such agreement may in fact express a rather simplistic view of the world and what it takes to reduce conflict. This is to be expected in the low power person as described above. Such a person is cognitive simple. For example, a prediction from Galtung's theory is that the peripheral person is incapable of cognition of alternatives and hence of differential evaluation. On the other hand, the low power person had probably been exposed to numerous hardships, making him generally insecure of the future, thus desiring peace by any means available.

Second, related to the above discussion is the possibility that peace agreement may simply reflect an acquiescence or agreement response set, developed as a result of a more general low self-esteem and personal insecurity pattern. In other words, the motivational pattern for the model "peace advocate" may be a function of low power expressed as cognitive rigidity and agreement response sets.

One way to determine whether the person low in power differentiates peace proposals would be to carry out factor analysis and determine what, if any, statistical independent dimensions (or peace ideologies) exist, then to complete a simple one-way analysis of variance between high, medium, and low groups on the predictor variables, analyzing for differences in peace agreement on each factor (or peace ideology) where the factor index is made up of all the separate peace proposals loading on that factor. A possible conclusion is that, if peace proposal agreement is found across independent dimensions, then the low power person is not differentiating the peace proposals.

Table 11.3 shows the results of the factor analysis and the analysis of variance. These factors can best be understood as peace ideologies and, although not mutually exclusive in the sense that people can subscribe to more than one, they are statistically independent as defined by orthogonal factor analysis. The number of countries in which the factors were found is indicated in parentheses behind the factor name.

The factor name is derived from what appears to be the common element shared by the peace proposals loading on that factor. Agreement with such a factor (or peace ideology) can be understood as peace through unity, and so forth for the other factors or ideologies.

Many of the factors appear rather similar in most countries. However, some seem to be more specific — maybe due to cultural, religious, or political peculiarities.

In all countries, there is a factor involving almost solely the three first peace items, those concerned with the individual and his relations in primary groups (family, school, work). This is referred to as an individualistic factor.

The first item in this factor — "more religious people" — is in Czechoslovakia, Poland, and Finland grouped together with "Private ownership." The content seems to be an antisocialist or capitalist ideology. Religion is following other dimensions in the socialist countries, and this indicates that the items may touch different sentiments and attitudes in different nations, depending upon their history. Still, or rather because of this, we do not feel that the content of the individualistic factor has changed when this item is missing in those countries.

The next factor reflects a supra-national aspect. The central elements in this factor are the three last peace proposals: "a world language," "peace-keeping forces," and "world state." We also frequently find proposals like "military alliances" and "unification

Table 11.2
Number of Significant (p<.05)
Pearson Product-Moment Correlations
between Peace Proposals and Predictor Variables

	Total	Positive	Negative
Czechoslovakia			
Social position	15	14	1
Activity	6	6	0
Alienation-satisfaction	3	1	2
Knowledge	9	8	1
Dogmatism	16	16	0
Finland			
Social position	10	10	0
Activity	10	10	0
Alienation-satisfaction	4	0	4
Knowledge	16	8	8
Dogmatism	19	19	0
Norway			
Social position	8	6	2
Activity	7	6	1
Alienation-satisfaction	7	0	7
Knowledge	8	5	3
Dogmatism	16	16	0
Yugoslavia			
Social position	8	5	3
Activity	7	6	1
Alienation-satisfaction	2	1	1
Knowledge	7	5	2
Dogmatism	16	16	0

Table 11.3
Peace Ideologies and the Number of Significant F Values across Countries for High, Middle and Low Groups on Predictor Variables

Peace Ideologies*	Social Position		Activity		Alienation-Satisfaction		Knowledge		Dogmatism**	
Liberal integration (6)	5	5	6	4	2	2	5	4	6	5
Federal integration (3)	2	1	1	1	1	1	1	1	2	2
Anti-imperialistic (4)	1	1	2	1	1	0	3	3	2	2
Humanitarian (5)	3	3	1	0	1	0	0	0	3	3
Individualistic (6)	2	2	2	1	0	0	4	4	4	4
Socialistic (1)	1	0	0	0	1	1	1	0	0	0
Capitalistic (1)	1	0	1	0	1	0	1	0	1	0
Nationalistic (1)	1	1	0	0	1	1	0	0	1	1

*Number of countries where peace ideologies are extracted as independent factors are shown in parentheses after factor name.

**First column represents number of significant F values (at least .05 level) and second column the number in the predicted direction.

of poor and small countries" together with this, and we give this factor the general heading federal integration. We also frequently find another factor which we term liberal integration, which is dominated by "increased trade and cooperation" and "improve UN." Socialist ideas often seem to go together with the first of these factors. The proposals "public ownership" and "more similarity of countries" seem to be the most central, and they are in some countries separated on a socialist factor. The same applies to "Unification of small and poor countries" which is then referred to as the factor of underdog unification.

An important factor seems to reflect an anti-imperialistic policy: "anticolonialism," "no international interventions." In some countries, this factor is mixed up with a generally humanitarian approach, such as "development aid," "no gap between poor and rich countries," "no hunger and poverty." When these items appear on an independent factor, this is then labeled humanitarian.

These last factors emphasize the importance of the structural inequalities often underlying conflict behavior. Other factors are protective (e.g., nationalistic, with items such as "keep national armies" and "self-sufficient countries"). In most countries, the items concerning the military also constitute a distinct militaristic factor.

Some factors appear just in some countries as independent clusters, namely one, economic dealing with the basis of owner-ship, and another, liberal, mainly based on "free choice of govern-ments" and "mixture of private and public ownership." The naming of the factors is only tentative and should not be interpreted too rigidly. Factors in all countries are not identical but are still quoted under the same heading, when the author considered the main content to be similar. These findings are summarized in Table 11.4, containing the main factors from all countries included in this study. If anything should be extracted from this brief bird's-eye view of the peace ideologies, it would be the striking similarity prevailing across national borders.

One overall observation can be made from Table 11.3. The low power person tends to agree more and the opposite extreme disagrees more, across all the independent factors. In other words, the peace ideologies do not discriminate between the people who are high in dogmatism, low in activity, knowledge, satisfaction, and belong to the periphery, from people who score at the other end of these indexes. Although some of the significant relationships were not in the predicted direction, this was mainly due to the non-linearity of the data and thus not due to evidence against the overall result, which supports the proposition that the low power person supports peace proposals across statistically independent dimensions.

This fact is evidence that we are dealing with a lack of discrimination and a response set which probably has very little relation to attitudes toward peace. It would appear that peace agreement is related to personality and social factors which are not conducive to or cannot fruitfully be employed as a base for peace action. These factors indicate an alienated and powerless position in the social structure, with collateral cognitive rigidity and feelings of powerlessness.

Power and pessimism-optimism. A person's view of the past, present, and future is a powerful indication not only of expectation, but also of potential for action. Part of the rationale is that a person who is

Table 11.4
The Most Frequent Factors of the Peace
Proposals in the Nations Studied

Factor	Nations									
	CS[1]	E[2]	GB[3]	IND[4]	J[5]	N[6]	NL[7]	PL[8]	SF[9]	YU[10]
Liberal integration	x	x	x			x	x	x	x	x
Federal integration	x	x	x	x	x	x	x	x	x	x
Anti-imperialistic	x	x	x	x	x	x		x	x	x
Humanitarian					x		x			x
Individualistic	x	x	x	x	x	x	x	x	x	x
Militaristic	x	x				x	x		x	x
Underdog unification	x	x	x	x	x		x			
Socialistic	x		x			x			x	
Capitalistic	x		x					x	x	
Liberal				x		x			x	
Economic		x			x					x
Nationalistic		x		x		x	x	x		

Explanation: x indicates that in fact these factors appear in one
cluster in the respective countries, but are split here
in order to fit into the general framework.

---

[1] CS = Czechoslovakia
[2] E = Spain
[3] GB = Great Britain
[4] IND = India
[5] J = Japan
[6] N = Norway
[7] NL = Netherlands
[8] PL = Poland
[9] SF = Finland
[10] YU = Yugoslavia.

optimistic about the future is likely to act accordingly and thus, in a
sense, fulfill his own prophecy. If it could be demonstrated that the
person who is high on subjective and objective power is optimistic, a
logical inference is that his (powerful) efforts will be directed toward
fulfilling his optimistic goals.

Table 11.5 shows the results of one-way analysis of variance between high, medium, and low groups on the predictor variables analyzing for differences on the Cantril scale.

The results clearly show that high activity, knowledge, satisfaction, and center position relate to optimism. The results for dogmatism are more complex. The past, present, and future of the individual's own life show that the low dogmatic persons are more optimistic than the high group, thus generally supporting hypothesis number two (H2). However, for country and the world, the significant F values are confounded by the nonlinearity of the data and in a few cases actually reverse the previous pattern (e.g., high dogmatic persons are more optimistic).

Table 11.5

Optimism-Pessimism and the Number of Significant
F Values* across Countries for High, Middle and
Low Groups on Predictor Variables

	Social Position		Activity		Alienation-Satisfaction		Knowledge		Dogmatism**	
Own Life										
Present	3	3	3	2	4	4	3	2	3	3
5 years ago	2	1	3	2	4	3	1	1	2	2
5 years from now	3	2	1	0	3	3	2	1	3	3
Year 2000	2	1	0	0	3	2	4	1	1	1
Country										
Present	2	2	2	0	3	3	1	1	3	0
5 years ago	3	3	1	1	2	2	0	0	2	0
5 years from now	2	1	1	1	4	4	2	0	1	0
Year 2000	2	1	1	1	4	3	2	1	1	0
World										
Present	2	1	1	0	3	3	0	0	2	0
5 years ago	3	1	1	0	2	2	2	1	1	0
5 years from now	2	1	2	1	3	3	2	0	1	0
Year 2000	2	1	0	0	3	3	1	1	1	0
TOTAL	28	18	16	8	38	35	20	9	21	9

*   Total number of possible significant F values is 5.

**   1st column is number of significant Fs; the 2nd column
is number in predicted direction.

One interpretation may be that high dogmatic individuals, because of low power, perceive their own lives in pessimistic terms. On the other hand, because of identification with sources of status and power in society, and because country and world may be more abstract concepts, it is possible for them to be more optimistic about these.

One inference which can be made is that there may be little if any relationship between agreement with peace proposals on the part of the low power person and actual action. On the other hand, due to the greater optimism of the high power person, one may expect that the proposals which he agrees with are much more meaningful, both because of his greater differential evaluation and because of the phenomena of the self-fulfilling prophecy (i.e., his optimism about the future is likely to be more closely related to action on behalf of the proposals with which he actually agrees).

Power and expectation of war. The prospect of war is probably one of the few persistent, ever-present anxieties disturbing much of mankind. Since weapons production is becoming increasingly sophisticated, the immediate and long-term future is indeed bleak, unless some constructive changes are made toward total disarmament. Who are the people that are pessimistic or optimistic in perceiving either war or disarmament in the future? This question concerns one of the most crucial issues facing man as he approaches the twenty-first century.

The findings reported in previous sections tend to suggest that low power individuals agree more with all types of peace proposals and are more pessimistic regarding the past, present, and future of their own lives and the existence of their country and the world, as compared to persons scoring at the opposite end of these indexes. Extrapolating from this, it is possible to predict that persons with these characteristics may also be more pessimistic regarding the prospects of war or disarmament in the future. If disarmament is still a realistic hope, then resources may be turned toward solving other pressing problems, such as the population explosion in the developing countries and the need to feed these growing populations.

Table 11.6 shows the significant F values between high, middle, and low groups on the predictor variables, analyzing for differences in expectations of war, armament, and disarmament in five years, twenty years, and by the year 2000. Table 11.7 shows the corresponding rank order of mean values with the highest mean value scored 1, middle 2, and lowest 3.

For social position the tables show seven significant relationships with all group means linear. In six of the seven, the center shows highest mean values, indicating an anticipation toward disarmament.

On the whole, therefore, it would appear that the center is more optimistic regarding the future, as compared to the periphery. Since the center, because of greater social and personal power, is capable of influencing national policy to a greater extent, this is fundamentally a positive sign. One possible explanation for the finding may lie in the personality and social characteristics of the center. Optimism about the future is probably related to the perceived ability to change the future in accordance with one's desires and expectations. Optimism may be functionally related to such perceived power.

Activity shows ten significant relationships: five are linear with high active groups showing highest mean values and thus having highest expectations of disarmament, while the other five are nonlinear with middle groups showing highest mean values. It should be noted, however, that there is no significant mean difference between high and medium groups for Netherlands, while there is no significant difference between high and low groups for Spain. While the latter complicates interpretation somewhat, the findings tend to lend support to the point that high active persons have greater expectations of disarmament, while low active persons are more pessimistic. On the one hand, participation in social activity reflects concern, but, in addition, expectations of successful involvement (why else be active?). Optimism may therefore be related to the perceived ability to influence the future successfully in accordance with one's hopes. This is likely the primary reason for the greater optimism of active persons.

The results for the alienation-satisfaction variable, however, are at best complex. Of the seven significant differences, five (for Netherlands and Spain) show highly alienated groups have the highest mean values, while the reverse is true for the significant relationships for Czechoslovakia and Great Britain. The only tentative conclusion

Table 11.6
Expectation of War and F Values* Across
Countries for High, Middle and Low Groups
On the Predictor Variables

Item	World Situation	Czechoslovakia	Finland	Great Britain	Netherlands	Norway	Yugoslavia	Spain
Social Position	5 years							57.7
	20 years				2.9	9.8	9.8	44.3
	Year 2000	3.0				4.0		45.4
Activity	5 years		5.5					6.0
	20 years	5.5			6.5	5.9		13.2
	Year 2000				8.7	6.3	3.7	13.1
Alienation-satisfaction	5 years							20.6
	20 years	3.1		4.2	2.8			22.1
	Year 2000				3.6			30.2
Knowledge	5 years							16.2
	20 years	4.9				11.5		34.2
	Year 2000	2.8	8.1		4.3	9.6	6.0	39.2
Dogmatism	5 years							5.9
	20 years		3.4		11.4	5.8		14.8
	Year 2000				13.4	4.4	3.2	13.1

* Significant at .05 level or beyond.

Table 11.7

Expectation of War and Rank Order of the Means for the Significant F Values

Item	World Situation	Czechoslovakia	Finland	Great Britain	Netherlands	Norway	Yugoslavia	Spain
Social Position	5 years							123
	20 years					123		123
	Year 2000	321			123	123		123
Activity	5 years		213					312
	20 years	123			123	123		312
	Year 2000				213	123	123	312
Alienation-satisfaction	5 years				123			123
	20 years	321		321	123			123
	Year 2000						123	123
Knowledge	5 years	123				123		123
	20 years					123		123
	Year 2000		123		123		123	123
Dogmatism	5 years	321			321	321		231
	20 years	321			321	321	321	231
	Year 2000		321		321	321		231

one can arrive at with this predictor is that predictability appears to be related to specific national patterns, and therefore overall interpretations are difficult.

Knowledge as a predictor variable indicates nine significant group mean differences, all linear, with high knowledge groups having highest mean values. In other words, persons high in knowledge about international systems, tend to expect the world to move toward disarmament, as compared to persons low in such knowledge. Knowledge reflects the cognitive ability to assimilate information and, in addition, the motivational concern to obtain such information. Thus, knowledge has both cognitive and motivational properties. It is unlikely that significant numbers of persons would go through the effort to obtain information were it not for the expectation that such knowledge would be useful in terms of some personal intervention. In this sense, knowledge reflects the personal power to intervene and the expectation that this intervention will be successful. This rationale may explain to some extent why high knowledge groups are more optimistic with respect to disarmament as compared to middle and low knowledge groups.

Dogmatism yielded eleven significant differences (with eight linear) showing low dogmatic persons being more optimistic, with three (for Spain) showing non-linear mean relationships with low dogmatic groups still having highest mean values. The overall results, then, seem to indicate that low dogmatic persons are, on the whole, more optimistic about the future and perceive the world as moving toward disarmament. Previous work has indicated that low dogmatic persons tend to have more adequate self concept, that is, tend to be high in self-esteem and personal security. Again, this, by implication, indicates that low dogmatic persons perceive the world as less threatening and, more important perhaps, perceive themselves as having the ability (power) to influence issues of importance toward some desired goal. This partially explains the higher optimism of the low dogmatic persons, with respect to war or disarmament in the future.

Summarizing, analysis with the five predictor variables seems to indicate that low power persons are on the whole more pessimistic with respect to disarmament in the future, supporting hypothesis number three (H3). The reason for this pessimism is partially found in the lack of power in such individuals and in the perceived inability to intervene successfully on issues which concern them. However, the significant results represent only a portion of the total number of relationships. The efficacy of the predictors must therefore be moderated by that fact.

THE INTERNATIONAL PATTERN OF AGREEMENT WITH THE PEACE PROPOSALS

The question in this section is the relative acceptance of the twenty-five peace proposals in the countries studied. Is the pattern of peace proposal agreement the same in the various countries, or is the acceptance of peace proposals idiosyncratic for each country?

How people of the various nations favored the peace proposals — Is there a basis for unity? Table 11.8 shows the percent agree minus percent disagree (relative acceptance) for the twenty-five peace proposals across the countries. In Table 11.9 the twenty-five peace proposals are ranked for the respective countries.

Table 11.10 shows the rankings of the ranges and means. As noted, the countries with highest inter-item disagreement (variability) are Czechoslovakia, Norway, and Netherlands, and least is found in Yugoslavia, Great Britain, and Spain. This measure may be viewed as a rough index of homogeneity of public opinion with respect to peace. This variable cannot be differentiated on the basis of ideology East or West. An exception is Spain, which is the most homogeneous country and, in addition, shows the highest overall peace agreement. The homogeneity can be attributed to the traditional religious, political, and economic institutions of that country. The highly positive attitudes toward peace are probably a function of the terrible civil war still in memory. Those nations showing highest peace agreement mean in addition to Spain are Netherlands and Yugoslavia; and the lowest means are found for Great Britain, Finland, and Norway.

Tables 11.11 and 11.12 show the international agreement on the five most and least popular items; unanimous agreement is noted on "no hunger and poverty." That is, in all the nations the reduction of hunger or poverty is viewed as one of the most popular peace proposals. Clearly, one reason for war, on which there is unanimous

Table 11.8

Percent Agree — Percent Disagree (Acceptance) for Twenty-Five Peace Items

Means and Ranges

	Czechoslovakia	Spain	Great Britain	Netherlands	Norway	Poland	Finland	Yugoslavia	TOTAL
1	-49	66	-26	14	-19	-1	2	36	23
2	65	80	10	71	51	51	49	38	415
3	83	90	60	83	65	48	75	72	576
4	83	59	10	57	54	75	44	82	464
5	94	92	84	91	90	80	90	87	708
6	94	66	77	78	79	58	74	76	592
7	94	68	68	30	65	81	84	82	602
8	64	64	40	73	25	37	20	63	386
9	-61	18	-4	-9	1	-47	17	-38	-114
10	74	78	72	78	41	65	86	70	564
11	30	5	-10	-51	-28	44	-11	33	12
12	85	77	69	84	77	72	84	80	628
13	27	39	47	22	47	24	78	31	315
14	26	41	45	38	4	27	17	6	204
15	94	63	61	48	58	89	71	87	571
16	26	2	-8	-21	1	41	22	54	117
17	1	36	23	27	6	6	42	-13	128
18	2	47	-23	-18	-56	-3	-45	38	-58
19	85	77	84	87	84	80	83	77	557
20	44	71	38	55	8	30	19	26	291
21	61	69	47	56	19	33	9	42	336
22	74	67	87	63	82	77	83	87	620
23	2	38	48	17	6	-5	40	-15	131
24	31	33	69	54	45	67	39	51	389
25	-5	16	13	4	-21	-9	-39	-4	-45
X̄	45	54	39	46	31	41	33	46	
Range	155	90	113	142	146	136	135	125	

Table 11.9
Ranks for the Twenty-Five Peace Proposals of Countries Participating in the Survey

	Czechoslovakia	Spain	Great Britain	Netherlands	Norway	Poland	Finland	Yugoslavia	Average
1	24	11.4	25	20	22	21	22	17	21
2	11	3	19.5	8	10	11	11	15.5	11
3	7.5	2	10	4	6.5	12	8	9	6
4	7	15	19.5	10	9	6	12	4.5	10
5	2.5	1	2.5	1	1	3.5	1	2	1
6	2.5	11.5	4	5.5	4	10	9	8	5
7	2.5	9	8	7	6.5	2	3.5	4.5	4
8	12	13	15	22	14	15	17	11	13
9	25	22	21	5.5	20.5	25	19.5	25	25
10	9.5	4	5	25	13	9	2	10	8
11	16	24	23	3	24	13	23	18	22
12	5.5	5.5	6.5	18	5	7	3.5	6	2
13	17	18	12.5	15	11	19	7	19	15
14	18.5	17	14	14	19	18	19.5	21	17
15	2.5	14	9	24	8	1	10	2	7
16	18.5	25	22	17	20.5	14	16	12	20
17	22	20	17	23	17.5	20	13	23	19
18	20.5	16	24	2	25	22	25	5.5	24
19	5.5	5.5	2.5	12	2	3.5	5.5	7	9
20	14	7	16	11	16	17	18	20	15
21	13	8	12.5	9	15	16	21	14	14
22	9.5	10	1	19	3	5	5.5	2	3
23	20.5	19	11	13	17.5	23	14	24	18
24	15	21	6.5	21	12	8	15	13	12
25	23	23	18	21	23	24	24	22	23

Table 11.10
Rankings of the Nations of Peace Proposal — Percent Agree-Disagree Ranges and Means

	Czechoslovakia	Spain	Great Britain	Netherlands	Norway	Poland	Finland	Yugoslavia
Range	1	8	7	3	2	4	5	6
X̄	4	1	6	2	8	5	7	2

Table 11.11
Inter-nation Agreement for Placing Peace Proposals into the Five Most Popular Categories

	Czechoslovakia	Spain	Great Britain	Netherlands	Norway	Poland	Finland	Yugoslavia
No hunger or poverty	X	X	X	X	X	X	X	X
No gap rich/poor countries	X	X	—	X	X	—	X	—
Trade exchange between countries	—	—	X	X	X	X	X	—
Choose governments freely	X	—	X	X	X	X	—	—
Stop intervening into internal affairs	X	—	—	—	—	⊤	X	X
Improve UN	—	—	X	X	—	X	—	X
More aid to developing countries	—	X	X	—	—	—	X	—
General and complete disarmament	X	—	—	—	—	X	—	X
Peace in family, school, work	—	X	—	—	X	—	—	—
Make individual less aggressive	—	X	—	—	—	—	—	—
No colonial system	—	—	—	—	—	—	—	—

Table 11.12

Inter-nation Agreement for Placing Peace Proposals into Five Least Popular Categories

	Czechoslovakia	Spain	Great Britain	Netherlands	Norway	Poland	Finland	Yugoslavia
Private ownership	X	X	X	X	X	X	—	X
World state	X	X	—	X	X	X	X	X
Self-sufficient countries	X	—	X	X	X	X	X	—
More religious	X	—	X	—	X	X	X	—
Public ownership	—	X	X	X	X	—	X	—
Withdraw from military alliances	—	X	X	X	—	—	—	—
Keep national armies	X	—	—	—	—	—	—	X
World language	—	—	—	—	—	X	—	X
Peace keeping forces	—	X	—	—	—	—	—	—
No colonial systems	—	—	—	X	—	—	—	—
Small countries unite	—	—	—	—	—	—	X	—
Member military alliance	—	—	—	—	—	—	—	X

agreement, is found in the hunger and/or poverty in the world. High inter-nation agreement was also found for "no gap between rich and poor countries" and "trade and exchange between countries."

There are some proposals which are more popular in the eastern countries. They are "general and complete disarmament" and "stop intervening into internal affairs." The popularity of the proposals is very likely tied to the ideology of coexistence in these countries. General and complete disarmament is essential for the success of Communism under conditions of economic and ideological competition with the Western countries. "Stop intervening into internal affairs" seems to be the Eastern way of saying "choose government freely." The latter is found among the popular proposals mainly in the Western countries (but also Czechoslovakia) and the former mainly in the Eastern countries (and Finland).

Perhaps both proposals are perceived as aimed toward the opposite ideological camp. The people in the east are saying, "Stop intervening into our affairs and let us build socialism without provocation;" and the people in the west are saying "Let each people choose its government freely," that is, "Let all people enjoy democratic parliamentarianism as we do." This indicates the importance of evaluating the peace proposals in terms of their semantic and ideological meaning in each country.

The least popular peace proposals (Table 11.12) show high inter-nation agreement on "private ownership," "world state," and "self-sufficient countries." Neither world domination, nor complete independence, nor the private ownership of the tools of production are seen as popular means of bringing about peace by the peoples of either East or West. It will be noted however, that "public ownership" is not among the five least popular proposals in either Czechoslovakia, Poland, or Yugoslavia. In fact, these countries have moderate positive values in Table 11.8 for "public ownership," indicating that a majority of the peoples of these countries agree with this proposal. The only other country which has a small positive value is Spain, which can be understood as a result of the Falangist or Marxist traditions in that country (or possibly a function of the acquiescence response).

The people of the NATO countries and Spain agree less with "withdrawal from military alliance," while the East countries agreed more. This suggests that there is a greater fear in the West of the East than vice versa. However, out of all the countries in the survey, only one (Yugoslavia) put "member of military alliances" in the least popular category, which corresponds rather well with official Yugoslavian policy.

There is no notable difference in homogeneity of opinion between east and west. However, the overall peace agreement mean for the Eastern group was 44 and the Western, 39, indicating, perhaps, a greater anxiety about war in the East. The pattern could also be explained by the more complex cognitive structures in the more developed and less authoritarian nations, which may allow a more critical evaluation of the peace proposals.

Table 11.13 shows the countries ranked on each of the twenty-five peace proposals. The results of these rankings substantiate well the previous discussion of differences between East and West as well as the individual country's pattern.

The five most popular peace proposals overall are:

> Abolish hunger and poverty
> Reduce gap between rich and poor countries
> Improve UN
> Stop intervening into internal affairs
> Choose governments freely

The five least popular proposals are:

> More religion
> Public ownership
> World state
> Self-sufficient
> Private ownership

International comparison of percent agree — percent disagree ranking of peace proposals. Did the various countries in our survey show similar patterns of peace proposal agreement; that is, are the same proposals favored in all the countries, or is each country idiosyncratic in its peace proposals acceptance? A partial answer to this question may be found in Table 11.14.

Table 11.14 shows the Spearman Rho correlations for ranking of the peace proposals based on percentages agree-disagree between eight countries. All the relationships are moderately high and significant except two. The two are the relationship between Spain and

Table 11.13
Countries Ranked on Each of Twenty-Five Peace Proposals
Using Percent Agree — Percent Disagree

	Czechoslovakia	Spain	Great Britain	Netherlands	Norway	Poland	Finland	Yugoslavia	Range (%)
1	8	1	7	3	6	5	4	2	115
2	3	1	8	2	4	4	6	7	70
3	2	1	7	2	6	8	4	5	42
4	1	4	8	3	6	5	7	2	73
5	1	2	6	7	3	8	3	5	14
6	1	7	4	3	2	8	6	5	36
7	1	5	5	8	7	4	2	3	64
8	2	2	5	1	7	6	8	4	53
9	8	1	4	5	3	7	2	6	79
10	4	2	5	2	8	7	1	6	45
11	3	4	5	8	7	1	6	2	95
12	1	5	8	2	5	7	2	4	16
13	6	4	2	8	2	7	1	5	56
14	5	2	1	3	8	4	6	7	41
15	1	5	6	8	7	2	4	3	46
16	3	5	7	8	6	2	4	1	75
17	7	2	4	3	5	5	1	8	55
18	3	1	6	5	8	4	7	2	103
19	2	7	3	1	3	6	5	7	10
20	3	1	4	2	8	4	7	6	63
21	2	1	4	3	7	6	8	5	60
22	6	7	1	8	4	5	3	1	24
23	6	3	1	4	5	7	2	8	63
24	8	7	1	3	5	2	6	4	38
25	5	1	2	3	7	6	8	4	55

Great Britain and Spain and Poland. Even these correlations, however, approximate significance. Strongest relationships (>.91) are
found for Czechoslovakia and Poland and Poland and Yugoslavia,
indicating ideological similarities in the eastern countries. There
seems to be more similarity between Eastern nations than between
Western ones. Typical analysis of correlations among national rankings of peace proposals, however, results in a single type!

Table 11.14
Spearman Rho Correlations for Rankings
of Peace Proposals Between Countries

Item

Czechoslovakia							
Spain	.67						
Great Britain	.71	.52					
Netherlands	.76	.83	.73				
Norway	.88	.68	.83	.84			
Poland	.91	.51	.66	.63	.81		
Finland	.75	.61	.79	.71	.88	.73	
Yugoslavia	.88	.55	.60	.63	.78	.91	.67

AN EXTENSION OF SOCIAL POSITION THEORY

In another chapter (Hartmann and Larsen, 1973) social position
theory was extended from an intra-national to an international
variable. It was suggested that, while each nation could be divided
into a center and periphery, the international community could
likewise be divided. Some nations are richer and more influential
than others. In our investigations we used indices of wealth and size[1]

---

1. We intended to use an activity index based on the number of memberships in
international governmental organizations (IGOs) and in international non-
governmental organizations (INGOs). Activity however correlated .92 with East-West
orientation. The more dissociated position of Eastern Europe in the international
community makes the activity index useless, so it was dropped. Wealth was measured
by three variables, gross domestic product per capita (GDP), gross energy consumed
(GEC), and number of television sets per capita. Size was measured by an index
composed of population size and GDP.

as assessments of a nation's relative "centralness" or "peripheralness." Certain conclusions may be drawn from the use of social position theory as a predictor of national peace attitudes. A center nation would have a stake in the status quo in order to maintain its privileged position. There would therefore be a greater tendency in center nations to agree with proposals which would favor the status quo or proposals which would enhance the positions of center nations. At the same time peripheral nations would have a larger proportion of peripheral people low in subjective and objective power. Extrapolating from the aforementioned findings of this chapter, greater overall peace agreement should be expected in peripheral nations. According to Galtung's theory, the center is pragmatic and logical. Proposals to which the center agrees more are therefore likely to be related in content and are likely to be non-absolutist in nature.

In summary, the hypotheses of Hartmann and Larsen are confirmed:

> There is a Center peace philosophy which is for *liberal integration,* which is related in content, and which is based on the existing structure. The Periphery shows a greater acquiescence to the proposals in general. Our main hypothesis about topdog nations giving most resistance to peace proposals threatening their high rank was found true for the wealth variable . . . the rich world mostly favors the inequalities in the world system and it mostly supports a structure that may lead to a dependency on other nations. There is also a slight trend to agree more with military institutions as an instrument of control of the international system, and this goes together with a greater tendency to accept interventions into the internal affairs of other countries. The wealthy nations are the most reluctant toward ideas of a supranational formation, while the poorer nations concentrate more on the individual level and are thus paying less attention to the social structures . . . .
>
> The samples in the Western nations are showing a greater inclination to accept military control, and the same tendency, though not so strong, is observed when it comes to dependence of other nations. Western nations agree slightly more with

supranational thinking but they are least attracted by the idea of strengthening UN. *The rich and also often the Western nations may be looked upon as the least eager to alter their status quo position in order to create a system of less inequality and less dominance.*

This results in a rather negative picture: The figures tell the story of the old ideological struggle between East and West concerning the economical system and further indicates a different attitude toward colonial systems partly as an effect of the earlier colonial history of East and West. Behind the stronger rejection of military institutions by the respondents in Eastern countries we may find a fear of Western military superiority. However, the alarming finding is this: *The top-dog nations, independent of their block dependence, are uniformly showing the attitude towards their underdogs that they wish to prolong the unequality.* Of course, one may argue that this is only a tendency and may point to the fact that the majority in all nations, for instance, supports most of the humanitarian peace proposals. This is true, but it is also difficult to go openly against such a good and reasonable policy! Finally it is a question of giving priority. When looking at our world today, we get the hunch that such policies do not have the necessary impact when decisions in the Center of the world system are made: The gap between rich and poor nations increases. The rich world is fighting their wars against liberation movements, as for instance in Indo-China, and concentrate their power, as for instance in the European Common Market. When looking around, one may be justified to state that *peace has still a long way to go.* And this exploration of attitudes may lead us to add: and a hard fight to win. (Pp. 19-20)

SOCIAL POSITION AND EXPECTED RELATIONS BETWEEN POTENTIAL CONFLICT GROUPS

Many believe that one source for conflict lies in basic differences between potential conflict groups. One possibility is that these differences may disappear in the foreseeable future. On the other hand, if basic problems are not solved along the way, those differences could sharpen and break out into open conflict. Since the way in which people perceive these probabilities may have an intimate relationship to their actual behavior, it is of some importance to differentiate individuals and groups on what is essentially an optimism-pessimism dimension, that is, the gradient which runs from believing that differences will disappear between potential conflict groups to believing that open conflict between them is inevitable.

The question asked the respondents in the various countries was: "Between now and the year 2000, what do you think is likely to happen in relations between (capitalist and socialist countries, rich and poor countries, and different races of the world)?" Each part of the question was followed with the following response categories: (1) differences will disappear; (2) the countries will accept the differ-

---

SOCIAL COST AND THE FUTURE

Social cost is essentially a power concept. The variables which measure power also define the relative vulnerability of people to rejection by significant others. Those who possess low levels of subjective and objective power are more vulnerable to rejection and, consequently, more easily manipulated. Those subjects who possess low power tend to acquiesce to a variety of peace proposals, while maintaining a pessimism about their lives and the possibility of conflict. Positive attitudes toward peace are not enough but must be linked to action for peace. There is an indiscriminate attitudinal reservoir for peace among those easily manipulated by social cost. The lower power people will agree with almost anything, as long as it leads to peace. Opinion leaders and other "significant others" can use this reservoir in working for the structural changes which are required for peace. Parallel to this effort, the ideology for peace will be accepted by the low power people if first articulated by those high in power. To understand the motivating power of social cost, it is necessary to assess all contemporary societies as structured along socio-economic lines. The implication of such an analysis is that those high in power initiate social change, and those low in power are vulnerable to social cost and manipulation.

ences and live in peaceful coexistence; (3) there will be major conflicts but not war; (4) there will be war between the countries.

The analysis was carried out for six countries (Czechoslovakia, Finland, Great Britain, Netherlands, Norway, Yugoslavia, and Spain). Each population was divided into high, middle, and low, on the social position variable. An analysis of variance was carried out between these groups, analyzing for differences between mean expected conflict scores. The results show that, for Czechoslovakia, Yugoslavia and Spain, the center tends toward greater expectations of conflict. The reverse, however, is true for Great Britain, Netherlands, and Norway, with respect to the relationship between capitalist and socialist countries. This result may suggest developmental differences, where the center has greater expectations of conflict in the developing countries. This difference is readily understood by evaluating the different roles of the center in developed and developing countries.

In developed countries, the center function is to protect the status quo. In developing countries, the center consists frequently of the elements who have led struggles for national independence, or in the case of Spain, supervised the destruction of the republic. The leading elements of developing nations have come to expect change through struggle. (It is interesting to note that the centers of Czechoslovakia and Yugoslavia fought opposite the current center of Spain in the civil war.) These past experiences, therefore, affect expectations of the future.

The second important factor which separates the countries with a higher expectation of conflict from the others is the militancy of their ideology. Britain, Netherlands, and Norway are all parliamentary democracies characterized by a commitment to gradual change. Czechoslovakia, Yugoslavia, and Spain are all characterized by a militant ideology in which changes in social systems have come about as a result of violent struggles. Related to this is the expectation that positive changes in the personal position of the center within a nation, and the nation's position within the world structure, are achieved through conflict. These differences undoubtedly interact to produce greater expectation of conflict in the latter group of countries.

SUMMARY

The general perspective of this chapter is that many of the findings of the study can be explained using power as an intervening variable between, on the one hand, the social and personality characteristics of the respondents, and on the other hand, the responses to questions dealing with peace proposals, optimism-pessimism, and expectations of war. Individuals low in social and personal power are more likely to acquiesce to peace proposals considered high in social desirability. At the same time they are also likely to be more pessimistic regarding their own lives and the condition of their country and the world. Since they possess little power to intervene actively in the future, they are also on the whole, more pessimistic about their own lives and the status of their country and the world, past, present, and future. This suggests that the greater peace agreement on the part of the low power person is partly a result of the inability to differentially evaluate the peace proposals in which the motivational processes of low self-esteem and powerlessness play an important part.

For many years in social science, it has been in vogue to concentrate on differences between people and groups. This has often led to a distorted view of social reality, overemphasizing differences in the minds of lay people and scholars alike. This error is an artifact of our approach to research, which focuses on differences and consequently reports only these. The focus on "differences" has facilitated the segregationist doctrine which keeps people alienated and apart. There are differences, of course, and some important ones, at that. However, as this research shows, there are also important international similarities in thinking, which must be given due weight if we are to understand the psychology of international behavior. The agreement patterns found in peace philosophy between different countries, exemplified in the high rank order correlations and similar peace proposal factors, are a major and important finding. We must reverse this emphasis on differences. As human beings wherever we live we have more in common than what separates us. This study has shown that there is a basis for developing an international consensus for achieving peace.

Assuming that there is some interaction between public opinion and government decision, it is important to identify those sectors of the population where the dissemination of peace research data and theory can do the most good in terms of action programs. The indirect evidence of this research (lack of differential evaluation of the low power person) suggests that this section of the population would be less effective as a basis for constructive peace action. However, the results also show a reservoir of good will toward peace as a concept which can be marshalled for change by opinion leaders.

The fact that high power individuals are more critical and perhaps show largely individualized patterns of agreement with peace proposals would suggest a greater differential evaluation of the various proposals. Because both cognitive and motivational processes have played their part in evaluating the peace proposals, there is likely to be a closer connection between peace agreement and action in this group. In addition, the high power person has greater resources in terms of both personal and social power. Therefore, the high power section of the population can more effectively be used as an action and pressure group on government decisions in the immediate future.

However, having the power to enact peace proposals does not necessarily imply intent to do so. Also, the opinions expressed in the center, although differentially evaluated, may nevertheless clash with the data of developing peace theory. Consequently, in the short-term future, it is important that educational efforts be directed toward the center, in order to convey the accumulated results of peace research. This is especially true since there is some evidence that the periphery, with some lag in time, tends to follow the opinion changes of the center (Galtung, 1964; Lazarfeld, Berelson, and Gaudet, 1948). Such an educational campaign would involve a thorough analysis of the communication sources that reach the center (newspapers, magazines, TV, and radio). But in addition to such an analytic tool, it is important to incorporate the results of research on social judgment, attitude formation, function, and change. Due to the phenomenon known as contrast-assimilation, it is necessary to know the modal stand in the center on any issue for which an educational campaign is mounted. Contrast-assimilation studies (Sherif and Hovland, 1965) have indicated that, if an attitudinal change is attempted too far away from the person's own stand on the issue, the individual will place the stimulus or communication even further away from his own stand and consequently reject it. On the other hand, if the communication is placed relatively close to the individual's stand on the issue, he is likely to perceive it as even closer and thus "assimilate" it.

If rather large changes are required in the center to make opinions conform with developing research and theory, it is clear that such change must be attempted in small steps. Any change attempted must be open and apparent to the individuals concerned. This would involve using reasoned arguments (there is some evidence that fear and emotional appeals are not effective anyway) and presenting the facts about why a given course of action is more desirable than another.

In all, then, this proposal is for using the center in the immediate future as a lever and guide for governments and to induce peace action indicated by established research and theory. The crisis of potential nuclear destruction must induce us to use the quickest and most effective method of conflict management. In the short term, the primary concern must be about the management of conflict (negative peace). The elimination of the threat of nuclear warfare must be first on the agenda. Without survival, it makes little sense to speak of the intermediate future and the distant "new society" peace education.

There is little doubt that psychological and social conditions interact and mutually reinforce each other. (By social is meant both intra- and inter-social interaction.) It is therefore imperative to think of peace education as operating on at least these two levels. In the intermediate future, the focus must be on improving the conditions of both the national and international periphery. Psychologically speaking, this would involve the periphery developing an increased awareness of social and political conditions in the world. Only by attaining such consciousness is it possible for the periphery to move toward a parity of power with the center and thereby obtain an equality in other psychological and social conditions (e.g., mental health and parity of wealth). In educational terms, strong support for broad humanities and liberal arts education is an important precondition for increased awareness among the periphery. The social condition which must accompany awareness is a parity of power, designed to reduce class and other categorical discrepancies.

The task of peace education is to move society toward a world free of hostile images. If the periphery become increasingly aware of social injustices and move toward a parity in power with the center; if Allport's four conditions of group and international interactions be enacted; and if the reverse conditions of the models for hostile international images be observed, thus lowering the social cost of interaction, the basis will be laid for the final goal of peace education: the synergetic integration of groups and cultures.

Epilogue: Tasks for the Future

The reader who has finished the journey through this book will undoubtedly still have questions unanswered. The topic of aggression is of great importance, and we do not pretend to know all the answers. Perhaps it is in the nature of complex topics that research creates more questions. This epilogue focuses on unsolved problems related to aggression. A last look at social cost and the future is taken; and, in a final exhortation, we question whether the future belongs to humanity, in the sense that we define it by our decisions, or whether we will let the events run their course and share a common fate of war and destruction.

The research tasks of the future must involve a reduction in our gaps of knowledge. In the prediction and control of aggression, we ought to move toward testing models and defining the proportion of aggressive behavior accounted for by each predictor variable. However, the aim of our efforts should be to move beyond research to policy decisions and action.

SPECULATIONS ON GAPS IN OUR KNOWLEDGE

There are a number of variables which do not have fully defined relationships to aggression. Some of these variables have not been completely tested in the laboratory or field, and some variables have yet to be examined. The proposed predictors of aggression include boredom, sex, age, intimacy, socio-economic class, punishment, situation versus personality, and ideology. A program of research covering these variables will move us closer to a comprehensive and valid model of aggression.

Boredom. One variable of obvious intuitive importance is boredom. Does boredom lead to aggression? The need for new experience (or some minimum stimulation) is important in the lives of most people. Is extensive boredom experienced as so frustrating that aggression becomes a desirable alternative? Has the sheer triteness and bleakness of the existence of many poor whites played a part in the lynching of blacks in the south? Did the war hysteria expressed in the pageantry of the Nazi rallies at Nuremburg fulfill a fundamental need of stimulation in that economically depressed era? When in need of stimulation, are people more easily carried away by the stirrings of great events promising aggression toward out-groups?

The drums and trumpets and majestic renditions of anthems serve to supplement the bleak life of many ordinary citizens. In the south, boredom and summer heat, combined with rationalizations that blacks are inferior and dangerous, may be the formula which produced horrid cases of lynchings. Is there an optimal level of stimulation below which people become restive and frustrated? Field experiments on deprived communities and self-reported boredom, as related to violence, are needed to test this relationship.

Changing sex and age roles. Human relationships are undergoing constant change. With the changing roles, how many of the traditional results showing males as being more aggressive are still valid? Low levels of female aggression are related to females' self-concepts of docility. As social conditions and norms change, traditional male and female differences must be viewed with skepticism. We know that violent crimes by females are rising more rapidly than those by males. To understand aggression, we must have our ears attuned to continual changes in social relationships.

We know next to nothing about the relationship of age to aggression. A hypothetical function relating age and aggression is curvilinear. Children and older people probably have not (on the average) the confidence or power to be as socially aggressive as those of middle-age. Although this may appear obvious to the reader, we need to remind ourselves that scientific investigation often finds the "obvious" to be untrue. In addition, we need to know more about the

other parameters related to aggression and age. Is frustration tolerance dependent upon age? Do outlets or targets of aggression depend
upon age?

The intimacy of the victim and aggressor. The relationship between
the aggressor and victim is an important variable in the formula
which produces aggression. Larsen, Lesh, and White (1974) completed a laboratory experiment of aggression modeled on Milgram's
obedience study (Milgram, 1963). The relative intimacy between the
subject and the victim was manipulated by arranging for informal
talks of varying lengths between the two, prior to the experiment. The
results showed that, the longer the subject talked with the victim, the
lower the level of shock administered.

We see many common-sense examples in life. The person who
would never be capable of plunging a knife into the chest of another
human being is perfectly capable of dropping bombs. Distance
reduces the impact of the suffering by interfering with the empathetic
processes. In the air war, the distance is both physical and psychological. At the altitude of modern bombers, one does not see what he hits,
and, in addition, the "enemy" is considered subhuman.

What are the factors that produce intimacy? This must be
thought of both as a question of the social environment and of human
empathy. What situations aid in reducing distance and in creating
empathy?

Socio-economic class and the modeling of aggression. We know
models are frequently capable of eliciting aggression. What we don't
know is how modeling is related to social class. In fact, a structural
approach to aggression has received little attention in the psychological literature. Perhaps we will find intervening variables between
modeling and aggression which are functions of social class.

Is the efficacy of modeling partly a function of intelligence,
critical social judgment, and cognitive complexity? Are the distribu-
tions of these variables partially dependent on socio-economic membership? Modeling is probably more effective with the uncritical and
simplistic person. It cannot be emphasized too strongly that, to
predict any behavior, the effect of social class membership must be
carefully evaluated.

Perhaps in the United States, class lines are blurred more than

elsewhere, but that does not exempt us from being cognizant of their socio-economic effects. The desire for equalitarian relationships on the part of most social scientists must not lead us to ignore unpleasant real differences. The effect of modeling and other variables on aggression, must be understood within a social structural framework.
The punishment function. What is the function relating punishment to aggression? Will mild punishment frustrate and, therefore, lead to higher levels of aggression? If severe punishment suppresses aggression, is that true only under conditions of superior power and surveillance? Severe punishment under conditions of superior power leads to displacement, frequently characterized by stereotyped hostility toward minority groups. We need to know more about the conditions which lead punishment to aggression.

Perhaps the severity of punishment is related to aggression and displacement in a linear manner. In this model, mild punishment is experienced as frustrating and less threatening and therefore leads to direct aggression. Severe punishment, however, instills fear as the primary emotional response and therefore produces displacement toward less threatening targets. Displacement remains at the core of stereotyped hostility, which underlies intergroup conflict.

Personality and the demands of the situation. A broader theoretical problem is the question of how much behavior is accounted for by situational conformity and how much by personality. The literature as a whole supports the predominant affect of situational pressures. What role does personality then play, if any? Are personality variables which reinforce pressures toward conformity the only ones which play a role in aggression? What traits aid resistance to conformity? How are they distributed in the psychological economy of the individual, and how are they distributed structurally in society? If, as may be suspected, only a fraction of a percent of the population possesses the ego strength to resist social pressures, personality is an unimportant variable. However, rigid operationalizations of personality and situational pressures are needed in order to gauge the relative importance of each.

Ideology as a reinforcer of aggression. Finally, of great importance is the relationship of ideological factors to aggression. This is an area which has been largely ignored, with the exception of Doob's (1964) work. Ideological factors frequently provide the justification for violence. Doob has noted the role of ideological concepts used as justifications in most historical wars. However, such concepts also play a role at the personal level; for example, the idea that vengeance or retribution is morally correct and just.

Perhaps the ideological component of stimulus equity aggression is the idea of equity or justice. Ideological concepts are frequently incorporated in the individual as assumptions about life. Consequently, acts covered by these assumptions are not questioned; on the contrary, the response is frequently automatic and immediate.

There is an apparent energy equity between most stimuli and responses. Is ideology partially responsible for this? "An eye for an eye, tooth for a tooth, life for a life" illustrates this ideological component. Ideological norms often dictate the form of retribution. In the Plains Indian culture, it is a norm that the relative of a brave killed must take a life from the tribe of the killer. Another ideological concept is that vengeance or retribution is a practical way of dealing with unacceptable behavior. Capital punishment is necessary because it serves as a deterrent to crime. Aggression by other nations must be punished, or it will lead to appeasement. The role of these ideological factors has not been investigated thoroughly.

THE PREDICTION AND CONTROL OF AGGRESSION

The purpose of scientific research in psychology is the prediction and control of behavior. To achieve this goal requires a movement away from single or double variable experiments to multiple variable models. Along with this change, we need a new concern for the relative importance of predictor variables, as expressed in the amount of variance they account for in aggression.

The models outlined in this book must be tested under a variety of circumstances. A comprehensive and refined model of aggression awaits interdisciplinary cooperation. The expanding knowledge will lead to a situation where we can, by various methods, control aggressive behavior. This suggests the importance of facing the moral question involved in behavior control. Psychologists have an uncanny interest in studying mainly the negative aspects of man's behavior. Studies on altruism should match those on aggression.

The proportion of aggressive behavior accounted for by predictor variables. In future research on aggression, we must focus on the amount of variance accounted for by each predictor variable and the roles of intervening variables and their interrelationships. Three key variables which affect the intensity and elicitation of aggression are: the value importance of the goal being obstructed, the degree of threat of punishment perceived in the situation if the individual aggresses, and the extent of group support which an individual can count on for his behavior. The aggression formula would read: The greater the support and the less the threat experienced, the more likely that the goal blockage will elicit aggression. On the other hand, if the goal represents important values, perhaps the individual would react despite threat or lack of support. To what extent are these variables dependent upon the situation? — This would partly influence the weight given to each of these factors.

How does the theoretical aggression threshold affect behavior? This is where personality traits may play a role. By sampling the variability in overt aggression, it would be possible to ascertain the average threshold for a given category of stimuli. Using these conditions, the following prediction formula for aggression reads: the value importance of the goal weight plus group support weight minus threat weight times average aggression threshold. This formula applies also to behavior between nations. Since international behavior is the behavior of the national decision makers, the same psychological and situational variables predict aggression.

We need to develop precise functional relationships between classes of stimuli and the average threshold of aggressive responses. In achieving this goal, we will find ourselves at the point of accurate prediction and control of behavior. At that juncture, we must evaluate the moral question of behavior control. Precisely what types of behaviors are primarily of therapeutic interest, and what types are the concern of society and social policy? Unless based on a sound and reasonable foundation, behavior control is bound to come under severe criticism and rejection.

Models as guidelines for research. Models of aggression are positioned midway between one-shot studies and scientific facts. Models are guidelines for research. A learning model of human aggression must move from a simple consideration of the effect of variables, in terms of statistical significance, to an evaluation of the proportion of behavior accounted for by the predictors of aggression. The question of nature versus nurture, for example, can be answered most fruitfully by determining the amount of variance accounted for by the predictor variables in these two categories.

Issues which ought to be dealt with in a future learning model of aggression include designs which test whether modeling produces imitation or catharsis. We also need a reformulation of the frustration-aggression hypothesis in cognitive expectancy terms as an alternative to the traditional drive formulations. Finally, in developing a learning model of human aggression, we must evaluate what results of animal studies can be extrapolated to human behavior. The resolution of these issues is important in moving toward a scientifically accurate model of human aggression.

Also needed is an accent on positive behavior. Perhaps it is in the nature of humans to focus greater attention on destructive aggressive behavior than positive altruistic behavior. Yet, altruism should be studied in its own right. The number of studies on altruism ought to match those on aggression. Social science must outline models of altruism in the future.

FROM PURE RESEARCH — TO POLICY IMPLICATIONS — TO ACTION

The history of scientific progress is one which has emphasized pure research. In many ways, this approach has reaped unexpected benefits for society. For example, rocket research originally had only a military purpose. From this grew the quest for the stars, and thus knowledge in interplanetary research has grown in geometric proportions. Knowledge in other fields (for example, in medicine) has also increased.

Yet research may have policy implications. The invention of the atomic bomb has changed forever the political and strategic relationships in the world. Is the world better off as a result of these changed relationships? This is a policy question which should have been evaluated, if it had been possible, in advance. To fail to evaluate the long-term effect of research is to abandon social responsibility. Policy considerations are important factors in any research program.

Policies to reduce aggression. The policies we are concerned with are those which will reduce aggression. Some are obvious now from the research cited in this book. For example, if we raise children to have high self-esteem and ego strength, they are less likely to be competitive and destructive. Everything which fosters personality integration and increases the individual's ability to withstand stress will reduce that person's predisposition to aggression. The sex differences in aggression suggest that roles for males should be re-evaluated. Perhaps if boys were shown the same affection and tenderness as girls and were not expected to display aggression, less hostility would be exhibited by males.

Models, especially parents, who act in an altruistic manner could make a significant contribution to the reduction of violence. If parents reward or condone aggression, they will probably raise aggressive children. If frustration is unavoidable, then it would be helpful to prepare for this possibility in advance. Expected and nonarbitrary frustration is easier to tolerate. If frustration is made to appear reasonable, less hostile feelings are elicited. In a broad sense, anything which can be done to reduce suffering and stress in the world would aid in reducing aggression.

By definition, aggression research is policy research. Psychology is engaged in the scientific venture of predicting and controlling human behavior. Humans have the ability of making choices and decisions. These choices must include an evaluation of what is desirable behavior. Aggression research should have policies for changing aggression.

Social action. Even policy research is not enough. In the rarefied atmosphere of universities, many scholars have maintained an aloofness from the pragmatic problems of life. This is best exemplified by the number of scientists who are totally involved in pure research. Yet action is the logical continuation of policy research. Scientists have a responsibility to join other concerned people in political and social action movements. Many do, but more are needed to wed the policy implications of their research to political work.

From our discussion, it is clear that much violence is camouflaged in the structural relationships of society. Deprivations which are a result of changeable inequities claim thousands of lives each year. Thousands of others live lives of despair in a mold from which there is no apparent escape. To focus our attention solely on open aggression and warfare overlooks this situation — equal in importance.

The effects of structural violence are often subtle, especially in a modern parliamentary democracy. This makes it very difficult to assign responsibility for structural violence and evoke change. But change must come to millions of deprived people throughout the world. The change must be a structural change, a change which establishes new relationships between people.

As in poker, what one person gains, another loses. Since structural change represents real gains for some and real losses for others, serious opposition may be expected from the latter. It would be naive to assume that structural change can be achieved without overcoming such resistance. Status quo forces who are reaping the benefits of inequity will undoubtedly use violence in their resistance to change. The serious question which faces those genuinely concerned with peace is: Is it better to tolerate brief historical periods of violence in order to overcome structural violence and induce change, or is it better to accept structural violence as a permanent feature of the world?

SOCIAL COST AND THE FUTURE

In this book, I have repeatedly appealed to the concept of social cost as an explanatory construct in aggression. There is a risk that any person who works with a concept becomes "ethnocentric" about it. This may be manifest in selective attention to data and research and enlarging the concept's importance beyond its place in psychology. Sometimes, however, it is necessary to be polemic in order to draw attention to a neglected area or point of view. It is my unswerving conviction that the effect of social approval or rejection from significant others has largely been overlooked in the study of aggression. Yet it would appear, as supported by available research, that this is a critical variable in the development and maintenance of hostility and, most important, in whether the hostility will be expressed in behavior.

We have seen how a number of variables are tied together by the social cost concept, in predicting the development and maintenance of hostile international images. Man's long dependency period is fundamental to the importance of social cost as a social motive. Man is, above all, social; the consideration of any behavior must begin with his gregarious nature. Conformity to situational pressures is explained to a large extent by social cost. True, for the German concentration camp guard, there were real terrors in refusing orders. But one of these real terrors was surely the possibility of being ostracized, punished, and removed from his social group. In understanding mass cruelty, the social cost of aggressive interaction cannot be ignored.

Social cost is neither negative or positive. The value of social cost depends upon the purpose for which this powerful motive is used. Without the control exerted by social approval or disapproval, there is nothing to guarantee that human relationships would not be destructive in our present society. Yet, the history of the human race has been replete with examples of social cost being employed in directing mass destruction. The world wars and the extermination of the Jews, specifically, could not have achieved their frightful proportions were it not for the conformity extracted by means of social approval and disapproval.

In our society today, social cost has become a powerful social motive, because most individuals are dependent for lengthy periods of time on a few significant others. If the self-concept of the child did not depend upon a few, but rather on many, the disapproval occasionally experienced would not be as threatening. The kibbutz system in Israel affords an opportunity to test this hypothesis. If the security of the child is not dependent upon the capricious decisions of a few adults, social approval would have less impact. A society which promotes acceptance of the individual on a broad level would reduce dependency and permit the freedom essential for actualizing self-relevant goals. In that society, the hopes for an enduring peace are permanently rooted.

EXHORTATION: COMMON FATE OR THE FUTURE AS A DECISION

Rotter (1966) described two kinds of people who differed in their beliefs as to who and what controlled their lives. For some, the locus of control is found in themselves. They decide their future and accept rewards or misfortune as a result of their behavior. Others feel that the happenings of their lives may be attributed to external factors. They use fate, chance, luck, or powerful others to explain the rewards of life or the difficulties they face. Such a basic attitude toward life is likely to have far-reaching behavioral consequences. Those who believe in internal control, for example, are more likely to change from smokers to non-smokers when presented with research results which link smoking to cancer (James, Woodruff, and Werner, 1965).

Apathy, in the sense of letting events run their course, is less likely among internals; and achievement of goals is therefore more likely. In the recent Coleman report (Coleman, Campbell, Hobson, McPartland, Mood, Weinfeld, and York, 1966) on equality of educational opportunity, the perception of control was a better predictor of achievement for children of minority groups than any other variable.

With respect to war, an external control orientation is expressed by such statements as: "Wars have been with us from the beginning and will always be with us," and, "Men are naturally hostile," Appeals to instinctive or genetic explanations of violence doom mankind to a perpetual state of hostility. Anyone vaguely familiar with psychology can recognize that in this conception lie the roots of the self-fulfilling prophecy. If the events are predetermined and cannot be changed by our actions, what is the sense of even trying?

The ultimate apocalyptic expression of external locus of control is found in the various conceptions of Armageddon. During this ultimate doomsday, presumably all infidel internals will be destroyed, and all believing externals will be saved. If the external locus of control concept is accepted in decision-making circles, events will likely someday take control over the goodwill of men. Conscious decisions must be made which will move the world toward integration and peace.

References

Abrams, L. Aggressive behavior in the authoritarian personality. *Dissertation Abstracts,* 1965, *25*(1), 16750.

Adams, B. N. Interaction theory and the social network. *Sociometry,* 1967, *30,* 64-78.

Adorno, T. W., Frenkel-Brunswik, E., Levinson, D. J., & Sanford, R. N. *The authoritarian personality.* New York: Harper, 1950.

Ainsworth, M. D., & Ainsworth, L. H. Acculturalization in East Africa, II, frustration and aggression. *Journal of Social Psychology,* 1962, *57*(2), 401-407.

Allison, J., & Hunt, D. E. Social desirability and the expression of aggression under varying conditions of frustration. *Journal of Consulting Psychology,* 1959, *23,* 528-532.

Allport, G. W. *Personality: A psychological interpretation.* New York: Holt, 1937.

Allport, G. W. *The nature of prejudice.* New York: Doubleday, 1958.

Allport, G. W. *Pattern and growth in personality.* New York: Holt, Rinehart and Winston, 1961.

Andrews, L. M., & Karlins, M. *Requiem for democracy.* New York: Holt, Rinehart and Winston, 1971.

Angell, R. C. Defense of what? *Journal of Conflict Resolution,* 1962, *6,* 116-124.

Ansbacher, H. L., & Ansbacher, R. R. *The individual psychology of Alfred Adler.* New York: Basic Books, 1956.

Arling, G. L., & Harlow, H. F. Effects of social deprivation on maternal behavior of rhesus monkeys. *Journal of Comparative and Physiological Psychology,* 1967, *64*(3), 371-377.

Aronfreed, J., & Paskal, J. Altruism, empathy and the conditioning of positive effect. Unpublished manuscript, University of Pennsylvania, 1965.

Ashley, N. R., Harper, R. S., & Runyon, D. L. The perceived size of coins in normal and hypnotically induced economic states. *American Journal of Psychology*, 1951, *64*, 654–672.

Atkinson, J. W. *An introduction to motivation*. Princeton, N. J.: Van Nostrand, 1964.

Azrin, N. H., Hake, D. G., & Hutchinson, R. R. Extinction induced aggression. *Journal of the Experimental Analysis of Behavior*, 1966, *9* (3), 191–204.

Azrin, N. H., Hutchinson, R. R., & Hake, D. G. Elicitation of aggression by physical blow. *Journal of the Experimental Analysis of Behavior*, 1965, *8* (3), 171–180.

Azrin, N. H., Hutchinson, R. R., & Sallery, R. D. Pain aggression toward inanimate objects. *Journal of the Experimental Analysis of Behavior*, 1964, *7* (3), 223–228.

Baldwin, J. D. The social behavior of adult male squirrel monkeys (*Saimiri sciureus*) in a semi-natural environment. *Folic Primates*, 1968, *9*, 281–314.

Bandura, A., Lipsher, D. H., & Miller, P. E. Psychotherapists' approach-avoidance reactions to patients' expressions of hostility. *Journal of Consulting Psychology*, 1960, *24*, 1–8.

Bandura, A., Ross, D., & Ross, S. A. Transmission of aggression through imitation of aggressive models. *Journal of Abnormal and Social Psychology*, 1961, *63*, 575–582.

Bandura, A., Ross, D., & Ross, S. Imitation of film-mediated aggressive models. *Journal of Abnormal and Social Psychology*, 1963, *66*, 3–11.

Bandura, A., & Walters, R. H. *Adolescent aggression*. New York: Ronald Press, 1959.

Bard, P., & Mountcastle, V. B. Some forebrain mechanisms involved in expression of rage with special reference to suppression of angry behavior. In R. L. Isaacson (Ed.), *Basic readings in neurophysiology*. New York: Harper & Row, 1964.

Barker, R., Dembo, T., & Lewin, K. Frustration and regression: An experiment with young children. In *Studies in child welfare*. Iowa City: University of Iowa Press, 1941.

Beeman, E. A. The effect of male hormone on aggressive behavior in mice. *Physiological Zoology*, 1947, *20*, 373-405.

Bell, D. (Ed.). *The radical right*. Garden City, N. Y.: Doubleday, 1963.

Berelson, B. R., & Steiner, G. A. *Human behavior: An inventory of scientific findings*. New York: Harcourt, 1964.

Berkowitz, L. Anti-semitism, judgmental processes, and displacement of hostility. *Journal of Abnormal and Social Psychology*, 1961, *62*, 210-215.

Berkowitz, L. *Aggression: A social psychological analysis*. New York: McGraw-Hill, 1962.

Berkowitz, L. Simple views of aggression. In A. Montagy (Ed.), *Man and aggression*. New York: Oxford University Press, 1973.

Berkowitz, L., & Daniels, L. R. Responsibility and dependency. *Journal of Abnormal and Social Psychology*, 1963, *66*, 429-436.

Bevan, W., Daves, W. F., & Levy, G. W. The relation of castration, androgen therapy, and pre-test fighting experience to competitive aggression in male C57BL/10 mice. *Animal Behavior*, 1960, *8*, 6-12.

Bixenstine, V. E., Potash, H. M., & Wilson, K. V. Effects of level of cooperative choice by the other player on choices in a prisoner's dilemma game. *Journal of Abnormal and Social Psychology*, 1963, *66*, 308-313.

Block, J., & Martin, B. C. Predicting the behavior of children under frustration. *Journal of Abnormal and Social Psychology*, 1955, *51*, 281-285.

Bogardus, E. S. Measuring social distances. *Journal of Applied Sociology*, 1925, *9*, 299-308.

Boulding, K. The prevention of World War III. In E. J. Hollins (Ed.), *Peace is possible*. New York: Grossman Publishers, 1966.

Boulding, K. Insight and knowledge in the development of a stable peace. In *No time but this present*. Studies preparatory to the 4th World Conference of Friends, 1967.

Bronson, R. H. Agonistic behavior in woodchucks. *Animal Behavior*, 1964, *12* (2), 470-478.

Brown, J. S., & Farber, I. E. Emotions conceptualized as intervening variables—with suggestions toward a theory of frustration. *Psychological Bulletin*, 1951, *48*, 465-495.

Brown, L. B. Aggression and denominational membership. *British Journal of Social and Clinical Psychology*, 1965, *4* (3), 175-178.

Brozan, N. Statement in the *New York Times*, June 25, 1974, p. 16.

Bruner, J. S., & Goodman, C. C. Value and need as organizing factors in perception. *Journal of Abnormal and Social Psychology*, 1947, *42*, 33-44.

Burnstein, E., & Worchel, P. Arbitrariness of frustration and its consequences for aggression in a social situation. *Journal of Personality*, 1962, *30* (4), 528-540.

Buss, A. H. *The psychology of aggression*. New York: Wiley, 1961.

Buss, A. H. Physical aggression in relation to different frustrations. *Journal of Abnormal and Social Psychology*, 1963, *67* (1), 1-7.

Buss, A. H., & Durkee, A. An inventory for assessing different kinds of hostility. *Journal of Consulting Psychology*, 1957, *21*, 343-348.

Campbell, A. Factors associated with attitudes toward Jews. In T. M. Newcomb & E. L. Hartley (Eds.), *Readings in Social Psychology*. New York: Holt, Rinehart and Winston, 1947. Pp. 518-527.

Cantril, H. *The psychology of social movements*. New York: Wiley, 1941.

Cantril, H. *The patterns of human concern*. New Brunswick, N. J.: Rutgers University Press, 1965.

Carmichael, S., & Hamilton, C. J. *Black Power: The politics of liberation in America*. New York: Vintage Books, 1967.

Carpenter, C. C. Aggressive behavior and social dominance in the six-lined race runner. *Animal Behavior*, 1960, *8*, 61-66.

Carthy, J. D., & Ebling, F. J. *The natural history of aggression*. New York: Academic Press, 1964.

Cartwright, D., & Harary, F. Structural balance: A generalization of Heider's theory. *Psychological Review*, 1956, *63*, 277-293.

Castell, R., & Ploog, D. Social behavior of squirrel monkeys: antagonisms between two groups. *Zeitschrift für Tierpsychologie*, 1967, *24* (5), 625-641.

Chesler, M., & Schmuck, R. Student reactions to the Cuban crisis and public dissent. *Public Opinion Quarterly*, 1964, *28*, 467-482.

Christiansen, B. *Attitudes toward foreign affairs as a function of personality*. Oslo, Norway: University of Oslo Press, 1959.

Christie, R., & Geis, F. *Studies in Machiavellianism*. New York: Academic Press, 1970.

Clark, G., & Sohn, L. B. *World peace through world law*. Cambridge: Harvard University Press, 1966.

Coelho, G. V. *Changing images of America: A study of Indian students' perceptions*. New York: Free Press, 1958.

Cofer, C. N., & Appley, M. M. *Motivation theory and research*. New York: Wiley, 1964.

Cohen, A. K. *Delinquent boys*. New York: Free Press, 1955.

Coleman, J. S., Campbell, E. Q., Hobson, C. J., McPartland, J., Mood, A. M., Weinfeld, F. D., & York, R. L. *Equality of educational opportunity*. Report from the Office of Education, Washington, D. C.: U. S. Government Printing Office, 1966.

Collias, N. E. Aggressive behavior among vertebrate animals. *Physiological Zoology*, 1944, *17*, 83–123.

Collias, N. E. Problems and principles of animal sociology. In C. P. Stone (Ed.), *Comparative psychology*. Englewood Cliffs, N. J.: Prentice-Hall, 1951.

Coopersmith, S. *The antecedents of self-esteem*. San Francisco: Freeman, 1967.

Crook, J. H. Primate societies and individual behavior. *Journal of Psychosomatic Research*, 1968, *12*, 11–19.

Crowne, D. P., & Marlowe, D. *The approval motive*. New York: Wiley, 1964.

Darley, J., & Latane, B. Diffusion of responsibility in emergency situations. Proceedings of the Annual Convention of the American Psychological Association, 1966.

Dart, R. A. The predatory transition from ape to man. *International Anthropological and Linguistic Review*, 1953, *1*, 1201–1219.

Davis, A. Child training and social class. In R. G. Barker et al.(Eds.), *Child behavior and development*. New York: McGraw-Hill, 1943.

Davis, A., & Havighurst, R. J. *The father of the man: How your child gets his personality*. Boston: Houghton Mifflin, 1947.

Davis, A., & Donenfeld, I. Extinction induced social interaction in rats. *Psychonomic Science*, 1967, *7* (3), 85–86.

De Charms, R., & Wilkins, E. J. Some effects of verbal expression of hostility. *Journal of Abnormal and Social Psychology*, 1963, *66*, 462–470.

Delgado, J. Cerebral heterostimulation in a monkey colony. *Science*, 1963, *141* (Whole No. 3576), 161–163.

Delgado, J. Social rank and radio stimulated aggressiveness in monkeys. *Journal of Nervous and Mental Diseases*, 1967, *144* (5), 383–390.

de Rivera, J. H. *The psychological dimension of foreign policy*. Columbus: Charles E. Merrill Pub. Co., 1968.

de Sola Pool, I. Effects of cross-national contact on national and international images. In H. C. Kelman (Ed.), *International Behavior*. New York: Holt, Rinehart and Winston, 1965.

Deutsch, M. Trust, trustworthiness, and the F scale. *Journal of Abnormal and Social Psychology*, 1960, *61*, 138–140.

Deutsch, M., & Collins, M. E. *Interracial housing: A psychological evaluation of a social experiment*. Minneapolis: University of Minnesota Press, 1951.

Dilger, W. C. Agonistic and social behavior of captive redpolls. *Wilson Bulletin*, 1960, *72*, 115–132.

Dittman, A. T., & Goodrich, D. W. A comparison of social behavior in normal and hyperaggressive preadolescent boys. *Child Development*, 1961, *32*, 315-327.

Doise, W. Intergroup relations and polarization of individual and collective judgments. *Journal of Personality and Social Psychology*, 1969, *12*, 136–143.

Doise, W., Csepeli, G., Dann, D., Gouge, C., Larsen, K. S., & Ostell, A. An experimental investigation into the formation of intergroup relations. Third European Summer School For Experimental Social Psychology, Konstanz, July 1971.

Doise, W., Csepeli, G., Dann, D., Gouge, C., Larsen, K. S., & Ostell, A. An experimental investigation into the formation of intergroup representations. *European Journal of Social Psychology*, 1972, *1*, 203–204.

Dollard, J., Doob, L. W., Miller, N. E., Mowrer, O. H., & Sears, R. R. *Frustration and aggression*. New Haven, Conn.: Yale University Press, 1939.

Doob, L. The behavior of attitudes. *Psychological Review*, 1947, *54*, 135–156.

Doob, L. *Patriotism and nationalism: Their psychological foundations*. New Haven, Conn.: Yale University Press, 1964.

Dreyer, P. I., & Church, R. *Psychonomic Science*, 1968, *10*, (7), 271–272.

Durbin, E. F. M., & Bowlby, J. *Personal aggressiveness and war*. New York: Columbia University Press, 1939.

Eckhardt, W. Planning for peace: An open letter to peace groups and other human relations groups. 1967, Mimeo, 4 pp. RPA Ref. No. 9130. Broadlawns Hospital, Des Moines, Iowa.

Ellison, G. D., & Flynn, J. P. Organized aggressive behavior in cats after surgical isolation of the hypothalamus. *Archives Italiennes de Biologie*, 1968, *106*, (1), 1–20.

Emery, F. E. Psychological effects of the western film: A study in television viewing. *Human Relations*, 1959, *12*, 195–232.

Endler, N. S., & Hunt, J. McV. Sources of behavioral variance as measured S-R inventory of anxiousness. *Psychological Bulletin*, 1966, *65*, 336–346.

Endler, N. S., & Hunt, J. McV. S-R inventories of hostility and comparisons of the proportions of variance from persons, responses, and situations for hostility and anxiousness. *Journal of Personality and Social Psychology*, 1968, *9*, 309–315.

Endler, N. S., Hunt, J. McV., and Rosenstein, A. J. An S-R inventory of anxiousness. *Psychological Monographs*, 1962, *76* (Whole No. 356).

Engley, A. H. Involvement as a determinant of response to favorable and unfavorable information. *Journal of Personality and Social Psychology*, Monograph 7, 1967, No. 3, Part 2, 1–15.

Epstein, R. Aggression toward outgroups as a function of authoritarianism and imitation of aggressive models. *Journal of Personality and Social Psychology*, 1966, *3*, 574–579.

Eron, L. D. Relationship of TV viewing habits and aggressive behavior in children. *Journal of Abnormal and Social Psychology*, 1963, *67* (2), 193–196.

Etkin, W. Cooperation and competition in social behavior. In W.

Etkin (Ed.), *Social behavior and organization among vertebrates.* Chicago: University of Chicago Press, 1964.

Etzioni, A. European unification: A strategy of change. *World Politics,* 1963, *16,* 32-51.

Eysenck, H. J. Primary social attitudes: A comparison of attitude patterns in England, Germany, and Sweden. *Journal of Abnormal and Social Psychology,* 1953, *48,* 563-568.

Falk, G. J. Status differences and the frustration-aggression hypothesis. *International Journal of Social Psychiatry,* 1959, *5,* 214-222.

Feierabend, I. K., & Feierabend, R. L. Aggressive behavior within politics, 1948-1962: A cross-national study. *Journal of Conflict Resolution,* 1966, *10,* 249-272.

Feierabend, I. K., & Feierabend, R. L. Conflict, crisis and collision: A study of international stability. *Psychology Today,* 1968, *1* (12), 26-32.

Feshbach, S. The drive-reducing function of fantasy behavior. *Journal of Abnormal and Social Psychology,* 1955, *50,* 3-11.

Feshbach, S., & Singer, R. D. *Television and aggression.* San Francisco: Jossey-Bass, 1971.

Festinger, L. *A theory of cognitive dissonance.* New York: Harper & Row, 1957.

Fiedler, F. E. Styles of leadership. *Harvard Business Review,* 1965, *43,* 115-122.

Fiedler, F., Warrington, W., and Blaisdell, F. Unconscious attitudes as correlates of sociometric choice in a social group. *Journal of Abnormal and Social Psychology,* 1952, *47,* 790-797.

Fischer, A. Sharing in preschool children as a function of amount and type of reinforcement. *Genetic Psychology Monographs,* 1963, *68,* 215-245.

Fischer, R. Fractionating conflict. Unpublished paper discussed in J. H. de Rivera, *The psychological dimensions of foreign policy.*

Fishman, C. G. Need for approval and the expression of aggression under varying conditions of frustration. *Journal of Personality and Social Psychology,* 1965, *2* (6), 809-816.

Frank, J. D. Group psychology and the elimination of war. In E. J. Hollins (Ed.), *Peace is possible.* New York: Grossman Publishers, 1966. Pp. 91-98.

Franus, E. Reactions of resistance and anger in a small child. Uniwesytet Jagiellonski Zeszyty Naukowe: *Psychologia I Pedagogika,* 1957, *1,* 137–163.

Frenkel-Brunswik, E., Levinson, D. J., & Sanford, R. N. The authoritarian personality. In T. M. Newcomb and E. L. Hartly (Eds.), *Readings in social psychology.* New York: Holt, Rinehart and Winston, 1947.

Freud, S. *A general introduction to psychoanalysis.* New York: Liveright, 1920.

Freud, S. Mourning and melancholia. In E. Jones (Ed.), *Collected Papers,* Vol. IV. London: Hogarth, 1925. Pp. 152–170.

Freud, S. *Beyond the pleasure principle.* Translated by James Strachey. New York: Liveright, 1950.

Freud, S. Why War? *The collected papers of Sigmund Freud.* Edited by Ernest Jones. New York: Basic Books, 1959.

Frisch, D. H. Scientists and the decision to bomb Japan. *Bulletin of Atomic Scientists,* 1970, *26* (6), 107–115.

Fromm, E. *Escape from Freedom.* New York: Holt, Rinehart and Winston, 1941.

Gaitskell, H. An eight point programme for world government. In E. J. Hollins (Ed.), *Peace is possible.* New York: Grossman Publishers, 1966. Pp. 141–150.

Gallup, G. G., Jr. Aggression in rats as a function of frustrative nonreward in a straight alley. *Psychonomic Science,* 1965, *3* (3), 99–100.

Galtung, J. Foreign policy opinion as a function of social position. *Journal of Peace Research,* 1964, 206–231.

Galtung, J. International TV panels in times of crisis. Paper presented at seminar "Policy Making and Television," Nordic TV Companies, Hango, Finland, Sept. 1968.

Galtung, J. Some basic assumptions of peace thinking. Mimeo. International Peace Research Institute, Oslo, Norway, 1969.

Galtung, J. Peace Research: Past experience and future perspectives. Submitted for publication. *Journal of Peace Research,* 1972.

Gillespie, J. R. Aggression in relation to frustration, attack and inhibition. *Dissertation Abstracts,* 1962, *22* (11), 4080–4081.

Gladstone, A. I. The possiblility of predicting reactions to international events. *Journal of Social Issues,* 1955, *11* (1), 21–28.

Goranson, R. E., & Berkowitz, L. Reciprocity and social responsibility reactions to prior help. *Journal of Personality and Social Psychology*, 1966, *3*, 227-232.

Haas, E. B. International integration: The European and universal process. *International Organization*, 1961, *15*, 366-392.

Hall, C. S., and Lindzey, G. *Theories of personality*. New York: Wiley, 1957.

Hamon, L. Peace research: Outline of an inquiry. *International Social Science Journal*, 1965, *17* (3), 420-441.

Haner, C. F., & Brown, P. A. Clarification of the instigation to action concept in the frustration-aggression hypothesis. *Journal of Abnormal and Social Psychology*, 1955, *51*, 204-206.

Hardy, K. R. An appetitional theory of motivation. *Psychological Review*, 1964, *71*, 1-18.

Harlow, H. F. Mice, monkeys, men and motives. *Psychological Review*, 1953, *60*, 23-32.

Harlow, H. F. Motivational forces underlying learning. In the Kentucky Symposium's *Learning theory, personality theory, and clinical research*. New York: Wiley, 1954.

Hartmann, A., & Larsen, K. S. Intranational and international social position and peace attitudes. In J. Galtung (Ed.), *Images of the year 2000 — A 12 nation cross-national study*. Hague: Mouton, 1976.

Hartmann, H., Kris, E., & Lowenstein, R. M. *Notes on the theory of aggression: The psychoanalytic study of the child*. New York: International Universities Press, 1949.

Hartup, W. W., & Himeno, Y. Social isolation versus interaction with adults in relation to aggression in pre-school children. *Journal of Abnormal and Social Psychology*, 1959, *59*, 17-22.

Hautojarvi, S., & Lagerspetz, K. The effects of socially-induced aggressiveness or nonaggressiveness on the sexual behavior of inexperienced male mice. *Scandinavian Journal of Psychology*, 1968, *9*(1), 45-49.

Hayden, T. Peace research USA, our generation against nuclear war. *Special Peace Research Supplement*. PRA Ref. No. 12778, 1967, *3* (2), 55-61.

Hayes, C. J. *The historical evaluation of nationalism*. New York: Macmillan, 1931.

Heath, R. Electrical self-stimulation of the brain in man. *American Journal of Psychiatry*, 1963, *120*, 571-577.

Heider, F. Attitudes and cognitive organization. *Journal of Psychology*, 1946, *21*, 107-112.

Heider, F. *The psychology of interpersonal relations.* New York: John Wiley & Sons, 1958.

Hilgard, E. R. *Theories of learning.* New York: Appleton-Century-Crofts, 1956.

Hokanson, J. E. Vascular and psychogalvanic effects of experimentally aroused anger. *Journal of Personality*, 1961, *29*, 30-39.

Hokanson, J. E., Burgess, M., & Cohen, M. F. The effects of three types of aggression on vascular processes. *Journal of Abnormal and Social Psychology*, 1963, *67* (3), 214-218.

Hokanson, J. E., & Shetler, S. The effect of overt aggression on physiological tension level. *Journal of Abnormal and Social Psychology*, 1961, *63*, 446-448.

Homans, G. C. *The human group.* New York: Harcourt, Brace and World, 1950.

Homans, G. C. *Social behavior: Its elementary forms.* New York: Harcourt, Brace and World, 1961.

Horney, K. *New ways in psychoanalysis.* New York: Norton, 1939.

Horney, K. *Our inner conflicts.* New York: Norton, 1945.

Horowitz, E. L., & Horowitz, R. E. Development of social attitudes in children. *Sociometry*, 1938, *1*, 301-338.

Hovland, C. I. *The order of presentation in persuasion.* New Haven, Conn.: Yale University Press, 1957.

Hovland, C. I., Harvey, O. M., & Sherif, M. Assimilation and contrast effects in reactions to communication and attitude change. *Journal of Abnormal and Social Psychology*, 1957, *55*, 244-252.

Hovland, C. I., Janis, I. E. (Eds.). *Personality and persuasibility.* New Haven, Conn.: Yale University Press, 1959.

Hovland, C., and Sears, R. Minor studies in aggression: VI. Correlation of lynchings with economic indices. *Journal of Psychology*, 1940, *9*, 301-310.

Hutchinson, R. R., Azrin, N. H., & Hunt, G. M. Attack produced by intermittent reinforcement of a concurrent operant response.

Journal of Experimental Analysis of Behavior, 1968, *11* (4), 489-495.

Hutchinson, R. R., Azrin, N. H., & Renfrew, J. W. Effects of shock intensity and duration on the frequency of biting attack by squirrel monkeys. *Journal of Experimental Analysis of Behavior*, 1968, *11* (1), 83-88.

Irving, L. F. Sex differences and the relationships between certain personality variables. *Psychological Reports*, 1957, *2*, 595-597.

James, W. H., Woodruff, A. B., & Werner, W. Effect of internal and external control upon changes in smoking behavior. *Journal of Consulting Psychology*, 1965, *29*, 127-129.

Janis, I. L., & Field, P. B. Sex differences and personality factors related to persuasibility. In I. L. Janis & C. I. Hovland (Eds.), *Personality and persuasibility*. New Haven, Conn.: Yale University Press, 1959.

Jersild, A. T., & Markey, F. V. Conflicts between preschool children. *Child Development Monographs*, No. 21, 1935.

Kagan, J. The measurement of overt aggression from fantasy. *Journal of Abnormal and Social Psychology*, 1956, *52*, 390-393.

Karli, P. New experimental data on interspecific aggressive behavior between rats and mice. *Journal of Physiology*, 1961, *3*, 383-384.

Karli, P., & Vergnes, M. New data on the neurophysiological bases of interspecific aggression between rats and mice. *Journal de Physiologie*, 1963, *55*, 272-273.

Katz, D. The functional approach to the study of attitude change. *Public Opinion Quarterly*, 1960, *24*, 163-204.

Katz, D. Nationalism and strategies of international conflict resolution. In H. C Kelman (Ed.) *International behavior*. New York: Holt, Rinehart and Winston, 1965. p. 366.

Katz, D., & Stotland, E. A preliminary statement to a theory of attitude structure and change. In S. Koch (Ed.), *Psychology: A study of a science*, Vol.3, New York: McGraw-Hill, 1959. Pp. 423-475.

Kaufmann, H. *Aggression and altruism*. New York: Holt, Rinehart and Winston, 1970.

Kelman, H. C. Processes of opinion change. *Public Opinion Quarterly*, 1961, *25*, 57-78.

Kenny, D. T. *An experimental test of the catharsis theory of aggression.* Ann Arbor, Mich.: University Microfilms, 1953.

Killian, L. M., & Grigg, C. M. *Racial crisis in America.* Englewood Cliffs, N. J.: Prentice-Hall, 1964.

Klineberg, O. Can world peace be taught? *Bulletin of Peace Proposals,* 1971, *2,* 128.

Komai, T., and Guhl, A. M. Tameness and its relation to aggressiveness and productivity of the domestic chicken. *Poultry Science,* 1960, *39,* 817-823.

Kosa, J. The rank order of peoples: A study in national stereotypes. *Journal of Social Psychology,* 1957, *46,* 311-320.

Krech, D., & Crutchfield, R. S. Elements of psychology. New York: Knopf, 1958.

Kregarman, J. J. Arbitrariness of frustration and aggression. *Dissertation Abstracts,* 1961, *22* (6), 2070.

Kregarman, J. J., & Worchel, P. Arbitrariness of frustration and aggression. *Journal of Abnormal and Social Psychology,* 1961, *62,* 183-187.

Lagerspetz, K. Genetic and social causes of aggressive behavior in mice. *Scandinavian Journal of Psychology,* 1961, *2,* 167-173.

Lagerspetz, K. Studies on the aggressive behavior of mice. *Annales Academiae Scientiarum Fennicae.* Series B. 1964, 1-131.

Lagerspetz, K., & Hautojarvi, S. The effect of prior aggressive or sexual arousal on subsequent aggressive or sexual reactions in male mice. *Scandinavian Journal of Psychology,* 1967, *8* (1), 1-6.

Lane, R. E. Political personality and electoral choice. *American Political Science Review,* 1955, *49,* 173-190.

Lansky, L. M., Crandall, V. J., Kagan, J., & Baker, C. T. Sex differences in aggression and its correlates in middle-class adolescents. *Child Development,* 1961, *32,* 45-58.

La Piere, A. T. Attitudes versus actions. *Social Forces,* 1934, *13,* 230-237.

Larsen, K. S. Authoritarianism, self-esteem and insecurity. *Psychological Reports,* 1969, *25,* 225-230.

Larsen, K. S. Aggression-altruism: A scale and some date on its validity. *Journal of Personality Assessment,* 1971, *35* (3), 275-281. (a).

Larsen, K. S. Racial prejudice and discrimination — The reasons why: Rokeach and Pettigrew in dialogue. *Bulletin of Peace Proposals*, 1971, *2*, 175-186. (b)

Larsen, K. S. Affectivity, cognitive style and social judgment. *Journal of Personality and Social Psychology*, 1971, *19* (1), 119-123. (c)

Larsen, K. S. Social cost versus belief incongruence and race as predictors of person type preferences across an intimacy dimension. Paper presented at annual meeting of the Western Psychological Association, Portland, April, 1972(a). Published as: Social cost and aggression. *Peace Research Reviews*, 1974, *5* (1).

Larsen, K. S. Determinants of peace agreements, pessimism-optimism, and expectation of world conflict: A cross national study, *Journal of Cross-Cultural Psychology*, 1972, *33*, 283-292. (b)

Larsen, K. S. Attributed power, response strategies, and non-zero sum game behavior. *Psychological Reports*, 1972, *30*, 821-822. (c)

Larsen, K. S. Emotional responses to frustration of approval seeking and personal identity. *Psychological Reports*, 1974, *34*, 403-405.

Larsen, K. S. Social cost, belief incongruence and race: Experiments in choice behavior. *The Journal of Social Psychology*, 1974, *94*, 253-267.

Larsen, K. S., Coleman, D., Forbes, J., & Johnson, R. Is the subject's personality or the experimental situation a better predictor of subject's willingness to administer shock to a victim? *Journal of Personality and Social Psychology*, 1972, *22* (3), 287-295.

Larsen, K. S., & Ommundsen, R. Social cost and prejudice. Submitted for publication, 1975.

Larsen, K. S., Lesh, B., & White, C. The effect of the subject-victim relationship and general authoritarianism on the subject's willingness to administer shock. *The Journal of Social Psychology*. In press, 1976.

Larsen, K. S., & Minton, H. L. Attributed social power — A scale and some validity. *The Journal of Social Psychology*, 1971, *85*, 37-39.

Larsen, K. S., & Schwendiman, G. Child-rearing habits, personality characteristics, and religious reference group as predictors of attitudes toward the war in Viet Nam. *Proceedings of Utah Academy of Sciences, Arts and Letters*, 1968, *45* (1), 35-41.

Larsen, K. S., & Schwendiman, G. Authoritarianism, self-esteem and insecurity. *Psychological Reports,* 1969, *25,* 229-230.

Larsen, K. S., & Schwendiman, G. Perceived aggression training as a predictor of two assessments of authoritarianism. *Journal of Peace Research,* 1970, *7,* 69-71.

Larsen, K. S., Schwendiman, G., & Stimpson, D. V. Change in attitude toward Negroes resulting from exposure to congruent and noncongruent attitudinal objects. *Journal of Peace Research,* 1969, *3,* 157-161.

Larsen, K. S., Simmons, D., & Coleman, D. Preference for conflict resolution strategies: A tridimensional predictive model. *Peace Research,* 1971, *3* (1), 1.

Lawler, J., & Laulicht, J. International integration in developing regions. *Peace Research Reviews,* 1970, *3,* 4.

Lazarfeld, P. F., Berelson, B. R., & Gaudet, H. *The people's choice.* New York: Columbia University Press, 1948.

Lazarus, R. S. *Patterns of adjustment and human effectiveness.* New York: McGraw-Hill, 1969.

Lefcourt, H. M., Barnes, K., Parke, R., & Swartze, F. Anticipated social censure and aggression-conflict as mediators of response to aggression induction. *Journal of Social Psychology,* 1966, *70* (2), 251-263.

Lefkawitz, M. M., Walter, L. O., & Eron, L. D. Punishment, identification, and aggression. *Merrill-Palmer Quarterly,* 1963, *9* (3), 159-174.

Lesser, G. S. The relationship between overt and fantasy aggression as a function of maternal responses to aggression. *Journal of Abnormal and Social Psychology,* 1957, *55,* 215-221.

Levi, W. On the causes of war and the conditions of peace. *Journal of Conflict Resolution,* 1960, *4,* 411-420.

Levin, H., & Sears, R. R. Identification with parents as a determinant of doll-play aggression. *Child Development,* 1956, *27,* 35-153.

Levine, S., & Conner, R. Endocrine aspects of violence. An unpublished staff report to the National Commission on the Causes and Prevention of Violence, December, 1969.

Levinson, D. J. Authoritarian personality and foreign policy. *Journal of Conflict Resolution,* 1957, *1,* 37-47.

Levison, P. K., & Flynn, J. P. The objects attacked by cats during stimulation of the hypothalamus. *Animal Behavior*, 1965, *13* (23), 217-220.

Lippitt, R., Polansky, N., Redl, F., & Rosen, S. The dynamics of power. *Human Relations*, 1952, *5*, 37-64.

Livson, N., & Mussen, P. H. The relation of ego control to overt aggression and dependency. *Journal of Abnormal and Social Psychology*, 1957, *55*, 66-71.

Lorenz, K. *On aggression*. New York: Harcourt, Brace and World, 1966.

Lovaas, O. I. Interaction between verbal and nonverbal behavior. *Child Development*, 1961, *32*, 329-336.

Lundy, R., Katkovsky, W., Cromwell, R., & Shoemaker, D. Self-acceptability and descriptions of sociometric choices. *Journal of Abnormal and Social Psychology*, 1955, *51*, 260-262.

Lyle, W. H., Jr., & Levitt, E. E. Punitiveness, authoritarianism, and parental discipline of grade school children. *Journal of Abnormal and Social Psychology*, 1955, *51*, 42-46.

Lysgaard, S. Adjustment in a foreign society: Norwegian Fulbright grantees visiting the United States. *International Social Science Bulletin*, 1955, 7, 45-51.

Magaziner, D. The reduction of hostility without catharsis. Paper presented at meetings of the Eastern Psychological Association. Philadelphia, April 1961.

Maple, T., & Matheson, D. W. *Aggression, hostility and violence*. New York: Holt, Rinehart and Winston, 1973.

Maslow, A. H. Deprivation, threat, and frustration. *Psychological Review*, 1941, *48*, 364-366.

Maslow, A. H. Conflict, frustration and the theory of threat. *Journal of Abnormal and Social Psychology*, 1943, *38*, 81-86.

Maslow, A. H. *Motivation and personality*. New York: Harper, 1954.

McClelland, D. C. *Personality*. New York: Sloane, 1951.

McDonald, A. L., & Heimstra, N. W. Modification of aggressive behavior of green sunfish with D-Lysergic acid diethylamide. *Journal of Psychology*, 1964, 57 (1), 19-23.

McDougall, W. *An introduction to social psychology*. London: Methuen, 1906.

Megargee, E. I. Undercontrolled and overcontrolled personality types in extreme and social aggression. *Psychological Monographs,* 1966, *80* (3).

Megargee, E. I., & Hokanson, J. E. *The dynamics of aggression.* New York: Harper and Row, 1970.

Mezei, L. Perceived social pressure as an explanation of shifts in the relative influence of race and belief on prejudice across social interactions. *Journal of Personality and Social Psychology,* 1971, *19,* 69-81.

Midlarsky, E., & Byran, J. H. Training charity in children. *Journal of Personality and Social Psychology,* 1967, *67,* 371-378.

Milgram, S. Behavioral study of obedience. *Journal of Abnormal and Social Psychology,* 1963, *67,* 371-378.

Milgram, S. Group pressure and action against a person. *Journal of Abnormal and Social Psychology,* 1964, *69,* 137-143. (a)

Milgram, S. Techniques and first findings of a laboratory study of obedience to authority. *Yale Scientific Magazine,* 1964. (b)

Milgram, S. Liberating effects of group pressure. *Journal of Personality and Social Psychology,* 1965, *1,* 127-134. (a)

Milgram, S. Some conditions of obedience to authority. *Human Relations,* 1965, *18,* 57-76. (b)

Milgram, S. The compulsion to do evil. *Patterns of Prejudice,* 1967, *1,* 3-7.

Miller, N. E. Theory and experiment relating psychoanalytic displacement to stimulus-response generalization. *Journal of Abnormal and Social Psychology,* 1948, *43,* 155-178.

Miller, N. E. Comments on theoretical models illustrated by the development of a theory of conflict. *Journal of Personality,* 1951, *20,* 82-100.

Miller, N. E. Liberalization of basic S-R concepts: Extensions to conflict behavior, motivation, and social learning. In S. Koch (Ed.), *Psychology: A study of a science,* Volume 2. New York: McGraw-Hill, 1959.

Miller, N. E., & Bugelski, R. Minor studies in aggression: The influence of frustrations imposed by the in-group on attitudes impressed toward out-groups. *Journal of Psychology,* 1948, *25,* 437-442.

Millon, T. *Modern Psychopathology*. Philadelphia: W. B. Saunders, 1969.

Minard, R. D. Race relationships in the Pacahonates coal field. *Journal of Social Issues*, 1952, *8* (1), 29-44.

Minton, H. L. Power as a personality construct. In B. S. Maher (Ed.), *Progress in Experimental Personality Research*, Vol. 4. New York: Academic Press, 1967.

Mischel, W. *Personality and assessment*. New York: Wiley, 1968.

Mischel, W. Continuity and change in personality. *American Psychologist*, 1969, *24*, 1012-1018.

Mischel, W., & Schopler, J. Authoritarianism and reactions to "Sputniks." *Journal of Abnormal and Social Psychology*, 1959, *59*, 142-145.

Mitchell, G. D. Persistent behavior pathology in rhesus monkeys following early social isolation. *Folia Primates*, 1968, *8*, 132-147.

Mitrany, D. The functional approach in historical perspective. *International Affairs*, 1971, *47*, 3.

Møller, G. W., Harlow, H. F., & Mitchell, G. D. Factors affecting agonistic communication in rhesus monkeys. *Behavior*, 1968, *31*, 339-357.

Montgomery, K. C. Exploratory behavior and its relation to spontaneous alternation in a series of maze exposures. *Journal of Comparative Psychology*, 1952, *45*, 50-57.

Moos, R. H. Sources of variance in responses to questionnaires and in behavior. *Journal of Abnormal Psychology*, 1969, *74*, 405-412.

Morris, R. T. *The two-way mirror*. Minneapolis: University of Minnesota Press, 1960.

Mulder, M., & Stemerding, A. Threat, attraction to group, and need for strong leadership. *Human Relations*, 1963, *16*, 317-334.

Muller, H. Means and aims in human genetic betterment. In T. M. Sonneborn (Ed.), *The control of human heredity and evolution*. New York: Macmillan, 1965.

Mussen, P. H., & Naylor, H. K. The relationship between overt and fantasy aggression. *Journal of Abnormal and Social Psychology*, 1954, *49*, 235-240.

Myer, J. S., & White, R. T. Aggressive motivation in the rat. *Animal Behavior*, 1965, *13* (5), 430-433.

Newcombe, H. Alternative approaches to world government. *Peace Research Reviews.* Monograph Series I, 2, 1967.

Newcomb, T. M. An approach to the study of communicative acts. *Psychological Review,* 1953, *60,* 393-404.

Ono, Y., and Uematsu, T. Seasonal variations of social behavior in Oryzias Lahipes. *Annals of Animal Psychology,* 1958, *8,* 63-70.

Osgood, C. E. *An alternative to war and surrender.* Urbana, Ill.: University of Illinois Press, 1962.

Osgood, C. E. *Perspectives in foreign policy.* Palo Alto: Pacific Books, 1966.

Osgood, C. E., & Tannenbaum, P. H. The principle of congruity in the prediction of attitude change. *Psychological Review,* 1955, *62,* 42-55.

Palmer, S. Frustration-aggression and murder. *Journal of Social Psychology,* 1960, *60,* 430-432.

Pastore, N. The role of arbitrariness in the frustration-aggression hypothesis. *Journal of Abnormal and Social Psychology,* 1952, *47,* 728-731.

Paul, J., & Laulicht, J. *In your opinion: Leaders' and voters' attitudes on defense and disarmament.* Clarkson, Ontario: Canadian Peace Research Institute, 1963.

Paulino, A. F. Dreams: Sex differences in aggressive content. *Journal of Projective Techniques and Personality Assessments,* 1964, *28* (2), 219-226.

Penfield, W. The interpretive cortex. *Science,* 1959, *129,* 1719-1725.

Pepitone, A., & Reichling, G. Group cohesiveness and the expression of hostility. *Human Relations,* 1955, *8,* 327-337.

Pettigrew, T. F. Personality and socio-cultural factors in inter-group attitudes: A cross-national comparison. *Journal of Conflict Resolution,* 1958, *2,* 29-42.

Pettigrew, T. F. In K. S. Larsen, Racial prejudism and discrimination — The reasons why: Rokeach and Pettigrew in dialogue. *Bulletin of Peace Proposals,* 1971, *2,* 175-186.

Phillips, B. H. Authoritarian, hostile and anxious students' ratings of instructor. *California Journal of Educational Research,* 1960, *11,* 19-23.

Pittman, D. J., & Handy, W. Patterns in criminal aggravated assault. *Journal of Criminal Law and Science,* 1966, *364,* 60-72.

Post, J. M. A study of an early class contact situation. *Journal of Human Relations,* 1959. *8,* 100-113.

Powell, J. T. The expression of aggression in introverts and extroverts: an experimental investigation. *Dissertation Abstracts,* 1966, *26* (10), 6172-6173.

Prosterman, R. L. Surviving to 3000: An introduction to the study of lethal conflict. Belmont: Duxbury Press, 1972.

Putney, S., & Middleton, R. Some factors associated with student acceptance or rejection of war. *American Sociological Review,* 1962, *27,* 655-667.

Rabbie, J. M., & Horwitz, M. Arousal of ingroup-outgroup bias by a chance or win loss. *Journal of Personality and Social Psychology,* 1969, *13,* 269-277.

Radke, M. J. Relation of parental authority to children's behavior and attitudes. University of Minnesota Institute of Child Welfare. Monograph No. 22, 1946.

Rapoport, A. *Strategy and conscience.* New York: Schocken, 1969. Pp. 277-282.

Rapoport, A. *Fights, games and debate.* Ann Arbor, Mich.: The University of Michigan Press, 1970.

Raser. J. R. The failure of fail-safe. *Transaction,* 1969, *6* (3), 12-19.

Raven, B. H. Social influence and power. In I. D. Steiner and M. Fishbein (Eds.), *Current studies in social psychology.* New York: Holt, Rinehart and Winston, 1965.

Redl, F., & Wineman, D. *The aggressive child.* New York: Free Press, 1957.

Restle, R., Andrews, M., & Rokeach, M. Differences between open and closed minded subjects on learning — set and oddity problems. *Journal of Abnormal and Social Psychology,* 1964, *68,* 648-654.

Roberts, W. W., & Keiss, H. O. Motivational properties of hypothalamic aggression in cats. *Journal of Comparative and Physiological Psychology,* 1964, *68* (2), 187-193

Roberts, W. W., Steinberg, M. L., & Means, L. W. Hypothalamic mechanisms for sexual, aggressive and other motivational behaviors in the opossum. *Journal of Comparative and Physiological Psychology,* 1967, *64* (1), 1-15.

Rokeach, M. *The open and closed mind.* New York: Basic Books, 1960.

Rokeach, M. Invited lecture at Oregon State University, August 1970.

Rokeach, M. *The nature of human values.* New York: Free Press, 1973.

Rokeach, M., & Mezei, L. Race and shared beliefs as factors in social choice. *Science,* 1966, *151,* 167-172.

Rood, J. P. Habits of the shorttail shrew. *Journal of Mammology,* 1958 *39,* 499-507.

Ropartz, P. The relation between olfactory stimulation and aggressive behavior in mice. *Animal Behavior,* 1968, *16* (1), 97-100.

Rosenberg, M. J. Images in relation to the policy process. In H. C. Kelman (Ed.), *International behavior.* New York: Holt, Rinehart and Winston, 1965.

Rosenberg, M. J., & Abelson, R. P. An analysis of cognitive balancing. In C. I. Hovland and I. L. Janis (Eds.), *Attitude organization and change.* New Haven, Conn.: Yale University Press, 1960. Pp. 112-163.

Rosenzweig, S. The experimental measurement of types of reactions to frustration. In H. A. Murray (Ed.), *Explorations in personality.* New York: Oxford Press, 1939.

Roth, R. M., & Puri, P. Direction of aggression and the non-achievment syndrome. *Journal of Counseling Psychology,* 1967, *14* (3), 277-281.

Rothaus, P., & Worchel, P. The inhibition of aggression under nonarbitrary frustration. *Journal of Personality,* 1960, *28,* 108-117.

Rotter, J. B. Generalized expectancies for internal versus external control of reinforcement. *Psychological Monographs.* 1966, 80 (Whole Nr. 609).

Sackett, G. P. Effects of rearing conditions upon the behavior of rhesus monkeys *(Macaca mulatta). Child Development.* 1965, *36,* 855-868.

Sampson, D. L., & Smith, H. P. A scale to measure world-minded attitudes. *Journal of Social Psychology,* 1957, *45,* 90-106.

Sawyer, J., & Guetzkow, H. Bargaining and negotiation in international relations. In H. C. Kelman (Ed.), *International Behavior*. New York: Holt, Rinehart and Winston, 1965.

Schmid, H. Politics and peace research. *Journal of Peace Research,* 1968, *3,* 217-272.

Scott, J. P. *Aggression.* Chicago: University of Chicago Press, 1958. (a)

Scott, J. P. *Animal Behavior.* Chicago: University of Chicago Press, 1958. (b)

Scott, J. P., and Fredericson, E. The causes of fighting in mice and rats. *Physiological Zoology,* 1951, *24,* 273-309.

Scott, W. A. Cognitive complexity and cognitive balance. *Sociometry,* 1963, *26,* 66-74.

Scott, W. A., & Withey, S. B. *The United States and the United Nations: The public view.* New York: Manhattan Pub., 1958.

Sears, R. R. Effects of frustration and anxiety on fantasy aggression. *American Journal of Orthopsychiatry,* 1951, *21,* 498-505.

Sears, R. R. Relation of early socialization experiences to aggression in middle childhood. *Journal of Abnormal and Social Psychology,* 1961, *63,* 461-465.

Sears. R. R., Maccoby, E. E., & Levin, H. *Patterns of child rearing.* Evanston, Illinois: Row, Peterson, 1957.

Seaver, B. The three definitions of peace. Friends coordination committee on peace. Philadelphia. Quoted in H. Newcomb, Alternative approaches to world government. *Peace Research Reviews,* 1967, *1,* 2.

Seay, B. M., Alexander, B. K., & Harlow, H. F. Maternal behavior of socially deprived rhesus monkeys. *Journal of Abnormal and Social Psychology,* 1964, *69,* 345-354.

Secord, P. F., Bevan, W., & Katz, D. The Negro stereotype and perceptual accentuation. *Journal of Abnormal and Social Psychology,* 1956, *53,* 78-83.

Seeman, M. On the meaning of alienation. *American Sociological Review,* 1959, *24,* 783-791.

Selltiz, C., & Cook, S. W. Factors influencing attitudes of foreign students toward the host country. *Journal of Social Issues,* 1962, *18* (1), 7-23.

Selye, H. *The stress of life.* New York: McGraw-Hill, 1956.

Seward, J. P. Aggressive behavior in the rat. III. The role of frustration. *Journal of Comparative Psychology,* 1945, *38,* 225-238.

Sheldon, W. H. (with collaboration of S. S. Stevens). *The varieties of temperament: A psychology of constitutional differences.* New York: Harper, 1942.

Sheldon, W. H. (with collaboration of S. S. Stevens & W. B. Tucker). *The varieties of human physique: An introduction to constitutional psychology.* New York: Harper, 1940.

Sherif, C. W., & Sherif, M. (Eds.). *Attitude, ego-involvement and change.* New York: Wiley, 1967.

Sherif, M. *In common predicament.* Boston: Houghton Mifflin, 1966.

Sherif, M., Harvey, O. J., White, B. J., Hood, W. R., & Sherif, C. W. *Intergroup conflict and cooperation: The robbers cave experiment.* Norman, Okla.: Institute of Group Relations, University of Oklahoma, 1961.

Sherif, M., & Hovland, C. I. *Social judgment.* New Haven: Yale University Press, 1965.

Siegel, A. E. Film-mediated fantasy aggression and strength of aggressive drive. *Child Development,* 1956, *27,* 365-378.

Siegel, A. E. The influence of violence in the mass media upon children's role expectations. *Child Development,* 1958, *29,* 35-36.

Siegel, H. S., & Siegel, P. B. *Animal Behavior.* 1961, *9* (3-4), 151-158.

Simmons, D. D., Larsen, K. S., & Fajardo, D. Pacifist-militarist allegiance, humanistic worldmindedness and peace proposal preferences. Paper presented at the annual meeting of the Peace Research Society (International), Vancouver, B. C., February 1972.

Simmons, J. L. *Deviants.* Berkeley: The Glendessary Press, 1969. Pp. 133-134.

Simpson, H. M., & Craig, K. D. Word associations to homonymic and neutral stimuli as a function of aggressiveness. *Psychological Reports,* 1967, *20* (2), 351-354.

Singer, J. D. Escalation and control in international conflict: A simple feedback model. *General Systems,* 1970, *15,* 163-172.

Skinner, B. *Walden two.* New York: Macmillan, 1948.

Smith, H. P., & Rosen, E. W. Some psychological correlates of worldmindedness and authoritarianism. *Journal of Personality*, 1958, *26*, 170-183.

Southwick, C. H. *Behavior*, 1967, *28* (1-2), 182-189.

Spilka, B., & Struening, E. L. A questionnaire study of personality and ethnocentrism. *Journal of Social Psychology*, 1956, *44*, 65-71.

Stein, D. D., Hardyck, J. A., & Smith, M. Brewster. Race and Belief: An open and shut case. *Journal of Personality and Social Psychology*, 1965, *1* (4), 281-289.

Stone, I. F. The pentagon and Peking. *The New York Review of Books*. March 1972.

Storr, A. *Human aggression*. New York: Atheneum, 1968.

Tajfel, H. Cognitive aspects of prejudice. *Journal of Social Issues*, 1969, *125*, 79-94.

Tajfel, H., Flament, L., Billig, M. G., & Brundy, R. P. Social categorization and intergroup behavior. *European Journal of Social Psychology*, 1971, *1*, 149-178.

Tedeschi, R. E., Tedeschi, D. H., Mucha, A., Cook, L., Mattis, P. A., & Fellows, E. Effect of various centrally active compounds on fighting behavior of mice. *Journal of Pharmacology and Experimental Therapeutics*, 1959, *125*, 28-34.

Thee, M. Will human sanity prevail? *Bulletin of Peace Proposals*, 1972, *1*, 3-4.

Thibaut, J. W. An experimental study of the cohesiveness of underprivileged groups. *Human Relations*, 1950, *3*, 251-278.

Thibaut, J. W., & Coules, J. The role of communication in the reduction of interpersonal hostility. *Journal of Abnormal and Social Psychology*, 1952, *47*, 770-777.

Thibaut, J. W., & Riecken, H. W. Authoritarianism, status and communication of aggression. *Human Relations*, 1955, *8*, 95-120.

Thompson, T., Travis, K., & Bloom, W. Aggressive behavior and extinction-induced response-rate increase. *Psychonomic Science*, 1966, *5* (9), 335-336.

Thorpe, L. P., & Johnson, V. Personality and social development in childhood and adolescence. *Review of Educational Research*, 1958, *28*, 422-432.

Tieson, N., & Mussen, P. H. The relation of ego control to overt aggression and dependency. *Journal of Abnormal and Social Psychology*, 1957, *55*, 66-71.

Tinbergen, N. On war and peace in animals and man. *Science*, 1968, *160*, 1411-1418.

Titus, H. E., & Hollander, E. P. The California F Scale in psychological research: 1950-1955. *Psychological Bulletin*, 1957, *54*, 47-64.

Torrance, E. P. Interpersonal aggression and submission in ability to endure pain and discomfort. *Journal of Social Psychology*, 1959, *48*, 205-210.

Toynbee, A. J. The reluctant death of national sovereignty. *Journal of Abnormal and Social Psychology*, 1961, *62*, 184-186.

Triandis, H. C., & Davis, E. E. Race and belief as determinants of behavioral intentions. *Journal of Personality and Social Psychology*, 1965, *2*, 715-725.

U Thant. United Nations, Office of Public Information, New York, Press Release SG/SM/1277, FAO, 2159, June 16, 1970.

U Thant. Address by the Secretary-General. *UN Monthly Chronicle*, 1971, *8* (5), 45-48.

Vernon, W., & Ulrich, R. *Science*, 1966, *152* (3722), 668-669.

Wake, F. R. Normal aggression and delinquency. *Bulletin of the Maritime Psychology Association*, 1959, *8*, 50-59.

Walters, R. H. Implications of laboratory studies of aggression for the control and regulation of violence. *Annals of the American Academy of Political and Social Science*, 1966, *364*, 60-72.

Washburn, M. Peace education is alive — but unsure of itself. *War/Peace Report*, November 1971.

Watten, J. M., & Maroney, R. J. *Journal of Social Psychology*, 1958, *48*, 223-233.

Wheeler, L. Toward a theory of behavioral contagion. *Psychological Review*, 1966, *73*, 179-192.

White, R. K., & Lippitt, R. *Autocracy and democracy: An experimental inquiry*. New York: Harper, 1960.

Whiting, J. M. W. The frustration complex in Kwoma society. *Man*, 1944, *44*, 140-144.

Whiting, J. M. W., and Child, I. L. *Child training and personality*. New Haven, Conn.: Yale University Press, 1953.

Williams, R. M., Jr. The reduction of integroup tensions. *SSRC Bulletin, No. 57.* New York: Social Science Research Council, 1947.

Willis, F. N., Jr. Fighting in pigeons relative to available space. *Psychonomic Science.* 1966, *4* (9), 315-316.

Wolfe, J. L., & Summerlin, C. T. Agonistic behavior in organized and disorganized rat populations. *Science,* 1968, *160* (3823), 98-99.

Woodworth, R. S. Reinforcement of perception. *American Journal of Psychology,* 1947, *60,* 119-124.

Worchel, P. Catharsis and the relief of hostility. *Journal of Abnormal and Social Psychology,* 1957, *55,* 230-243.

Wurtz, K. R. Some theory and data concerning the attenuation of aggression. *Journal of Abnormal and Social Psychology,* 1960, *60,* 134-136.

Wyer, R. S., Jr., Weatherley, D. A., & Terrell, G. Social role, aggression and academic achievement. *Journal of Personality and Social Psychology,* 1965, *1* (6), 645-649.

Zimbardo, P. G. Involvement and communication discrepancy as determinants of opinion conformity. *Journal of Abnormal and Social Psychology,* 1960, *60,* 86-94.

Zuckerman, S. *The social life of monkeys and apes.* New York: Harcourt, Brace & World, 1932.

Index

About the Author

KNUD S. LARSEN has dedicated his life to the optimistic hope that peace between nations can be achieved. An associate professor at Oregon State University since 1974, he also is a research associate of the International Peace Research Institute of Oslo, Norway. He serves on the Board of Social Issues of the Oregon State Psychological Association and is a permanent corresponding member of the editorial committee of the *Bulletin of Peace Proposals*.

He also is a research fellow in psychology of the Australian Institute of Aboriginal Studies, Canberra, and currently is conducting studies in aboriginal decision-making processes.

Dr. Larsen received his early education in Denmark's schools and came to California in 1956, where he attended high school. He received B.A. and M.A. degrees from California State University at Los Angeles and a doctorate in social psychology from Brigham Young University.

He was a probation counselor for Los Angeles County while attending school and in 1968 went to Oslo as a researcher for the International Peace Research Institute.

His research paper on "Images of the World in the Year 2000" was read at the plenary meeting, Year 2000 Project, held in Prague. He has published widely in scientific journals on the subjects of peace and conflict research, social cost, social judgment and discriminatory behavior, attitude change, and on varied other subjects.